MEASURING LITERACY

PERFORMANCE LEVELS FOR ADULTS

Committee on Performance Levels for Adult Literacy

Robert M. Hauser, Christopher F. Edley, Jr., Judith Anderson Koenig, and Stuart W. Elliott, editors

Board on Testing and Assessment

Center for Education

Division of Behavioral and Social Sciences and Education

NATIONAL RESEARCH COUNCIL
OF THE NATIONAL ACADEMIES

D1219425

THE NATIONAL ACADEMIES PRESS
Washington, D.C.
www.nap.edu

THE NATIONAL ACADEMIES PRESS 500 Fifth Street, N.W. Washington, DC 20001

NOTICE: The project that is the subject of this report was approved by the Governing Board of the National Research Council, whose members are drawn from the councils of the National Academy of Sciences, the National Academy of Engineering, and the Institute of Medicine. The members of the committee responsible for the report were chosen for their special competences and with regard for appropriate balance.

This study/publication was supported by Cooperative Agreement No. R215U990016 between the National Academy of Sciences and the U.S. Department of Education. Additional funding was provided by an award from the Presidents' Committee of The National Academies. Any opinions, findings, conclusions or recommendations expressed in this publication are those of the authors and do not necessarily reflect the views of the organizations or agencies that provided support for the project.

Library of Congress Cataloging-in-Publication Data

Measuring literacy : performance levels for adults / Committee on Performance Levels for Adult Literacy ; Robert M. Hauser ... [et al.], editors.
    p. cm.
  Includes bibliographical references.
  ISBN 0-309-09652-9 (pbk.) — ISBN 0-309-55015-7 (pdf) 1. Functional literacy—United States—Evaluation. I. Hauser, Robert Mason. II. National Research Council (U.S.). Committee on Performance Levels for Adult Literacy.
  LC149.7.M4 2005
  302.2'244—dc22

                          2005021251

Additional copies of this report are available from the National Academies Press, 500 Fifth Street, N.W., Lockbox 285, Washington, DC 20055; (800) 624-6242 or (202) 334-3313 (in the Washington metropolitan area); Internet, http://www.nap.edu.

Printed in the United States of America

Suggested citation: National Research Council. (2005). *Measuring literacy: Performance levels for adults*. Committee on Performance Levels for Adult Literacy, R.M. Hauser, C.F. Edley, Jr., J.A Koenig, and S.W. Elliott, editors. Board on Testing and Assessment, Center for Education. Division of Behavioral and Social Sciences and Education. Washington, DC: The National Academies Press.

THE NATIONAL ACADEMIES
Advisers to the Nation on Science, Engineering, and Medicine

The **National Academy of Sciences** is a private, nonprofit, self-perpetuating society of distinguished scholars engaged in scientific and engineering research, dedicated to the furtherance of science and technology and to their use for the general welfare. Upon the authority of the charter granted to it by the Congress in 1863, the Academy has a mandate that requires it to advise the federal government on scientific and technical matters. Dr. Ralph J. Cicerone is president of the National Academy of Sciences.

The **National Academy of Engineering** was established in 1964, under the charter of the National Academy of Sciences, as a parallel organization of outstanding engineers. It is autonomous in its administration and in the selection of its members, sharing with the National Academy of Sciences the responsibility for advising the federal government. The National Academy of Engineering also sponsors engineering programs aimed at meeting national needs, encourages education and research, and recognizes the superior achievements of engineers. Dr. Wm. A. Wulf is president of the National Academy of Engineering.

The **Institute of Medicine** was established in 1970 by the National Academy of Sciences to secure the services of eminent members of appropriate professions in the examination of policy matters pertaining to the health of the public. The Institute acts under the responsibility given to the National Academy of Sciences by its congressional charter to be an adviser to the federal government and, upon its own initiative, to identify issues of medical care, research, and education. Dr. Harvey V. Fineberg is president of the Institute of Medicine.

The **National Research Council** was organized by the National Academy of Sciences in 1916 to associate the broad community of science and technology with the Academy's purposes of furthering knowledge and advising the federal government. Functioning in accordance with general policies determined by the Academy, the Council has become the principal operating agency of both the National Academy of Sciences and the National Academy of Engineering in providing services to the government, the public, and the scientific and engineering communities. The Council is administered jointly by both Academies and the Institute of Medicine. Dr. Ralph J. Cicerone and Dr. Wm. A. Wulf are chair and vice chair, respectively, of the National Research Council.

www.national-academies.org

COMMITTEE ON PERFORMANCE LEVELS
FOR ADULT LITERACY

v

Foreword

In the summer of 2002, the National Center for Education Statistics approached the Board on Testing and Assessment (BOTA) of the National Academies with a request for assistance in setting performance standards for their upcoming assessment of adults' literacy skills. This was a unique request for BOTA. Over the years, BOTA had explored and provided advice on a variety of issues related to setting performance standards on educational achievement tests—from discussions of the standards-based reform movement in education and its effects on various groups of student to recommendations for best practice in setting performance standards for the National Assessment of Educational Progress. Undertaking the process of actually setting performance standards, however, was a new endeavor for BOTA.

Setting performance standards is an inherently judgmental task. The process involves determining the number and nature of the performance levels used for reporting the test results (such as "proficient" or "below basic"), the descriptions of the levels, and the test scores used to demark the range of scores associated with each performance level. A variety of standard-setting procedures are documented in the measurement literature, procedures that lay out the methodologies and best practices, but all ultimately rely on the judgments of testing experts, policy makers, and other stakeholders and users of the test results. The answers to questions such as "How much literacy is enough?" or "What constitutes a literacy problem?"—either for an individual or for society as a whole—are not exclusively technical. Bringing scientific principles to the process of collecting and summarizing judgmental information was a daunting challenge.

Consistent with its mission, BOTA accepted this request. Formed to provide scientific advice to policy makers and the public about critical issues related to testing and assessment, BOTA draws on the interdisciplinary expertise of its members to bring a wide variety of perspectives to bear on such complex problems. Members of BOTA welcomed this opportunity to demonstrate a scientific approach to the problem and offer advice about two critical and timely issues: how to help describe and understand the literacy skill levels of adults in this country and how to set performance standards in a meaningful and technically valid way.

Under the auspices of BOTA, the Committee on Performance Levels for Adult Literacy was formed as an interdisciplinary panel of 17 members with expertise in the areas of adult education and adult literacy, economics, educational measurement and standard setting, law, political science, and sociology. BOTA remained actively involved with this work, with four members of BOTA serving on the committee, two of whom served as committee co-chairs. Members of BOTA provided ongoing oversight for the work in formulating the committee's charge and overall approach to its tasks, identifying individuals to serve on the committee, offering feedback to the committee, and reviewing the draft report and recommendations.

The committee was convened in December 2002 and held six meetings. During the course of its work, the committee solicited feedback from stakeholders using a variety of mechanisms, including a public forum held in February 2004. The committee also convened two standard-setting sessions, in July and September 2004, which involved experts in adult literacy, adult education, teaching, and other relevant fields. This report presents the findings and recommendations that resulted from these activities and the committee's deliberations. It is BOTA's hope that this report will be of use to a variety of audiences: the U.S. Department of Education in its final decision making about performance standards for its adult literacy assessments and plans for future assessments; policy makers and practitioners in the adult literacy field as they make programmatic decisions; and the psychological measurement community as they grapple with the complex technical and judgmental issues involved in the task of setting valid performance standards in similar situations.

BOTA extends its sincere appreciation to the committee for its hard work on this challenging project, and particularly to Christopher Edley, Jr., and Robert Hauser, who served as co-chairs.

Lauress L. Wise, *Chair*
Board on Testing and Assessment

Acknowledgments

The work of the Committee on Performance Levels for Adult Literacy benefited tremendously from the contributions of many people, and the committee is grateful for their assistance and support.

First, we wish to acknowledge the National Center for Education Statistics (NCES), which sponsored this project. We think that the leadership of the NCES was wise, both to pursue improvements in standard setting and—as a statistical agency—to choose an impartial external body to establish its reporting standards. The committee thanks Gary Phillips for his willingness to initiate the study and extends its heartfelt thanks to Peggy Carr for her interest in this important topic and her constant support throughout the project. During the course of this project other NCES staff members, including Sheida White and Andrew Kolstad, gave generously of their time. We thank each of them for the wealth of information they provided and their prompt answers to all of the committee's questions.

The American Institutes for Research (AIR) served as contractor to NCES for work on National Assessment of Adult Literacy (NAAL), and many of its staff were generous with both advice and assistance. Mark Kutner was an invaluable resource to the committee, and we are grateful for his responsiveness to all of the committee's requests. We also thank AIR staff members Stephan Baldi, Elizabeth Greenburg, and Eugene Johnson for their ongoing assistance and readiness to answer the committee's questions.

Special thanks are also due to Irwin Kirsch, who led the work on the 1992 National Adult Literacy Survey (NALS) at the Educational Testing Service. Irwin was a tremendous resource to the committee as they worked to reconstruct and understand procedures that had been used to determine the performance levels for the earlier literacy assessment. His fact-checking of report text that documented these processes was a great help to the committee.

Early in its tenure, the committee commissioned a literature review of studies conducted on NALS. We thank M. Cecil Smith of Northern Illinois University for his thorough review of the literature, which provided an important part of the foundation for the committee's work.

The committee held an information-gathering meeting to learn about international assessments of adult literacy, and we are grateful to presenters at this meeting, including Mariann Lemke of the U.S. Department of Education; Scott Murray then of Statistics Canada; and Irwin Kirsch of Educational Testing Service.

At the fourth meeting, the committee convened a public forum. The insights provided by the participants were very useful in helping the committee determine the performance levels. For this, we are grateful to Cynthia Baur, U.S. Department of Health and Human Services; Beth Beuhlmann, U.S. Chamber of Commerce, Workforce Preparation; Richard Colvin, Hechinger Institute; Leslie Farr, Ohio State University; Milton Goldberg, Education Commission of the States; Anne Lewis, freelance journalist; Richard Long, International Reading Association; Christopher Mazzeo, National Governors Association; Gemma Santos, Miami Dade Public Schools; Tony Sarmiento, Senior Service America, Inc.; Linda Taylor, Comprehensive Adult Student Assessment System; and Robert Wedgeworth, Proliteracy Worldwide.

Representatives from five state departments of adult education also provided feedback about performance levels and about how NAAL results would be used in their states. We thank Bob Bickerton, Donna Cornelius, and Ann Serino, Massachusetts Department of Education; Steve Coffman, Missouri Department of Education; Cheryl King and Reecie Stagnolia, Kentucky Department of Education; Tom Orvino, New York Department of Education; and Linda Young, Oklahoma Department of Education.

The committee is indebted to the individuals who assisted with the bookmark standard-setting sessions, held in July and September 2004. We particularly thank Richard J. Patz, of R.J. Patz, Inc., who led the standard-setting procedures. His expertise and guidance were key to the success of the standard settings. We are also grateful to Jeff Hauger and April Zenisky, University of Massachusetts, Amherst, and Andrew Poggio, University of Iowa, who assisted with managing the standard-setting sessions. Their assistance was key in making the sessions run smoothly.

Special thanks are due to the many individuals who served as panelists for the bookmark standard-setting sessions. The committee truly appreciates their hard work and keen insights. The panelists included Eunice Askov,

Pennsylvania State University; Marjorie Ball, Mississippi State Penitentiary; Roxanne Bauer, Indianapolis Public Schools; Michelle Blantz, South Georgia Technical College; Rhodella Brown, Daytona Beach Community College, Florida; Miriam Burt, Center for Applied Linguistics; Laura Chenven, AFL-CIO Working for America Institute; Suzanne Cimochowski, EASTCONN; Marie Cora, Hotspur Partners, LLC; Christopher Coro, Northampton Community College, Pennsylvania; Susan Cowles, Oregon State Department of Community Colleges and Workforce Development; Shari Crockett, Regional Office of Education, Illinois; Lansing Davis, New Jersey State Employment and Training Commission; Kim Donehower, University of North Dakota; Suzanne Elston, Bradley County Adult Education, Tennessee; Leslie Farr, Ohio State University; Sharon Floyd, Saginaw Public Schools; Janet Geary, North Kansas City School District; Karen Gianninoto, Salisbury State University; Kimberly Gibson, Sierra College; Suzanne Grant, Arlington Public Schools, Virginia; Anne Greenwell, Jefferson County Public Schools, Kentucky; Christina Gutierrez, T.C. Williams High School, Virginia; Nancy Hampson, San Diego Community College District; James Harris, Caliber Associates; Roberta Hawkins, Shorewood High School, Washington; Fran Holthaus, Upper Valley Joint Vocational School, Ohio; Sally House, Central Mississippi Correctional Facility; Brenda Jeans, Beauregard Parish School Board, Louisiana; Paul Jurmo, New York University; Judy Kihslinger, Waukesha County Technical College, Wisconsin; Terry Kinzel, Big Bend Community College, Washington; Jaqueline Korengel, Commonwealth of Kentucky; Nathan Kuncel, University of Illinois at Urbana-Champaign; Diane Lindahl, Western Wisconsin Technical College; Ardith Loustalet, St. Vrain Valley School District, Colorado; Alfredo Lujan, Monte del Sol Charter School, New Mexico; Sanford Marks, Community College of Southern Nevada; Peggy McGuire, University of Tennessee; Maureen Meehan, University of Illinois at Chicago; Doug Molitor, 3M; Donald Mott, Wilson Mott & Associates, North Carolina; Vivian Mott, East Carolina University; Bill Muth, U.S. Federal Bureau of Prisons; Connie Nelson, Massachusetts Worker Education Roundtable; Donna Nola-Ganey, Louisiana Department of Education; Peg Perri, Western Wisconsin Technical College; Rebecca Rogers, Washington University, St. Louis; Teresa Russell, independent consultant; Sally Sandy, Parkway School District, Missouri; Kathleen Santopietro Weddel, Colorado Department of Education; Diane Schroeder, St. Charles Community College, Missouri; Don Seaman, Texas Center for the Advancement of Literacy and Learning; Jane Siveria, Florida Department of Education; Cristine Smith, World Education, Inc.; Maggie Sokolik, University of California, Berkeley; Linda Stacy, Owens Community College, Ohio; Linda Taylor, Comprehensive Adult Student Assessment System; Ray Thompson,

Middle Georgia Technical College; Patricia Thorpe, University of Phoenix; Fran Tracy-Mumford, Delaware Department of Education; Karen Valbrun, Georgia State Department of Technical and Adult Education; Denise Weiner, Delaware Department of Education; Lynne Weintraub, Jones Library; Ira Yankwitt, Literacy Assistance Center; and Linda Young, Oklahoma State Department of Education.

Senior staff members of the National Research Council (NRC) helped the committee move this project forward. Michael Feuer enthusiastically backed the project and lent his wisdom and advice at key stages. Patricia Morison provided sage advice throughout this project and made valuable comments on several versions of the report. Eugenia Grohman's knowledge and experience with NRC's procedures and the committee process were of great assistance. We thank Christine McShane for her expert editing assistance and Yvonne Wise for her work in moving this report through the publication process. The committee is indebted to Kirsten Sampson Snyder for ably guiding the report through the NRC review process.

Special thanks are due to Michael DeCarmine for his masterful handling of the logistical aspects of this project. In addition to handling the responsibilities associated with organizing committee meetings, Michael very capably managed the logistics of holding the July standard-setting session with 45 participants. He was also of great assistance to the committee by attending and reporting on his observations of the training sessions for NAAL survey administrators.

We also thank Lisa Alston, who provided support throughout the project. We are grateful to Dorothy Majewski, who assumed responsibility for organizing the second standard-setting session. The committee also appreciates the assistance of Teresia Wilmore and Dionna Williams, who ably stepped in to assist at various stages of the project.

Many other NRC staff contributed to the success of this project. We thank Connie Citro for her wealth of experience with standard setting in other contexts. Connie provided advice throughout the project. The committee sincerely appreciates the analytical assistance provided by Lynne Steuerle Schofield. Lynne's statistical expertise and careful attention to detail contributed greatly to the substance and quality of this report. Lori Houghton Wright played a major role in organizing and managing the standard settings and contributed greatly to their overall success. We also appreciate Lori's assistance in helping to produce this report. We thank Andrew Tompkins for his work in observing and reporting on the training procedures for NAAL interviewers and his shrewd research assistance.

It has been most rewarding for us to work with our coeditors, Judith Koenig and Stuart Elliott. They kept everyone on track, drew wisely on various areas of expertise to create an effective division of labor within the committee, initiated and coordinated contacts with all of the parties to the project, and shouldered the major share of report preparation. We cannot imagine more professional and enjoyable colleagues.

Above all, we thank the committee members for their dedication and outstanding contributions to this study. They drafted text, prepared background materials, reviewed numerous versions of this report, and gave generously of their time throughout the course of this three-year project. Both of us are novices in comparison to any of them in matters relating to adult education, adult literacy, and the measurement of literacy. Their varied expertise—and their patience with us—were essential to the report and to our growing appreciation of the importance and complexity of these matters.

This report has been reviewed in draft form by individuals chosen for their diverse perspectives and technical expertise, in accordance with procedures approved by the NRC's Report Review Committee. The purpose of this independent review is to provide candid and critical comments that will assist the institution in making its published report as sound as possible and to ensure that the report meets institutional standards for objectivity, evidence, and responsiveness to the study charge. The review comments and draft manuscript remain confidential to protect the integrity of the deliberative process.

We wish to thank the following individuals for their review of this report: Terry C. Davis, Department of Medicine and Pediatrics, Louisiana State University Health Sciences Center-Shreveport; Reynaldo F. Macias, Department of Chicana and Chicano Studies and the César E. Chávez Center for Interdisciplinary Instruction, University of California, Los Angeles; Mark D. Reckase, Departments of Counseling, Educational Psychology, and Special Education, Michigan State University; Stephen Reder, Department of Applied Linguistics, Portland State University; Loretta A. Shepard, School of Education, University of Colorado at Boulder; Sondra G. Stein, Policy Oversight, Equipped for the Future (EFF) Work Readiness Credential, Washington, DC; Sandy Strunk, Community Education, Lancaster Lebanon Intermediate Unit 13, East Petersburg, PA; Andrew Sum, Center for Labor Market Studies, Northeastern University; Daniel Wagner, National Center on Adult Literacy/International Literacy Institute University of Pennsylvania; Lauress (Laurie) Wise, President's Office, Human Resources Research Organization (HumRRO), Alexandria, VA.

Although the reviewers listed above have provided many constructive comments and suggestions, they were not asked to endorse the conclusions or recommendations nor did they see the final draft of the report before its release. The review of this report was overseen by P. David Pearson, Graduate School of Education, University of California, Berkeley, and Stephen E. Fienberg, Department of Statistics, Carnegie Mellon University. Appointed by the NRC, they were responsible for making certain that an independent examination of this report was carried out in accordance with institutional procedures and that all review comments were carefully considered. Responsibility for the final content of this report rests entirely with the authoring committee and the institution.

Christopher F. Edley, Jr., and Robert M. Hauser, *Co-Chairs*
Committee on Performance Levels for Adult Literacy

Contents

Executive Summary

In today's society, literacy is an essential skill, one that helps people thrive individually, socially, and economically. Literacy is important for all aspects of life, from handling personal affairs, to engaging in the workforce, to participating in a democratic society. Literacy skills are critical both for individuals' functioning and for a well-functioning society. Literacy has an impact on a nation's economic status, the well-being of its citizens, the capabilities of its workforce, and its ability to compete in a global society. Deficiencies in literacy and mismatches between the skills of citizens and the needs of an economy can have serious repercussions.

Policy makers rely on assessments of literacy to evaluate both the extent of such mismatches and the need for services that provide basic literacy skills to adults. Such assessments can provide the foundation and impetus for policy interventions. The National Adult Literacy Survey (NALS) was designed to provide such information.

NALS was a household survey of a nationally representative sample of 26,000 adults age 16 and older conducted by the U.S. Department of Education in 1992. It built on two prior literacy assessments that were more limited in scope, the 1985 Young Adult Literacy Survey of 21- to 28-year-olds and a national survey of job seekers in 1990.

The 1992 assessment was designed to assess adults' ability to apply their literacy skills to everyday materials and tasks. NALS measured three dimensions of functional literacy using a wide array of tasks and materials encountered in daily life. Prose literacy measured skill in understanding information presented in continuous texts (e.g., a newspaper article). Document literacy reflected skill in using information presented in graphs, figures, and tables (e.g., a bus schedule). Quantitative literacy assessed skill with using arithmetic operations on numbers presented in scenarios, texts, or documents (e.g., a product advertisement). Performance on NALS reflected both the difficulty of the tasks and the complexity of the materials.

To provide information that could more easily be understood and used by policy makers and the public, the test designers grouped scores on NALS into five performance levels. Brief descriptions of the levels were provided and the percentage of adults whose scores fell into each performance level was reported along with summary measures of the scores.

A decade later, the Department of Education implemented plans for a successor to NALS, called the National Assessment of Adult Literacy (NAAL), conducted in 2003. NAAL was designed to produce some new information while retaining enough consistency with the 1992 assessment to evaluate trends over the ensuing decade. NAAL includes additional health related materials intended to yield a measure of health literacy in addition to scores in prose, document, and quantitative literacy. Two other components were added to increase the information gathered about adults with low-level English literacy skills: the Fluency Addition and the Adult Literacy Supplemental Assessment (ALSA). In preparation for release of NAAL results, the Department sought advice from the National Research Council's Board on Testing and Assessment about developing performance levels for the assessment.

PROBLEM STATEMENT

NALS was intended to describe the range of English literacy skills of adults in the United States. The performance levels used to report the 1992 results were designed as a means for communicating about adults' literacy skills, but they were not meant to reflect policy-based judgments about expectations for adult literacy. That is, the procedures used to develop the assessment did not involve identifying the level of skills adults need in order to function adequately in society. When findings from the 1992 survey were released, however, the performance levels were interpreted and discussed as if they represented standards for the level of literacy adults should have. The lowest two levels were referred to as inadequate, so low that adults with these skills would be unable to hold a well-paying job. The results of the assessment and these sorts of unsupported inferences about the results provoked widespread controversy in the media and among experts in adult literacy about the extent of literacy problems in the country.

In response to the department's request for advice, the Committee on Performance Levels for Adult Literacy was established and charged to:

• Review and evaluate the procedures for determining the performance levels for the 1992 National Adult Literacy Survey and

• Recommend a set of performance levels for the 2003 National Assessment of Adult Literacy that are valid, appropriate, and permit comparisons between the 1992 and the 2003 results.

Through a process detailed below, the committee has determined that five performance levels should be used to characterize the status of English language literacy in the United States: nonliterate in English, below basic literacy, basic literacy, intermediate literacy, and advanced literacy.

DETERMINING THE 1992 PERFORMANCE LEVELS AND CUT SCORES

The process for determining the 1992 performance levels is described in the technical manual for NALS. The test designers developed a process for determining the levels that drew on analyses conducted with the earlier literacy assessments. The process involved making judgments about features of the test questions that contributed to their complexity (e.g., the amount of distracting information) and rating the items according to these features. The questions were rank-ordered from least to most difficult according to a statistical estimate of each question's difficulty. The listing of questions was visually inspected for natural break points in the complexity ratings. Four break points were identified and converted to scale scores that became the cut scores used to separate the five performance levels. Narrative descriptions characterized the cognitive complexity of the items constituting each level.

The statistical estimate of each question's difficulty used to rank-order the questions was calculated to represent a certain chance of responding correctly. In the language of test design, this chance is called a "response probability." The choice of a specific response probability value is an important decision because it affects the value of the cut scores used to separate the performance levels: the cut scores could be higher or lower simply as a consequence of the response probability selected. In 1992, the test designers chose to use a response probability of 80 percent for NALS. This decision has been the subject of debate, largely centering on whether it led to overly high cut scores, thus underestimating the literacy of adults in the United States.

Like many decisions made in connection with developing a test, the choice of a response probability value requires both technical and nontechnical considerations. The decision should be based on the level of confidence one wants to have that examinees have truly mastered the content and skills assessed, but it should also reflect the objectives for the test, the ways the test results are used, and the consequences associated with these uses. Choice of a response probability value requires making a judgment, and reasonable people may disagree about which of several options is most appropriate.

Committee's Evaluation

Some of the more important details about the process for determining the 1992 performance levels were not specified in the NALS technical manual, such as who participated in producing the complexity ratings and exactly how decisions were made about the break points. Although the test designers appear to have selected a response probability of 80 percent to represent the concept of mastery, as is sometimes used in the field of education, the reasons for this choice were not fully documented in the technical manual. It is therefore difficult to fully understand the process and how it was carried out.

It is our opinion that a more open and public process combined with more explicit documentation would lead to better understanding of how the performance levels were determined and what inferences could be based on them. An open process would be in line with currently accepted guidelines for educational and psychological testing.

There is a broad literature on procedures for developing performance levels and setting cut scores. This literature documents the methods and ways to systematize the process of setting cut scores. Use of established procedures for setting cut scores allows one to draw from the existing research and experiential base and facilitates communication with others about the general process. We therefore decided to pursue use of these methods in our process for determining performance levels and cut scores.

DEVELOPING NEW PERFORMANCE LEVELS

Based on our review of the procedures used for determining the 1992 performance levels, we decided to embark on a systematic process to determine a new set of performance levels. We established as overriding principles that the process should model exemplary practices, be conducted in an open and public way, and be explained in a manner that permits replication and invites constructive criticism. Our range of options for new performance levels was substantially narrowed, however, by prior decisions about test development, the scope of content and skills to be covered, and the background information gathered from assessment participants.

Typically, when the objective of a test is to report results according to performance levels, the desired performance categories are articulated early in the development phase and serve as the foundation for test development. With the number of levels and their descriptions laid out in advance, development efforts can focus on constructing items that measure the skills described by the levels and in sufficient number to provide reliable results, particularly at the boundaries between performance levels.

Determining performance levels after the test development process is complete does not represent exemplary practice. Furthermore, because the assessment was not designed to provide information about what adults need to function adequately in society, there was no way for us to develop performance levels that would support such inferences. Nevertheless, we agreed to assist with the challenging problems of communicating about adults' literacy skills and improving understanding of the findings. We sought to determine performance levels that would describe adults' literacy skills and be relevant to public policy on adult literacy.

The decision to design a new set of performance levels meant that the committee needed to address questions related to the number of levels, the cut scores for the levels, and whether separate performance-level descriptions should be developed for each of the three literacy scales. Feedback from stakeholders suggested they seek answers to four policy-related questions. They want to know what percentage of adults in the United States:

• Have very low literacy skills and are in need of basic adult literacy services, including services for adult English language learners.
• Are ready for GED (general educational development) preparation services.
• Qualify for a high school diploma.
• Have attained a sufficient level of English literacy that they can be successful in postsecondary education and gain entry into professional, managerial, or technical occupations.

The committee's process for determining the performance-level descriptions involved a combination of data analyses, stakeholder feedback, and review of the test specifications and actual test questions. Our analytic work revealed very high correlations among the three literacy scales, which suggested that a single literacy score combining the three scales would be sufficient for reporting the assessment results. Stakeholder feedback indicated that the three literacy scores provide information that is useful for other purposes. We therefore developed performance-level descriptions that include both an overall description for each level as well as descriptions specific to the prose, document, and quantitative literacy scales.

Based on our information-gathering activities and analytic work, we recommend the use of five performance levels that correspond to the policy-related questions identified by stakeholders.[1] We remind the reader that these performance levels are not intended to represent standards for what is required to perform adequately in society because the assessments were not developed to support such inferences.

RECOMMENDATION 4-1: The 2003 NAAL results should be reported using five performance levels for each of the three types of English literacy: Nonliterate in English, below basic literacy, basic literacy, intermediate literacy, and advanced literacy.

A brief description of each level appears below:

> **Nonliterate in English:** may recognize some letters, numbers, or common sight words in everyday contexts.
>
> **Below Basic Literacy:** may sometimes be able to locate and use simple words, phrases, and numbers in everyday contexts and perform simple one-step arithmetic operations.
>
> **Basic Literacy:** is able to read simple words, phrases, and numbers in everyday contexts when the information is easily located and able to solve one-step problems.
>
> **Intermediate Literacy:** is able to read and use written materials to locate information in denser, less commonplace texts, summarize information, draw simple inferences, and make use of quantitative information when the arithmetic operation is not easily inferred.
>
> **Advanced Literacy:** is able to read and use more complex written material to integrate multiple pieces of information, perform analytical tasks, draw more sophisticated inferences, and make use of quantitative information when more complex relationships are involved.

Each performance level was intended to correspond to one of the policy-related questions suggested by stakeholders, with the exception that the two lowest levels both address the first question. The reason for this is attributable to differences between the 1992 and 2003 assessments. Because a significant number of 1992 participants were unable to complete any of the NALS questions, the supplemental ALSA was added in 2003 as a separate low-level component. A set of screening questions was used to determine which component, ALSA or NAAL, participants should take; the nonliterate in English category encompasses those who were assigned to take ALSA. This screening procedure was not used in 1992, however, so no one from the earlier assessment can be classified into the nonliterate in English category. Thus, the nonliterate in English and below basic catego-

---

[1]Recommendation numbers refer to the report chapter in which they are made and the sequence in which they appear in the chapter.

ries will need to be combined to permit comparisons between NAAL and NALS.

In identifying these levels, we were conscious of the fact that one of the audiences for NAAL results will be adult education programs, which are for the most part guided legislatively by the Workforce Investment Act of 1998, Title II, Adult Education and Family Literacy Act. This act mandates the National Reporting System (NRS), which specifies a set of education functioning levels used in tracking progress of adult education program enrollees. Although it was not possible to establish a one-to-one correspondence between the NAAL and NRS levels, there appears to be a rough parallel between nonliterate in English and the NRS beginning literacy level; between below basic and the NRS beginning basic and low intermediate levels; and between basic and the NRS high intermediate level.

Setting Cut Scores

The literature on setting achievement levels documents the strengths and weaknesses of various methods of setting cut scores. A review of these critiques quickly reveals that there are no perfect methods. Like the cut score-setting process itself, choice of a procedure requires making an informed judgment about the most appropriate method for a given assessment situation. Based on our review, we decided to use the bookmark standard-setting method and to evaluate the reasonableness of the resulting cut scores by comparing them with data from the assessment's background questionnaire. We held two bookmark standard-setting sessions, in July 2004 to examine the NALS data and in September 2004 using the NAAL data.

Given the public debate about the response probability value chosen for NALS, we decided to examine the impact of three commonly used response probability values (50, 67, and 80 percent) on the July bookmark standard-setting process. Analyses of the results from the July standard setting revealed that use of different response probability values produced different cut scores. The committee considered this finding, along with feedback from panelists, as well as other factors (e.g., the uses of the assessment results) to inform their choice of response probability values for the September standard setting. Panelist feedback about applying a probability level of 50 percent tended to be negative, which contributed to our view that it was not a viable option. The committee judged that a probability level of 80 percent was overly stringent given the uses of the assessment results. We therefore decided that the September bookmark panelists should use a moderate response probability level of 67 percent, the value generally recommended in the literature by the developers of the bookmark procedure. This is not to suggest that a response probability of 67 percent would be appropriate for all situations in which cut scores must be set. We acknowledge that some stakeholders for the present assessment, such as those in the health field, would argue for a response probability of 80 percent to reflect the critical importance of correctly using health-related materials to accomplish health tasks.

We examined the cut scores that emerged from the bookmark procedures in relation to relevant background information and made slight adjustments. We make the following recommendation with regard to the cut scores for the performance levels:

RECOMMENDATION 5-1: The scale-score intervals associated with each of the levels should be as shown below for the prose, document, and quantitative dimensions of literacy.

	Nonliterate in English	Below Basic	Basic	Intermediate	Advanced
Prose:	Took ALSA	0-209	210-264	265-339	340-500
Document:	Took ALSA	0-204	205-249	250-334	335-500
Quantitative:	Took ALSA	0-234	235-289	290-349	350-500

We note that although these scale-score intervals reflect extensive data collection, statistical analysis, and informed judgment, their precision should not be overemphasized. If another standard setting was held with different panelists, it is likely that the cut scores would vary to some extent.

Initially, the committee hoped to set cut scores for an overall score that combined the three literacy areas. This was not possible, however, because the statistical procedures used to estimate each question's difficulty level were not run in a way that would allow the combination of questions from the different literacy areas. Thus, although we provide a set of overall performance levels that combine the descriptions for each literacy area, cut scores could not be set on an overall scale.

We note that there are significant problems at both the lower and upper ends of the literacy scale. At the lower end of the scale, the problems relate to the test designers' decision to develop ALSA as a separate component and to not place ALSA and NAAL scores on the same scale. With regard to the upper end of the scale, feedback from the bookmark panelists, combined with our review of the items, suggests that the assessment does not adequately cover the upper end of the distribution of literacy skills. We note that there is growing public concern about readiness for college-level work and preparedness for entry into technical and professional occupations, but

NAAL, as currently designed, will not allow for detection of problems at that level. It is therefore with some reservations that we include the advanced category in our recommendation for performance levels, and we leave it to the Department of Education to ultimately decide on the utility and meaning of this category.

With regard to these issues, we recommend:

RECOMMENDATION 5-2: Future development of NAAL should include more comprehensive coverage at the lower and upper ends of the continuum of literacy skills. At the lower end, the assessment should include evaluation of the extent to which individuals are able to recognize letters and numbers and read words and simple sentences, to allow determination of which individuals have the basic foundation skills in literacy and which individuals do not. This assessment should be part of NAAL and should yield information used in calculating scores for each of the literacy areas. At the upper end of the continuum of literacy skills, future development should include assessment items necessary to identify the extent to which policy interventions are needed at the postsecondary level and above.

OTHER ISSUES

Communicating Survey Results

Experience with the initial release and subsequent media coverage of the 1992 NALS results highlighted the critical importance of clearly communicating assessment results so they are interpreted correctly and are useful to the various audiences concerned about adult literacy in the United States. The substantive challenge will be to convey the message that literacy is not a unidimensional concept or an all-or-nothing state. That message will be most understandable and useful to the public and policy makers if it is anchored in the competencies and life circumstances associated with each performance level and each of the three literacy areas.

We therefore encourage the Department of Education to present the NAAL results with implications of their relevance for different contexts in which adults function, such as employment and the workplace, health and safety, home and family, community and citizenship, consumer economics, and leisure and recreation as well as the different aspects of life affected by literacy.

In addition, the department should prepare different versions of the performance-level descriptions that are tailored to meet the needs of various audiences. Simple descriptions of the performance levels should be prepared for general audiences to enhance public understanding. More detailed descriptions should be developed to be responsive to the needs of other users. The report includes several versions of performance-level descriptions that could serve as a starting place for such efforts.

Policy Interventions for Low-Literate Adults

With the development of ALSA in 2003, specific attention was focused on the skills of low-literate adults, and one would expect that many services will be directed at the needs of this group. The nonliterate in English and below basic categories are likely to be heterogeneous, encompassing English speakers who have weak literacy skills, non-English speakers who are highly literate in their native languages but not in English, and non-English speakers who are not literate in any language. Distinctly different services and strategies will be needed for these groups.

Reports of the percentages of adults in the nonliterate in English and below basic categories should distinguish among native English speakers and non-English speakers. This will allow for more appropriate conclusions to be drawn about the extent of literacy problems among native English-speaking adults and the share of adults in the United States who are still learning English and therefore cannot handle literacy tasks in English.

Exemplifying the Performance Levels

Presentations of the 1992 results included samples of released NALS items that illustrated the skills represented by each of the performance levels. Items were used to exemplify (or were "mapped" to) the performance level at which there was an 80 percent probability of an examinee's responding correctly. Mapping procedures are useful for communicating about test performance, but we suggest that the department carefully consider the ways in which released items are used to illustrate the skills represented by the performance levels. The simplest displays should avoid the use of response probabilities and just indicate the proportion of people in a given level who can do the item. If the department decides to use an item-mapping procedure, we suggest that presentations include more than one response probability for each item (e.g., 80 and 60 percent) and encourage use of displays that emphasize that individuals at every score point and each performance level have some probability of responding correctly to each item. This will stimulate understanding of the strengths and weaknesses of those scoring at each level.

Developing a Dissemination Strategy

To ensure that an accurate, nuanced message is effectively conveyed, the department should consider a variety of dissemination strategies beyond publication of the results, press releases, and news conferences. This should include information on the type of literacy that is assessed and recognition that many of the individuals who score in the lowest levels are English learners. We encourage the department to enlist the services of communication professionals to develop materials that present a clear and accurate message; to pilot test the interpretation of those materials with focus groups; and to revise them as appropriate before release. A briefing strategy should be developed that includes prebriefings for department policy makers and congressional staff. These groups should be briefed in detail on the supportable inferences from the findings before the official release of NAAL results.

Future Literacy Assessments

The committee understands that there are currently no plans to conduct a follow-up to NAAL. In our judgment, ongoing assessment of the literacy skills of this nation's adults is important, and planning for a follow-up to NAAL should begin now. In an effort to be forward looking, we offer several suggestions for ways to improve the assessment instrument and expand on the literacy skills assessed.

Demand-Side Analysis of Critical Skills

It is clear from the conclusions drawn about the 1992 results that stakeholders expected the findings to inform them about the percentages of adults whose literacy skills were adequate to function well in society. Although NALS was not designed for this purpose, an assessment could be designed to support interpretations about the skills adults need and should have. Many testing programs, such as those used to make credentialing decisions, begin the development process by gathering information from experts in the specific fields about the skills and capabilities essential to successful performance. NALS and NAAL currently draw items from six contexts of daily life. An alternate approach to test development would analyze the literacy demands in each context and identify the essential proficiencies. The standard-setting process could then articulate the level of skills required to adequately function in the six areas. Each new version of NAAL should update the items to reflect current literacy requirements and expectations in each context but also retain some time-invariant items to allow for trend analysis.

We therefore suggest that the department work with relevant domain-specific experts, stakeholders, and practitioners to identify the critical literacy demands in at least six contexts: work, health and safety, community and citizenship, home and family, consumer economics, and leisure and recreation. Future generations of NAAL should be designed to measure these critical skills and should be developed from the outset to support standards-based inferences about the extent to which adults are able to perform these critical skills.

Feedback from experts in each of the contexts could also be used to expand the information collected on the background questionnaire, following the procedures used to design additional questions about individuals' health and safety habits on the 2003 background questionnaire. Similar procedures could be used to link demand-side analyses with the construction of the background questionnaire items for each context. This approach would also facilitate the validation of performance standards.

Broadening the Scope of Coverage

Several decisions made during the design of NAAL served to narrow its focus and the type of information obtained. In our view, future generations of NAAL could be broadened in terms of content coverage and sampling procedures.

Quantitative literacy, as conceived for NALS and NAAL, evaluates relatively basic arithmetic skills but commingles evaluation of mathematics skills with reading and locating information in texts. Other adult literacy assessments (e.g., the Adult Literacy and Lifeskills Survey) have moved to include a more mathematically based numeracy component. Neither NALS nor NAAL was meant to be a formal test of mathematical proficiency in higher level domains, and we are not suggesting that this should be the case. We think, however, that the mathematical demands of a technological society require more than a basic grasp of whole numbers and money as reflected in NAAL.

The department should consider revising the quantitative literacy component on future assessments of adult literacy to include a numeracy component assessed as a separate construct, less tied to prose or document literacy but still reflective of the types of tasks encountered by adults in everyday life situations. The numeracy skills to include on the assessment should be identified as part of an analysis of critical literacy demands in six content areas. The types of numeracy skills assessed on the Adult Literacy and Lifeskills Survey could serve as a starting place for identifying critical skills.

Currently NAAL collects background information only from those who speak sufficient English or Spanish to understand and respond to the screening and background questions. No information is collected about those who do not speak English or Spanish, unless an interpreter happens to be present at the time of the assessment, and even then the information collected is only about age, ethnicity, and gender. We recognize that NAAL is intended to be an assessment of English literacy skills and that assessing competence in other languages is not the goal. Nevertheless, it is important to paint a nuanced picture of the skills and backgrounds of the entire population. If background questions were asked in a language newcomers could understand, the range of information obtained would be much broader, and policy makers would gain a more accurate picture of the literacy needs in this country.

The department should seek to expand the information obtained about non-English speakers in future assessments of adult literacy, including background information about formal education, training and work experience here and abroad, and self-reports about the use of print materials in languages other than English. Efforts should also be made to be more structured in collecting background information about individuals who speak languages other than English and Spanish and to better address the challenges of translation.

For NALS and NAAL, literacy has been construed in a specific way. The concept of literacy changes over time, however, as expectations for knowledge and skill levels increase, and it changes with the advent of new mediating technologies. We suggest that the definition of literacy be reconsidered and possibly broadened for future assessments of adults' literacy skills. Issues that should be considered in developing the definition include assessment of writing and composition skills; assessment of technology mediated literacy skills; and the role of computers, the Internet, and technology in evaluating literacy skills.

CONCLUSION

The committee has suggested some far-reaching recommendations for future literacy assessments. Most notably, we recommend an alternative approach to test development, one that considers the tasks of daily living to identify the critical literacy demands that will guide development of the item pool. This approach could change the nature of the assessment, the test administration processes, and the meaning of the results. We recognize that such extensive modifications of the assessment would make it difficult to measure trends in adult literacy, which is also an important goal. These competing goals must be carefully weighed in the design of future assessments. Regardless of whether any of the proposed changes are implemented, the committee recommends that, in the future, the process of developing the performance levels be carried out concurrently with the process of designing the assessment and constructing the items.

1

Introduction

In 1992, the U.S. Department of Education sponsored the first nation-wide assessment of adults' English literacy skills. This assessment, called the National Adult Literacy Survey (NALS), was a household survey of a nationally representative sample of 26,000 adults aged 16 years and older. A decade later, the Department of Education implemented plans to revise and readminister the assessment. The revised assessment, renamed the National Assessment of Adult Literacy (NAAL), was designed to produce some new information while retaining enough consistency to allow comparisons with the 1992 results to evaluate trends in adults' literacy skills over the ensuing decade. The department requested that the National Research Council (NRC) provide advice about creating performance levels for reporting the assessment results. This report details the work and findings of the Committee on Performance Levels for Adult Literacy. In this chapter, we first provide a description of the problem and then lay out the context for the committee's work and its approach to its charge.

PROBLEM STATEMENT

NALS measured literacy skills using a wide array of tasks that reflected the types of materials and demands that adults encounter in their daily lives. The assessment measured three types of literacy: (1) prose literacy was a measure of skill in using information presented in textual formats (e.g., a newspaper article); (2) document literacy reflected skill in using information presented in graphs, figures, and tables (e.g., a bus schedule); (3) and quantitative literacy measured skill with using and performing arithmetic operations on numbers presented in texts or documents (e.g., in a bar graph).

NALS was intended to profile and describe the English literacy skills of adults in the United States. It was not designed, however, to indicate whether or not any particular level of skills was adequate. That is, the test development process did not involve identifying the level of skills adults need in order to function adequately in society. Thus, it was not intended to support inferences about what constitutes an adequate level of literacy.

To provide information that could be more easily understood and used by policy makers and the public, the test designers grouped scores into five categories, or performance levels (called NALS Level 1, NALS Level 2, NALS Level 3, etc.). Brief descriptions of the levels were provided, and the results were reported by scores as well as by the percentage of those surveyed whose scores fell into each performance level.

The performance levels used for reporting NALS results were intended simply to describe adults' literacy skills, not to suggest a level of performance that could be regarded as sufficient to function in society. When findings from the 1992 survey were released, however, many unsupported inferences were made about the results. The five performance levels were interpreted and discussed by policy makers, the media, and the public as if they represented standards for the level of literacy that adults should have. Some, for example, referred to the lowest two levels as "inadequate," so low that adults with these skills would be unable to hold a well-paying job (Gray, 1993; Kaplan, 1993). As many as 47 percent of adults in the United States, or about 90 million people, fell into these bottom two levels. In his September 8, 1993, press release, Secretary of Education Richard W. Riley stated that "the vast majority of Americans . . . do not have the skills they need to earn a living in our increasingly technological society," which led to such headlines as "Literacy of 90 Million is Deficient" (Jordan, 1993). The results of the assessment and these unsupported conclusions about the results provoked widespread controversy in the media and among experts on adult literacy about the extent of literacy problems in the country.

According to the assessment designers, however, NALS was not intended to provide firm answers to questions about the literacy skills essential for individuals to succeed in society. The procedures for designing the test did not involve identifying what adults need to know and be able to do to adequately function in society and to obtain a well-paying job. The performance levels were designed to demonstrate the range of literacy demands placed on adults as part of their daily lives but not to shed light on the types of literacy demands associated with particular contexts of life. For example, the performance levels were not intended to support conclusions about the specific levels of English literacy required to obtain, remain, or advance in a particular occupation, to manage a household, or to obtain legal or community services (Kirsch et al., 1993). In addition, the process for determining the performance levels did not involve procedures typically used for setting standards. Thus, although policy makers and the press interpreted NALS performance levels as if they represented standards for what adults should know and be able to do, these sorts of interpretations are not aligned with the purpose of the assessment.

In preparation for the release of the 2003 results, the Department of Education decided to focus specific attention on how NAAL results should be reported and interpreted. The department sought advice from the NRC and requested that its Board on Testing and Assessment (BOTA) recommend performance levels to use in reporting NAAL results. The Committee on Performance Levels for Adult Literacy was established to provide this advice. The committee included individuals with a broad array of expertise, including adult education, educational measurement and standard setting, English for speakers of other languages, literacy and literacy measurement, psychology, political science, public health, sociology, statistics, and survey methodology. The committee was charged to:

- Review and evaluate the processes and procedures used for determining the performance levels for the 1992 NALS and
- Recommend a set of performance levels for the 2003 NAAL that are valid and appropriate and permit comparisons between the 1992 and 2003 results.

In this report, we use several terms that need to be defined:

Performance level: a range of test scores that reflect similar levels of knowledge, skills, and capabilities as measured on a test.
Performance-level description: the description of the knowledge, skills, and capabilities test takers need to demonstrate in order to be classified into a specific performance level.
Cut score: the score that separates one performance level from another performance level.
Standard setting: the procedures used to determine the cut scores. Many standard-setting methods rely on judgments made by a set of panelists selected for their expertise in subject areas evaluated on the test; they use established systematic procedures for collecting these judgments. Other methods make use of statistical information describing discrimination based on the test scores between existing externally defined groups (e.g., *masters* and *nonmasters*).

In addition, there are a number of agencies involved in this work:

• National Center for Education Statistics (NCES): the statistical agency of the U.S. Department of Education that provided oversight for NALS and NAAL.

• Educational Testing Service (ETS): one of the contractors to NCES that assisted with work on NALS.

• American Institutes for Research (AIR): one of the contractors to NCES that assisted with work on NAAL.

• Westat: one of the contractors to NCES that assisted with work on both NALS and NAAL.

• NRC: the organization that NCES requested to recommend performance levels for NAAL.

• BOTA: the NRC board that provided oversight for the Committee on Performance Levels in Adult Literacy.

OVERARCHING GOALS

When BOTA agreed to take on this project, it set an overarching goal for the committee's work: to demonstrate a process for determining performance levels and the associated cut scores that represents exemplary practice. The board provided oversight for the committee's work and encouraged the committee to approach the process in an open manner that would enhance public understanding of the results and to use a scientifically informed process that would result in performance levels that are valid and defensible.

Throughout its work, the committee sought to model exemplary practices. However, as with much in the assessment field, one must always strike a balance between idealistic goals and practical constraints. For any testing program, practical and resource considerations limit efforts to strive for the ideal. For the committee, the challenge was to design a process for developing performance levels retroactively.

To explain, the committee's work began late in 2002, just before the actual data collection for NAAL was scheduled to begin. By that time, most of the decisions about NAAL had already been made. This placed certain limitations on our work and substantially narrowed the range of options available to us as we tried to develop new performance levels. For example, when we began our work, development of the tasks that make up the literacy assessment was finished, and the background questionnaire administered in conjunction with NAAL had already been finalized. This meant that our choices about new performance levels were limited due to prior decisions about test development, the scope of the content and skills to be covered, and the range of difficulty of the items included on the assessment. In addition, any analyses we chose to conduct to evaluate the relationships between new performance levels and background characteristics (i.e., to appraise the reasonableness and validity of the cut scores associated with the performance levels) were restricted by predetermined choices about the questions included on the background questionnaire.

Developing performance levels retroactively, as the time constraints on the committee required, clearly is not best assessment practice. Despite our reservations, we accepted the charge to assist the Department of Education with the challenging problem of communicating about adults' literacy skills and improving understanding and interpretation of NAAL findings.

LIMITATIONS ON INFERENCES ABOUT LITERACY SKILLS

Prior decisions during the test development phase and the process of developing administrative procedures also affect the inferences that can be based on NALS and NAAL results, regardless of the performance levels used for reporting. The first limitation is posed by the definition of literacy that guided test development. As has long been recognized by researchers and practitioners in the field of literacy studies, literacy can be defined in a variety of ways. In recognition of the understanding that literacy is not a unitary construct, it has become customary in the field to speak of "multiple literacies" rather than "literacy" (see Wagner, 2004, for further discussion of this issue). It follows, then, that any assessment will be able to test some types of literacy but not others.

The version of literacy that is tested through NAAL is based on an information-processing view of reading and cognition. Therefore, the difficulty of test items is varied along such parameters as the density of information and the complexity of the text structure, factors that would affect the ease or difficulty of reading. For example, if the information required to answer a question about a paragraph is found in the first sentence of that paragraph, the literacy task is presumed to be easier than if a person is required to read further or to sort through distracting information. This information-processing view of what makes reading easy or difficult, or more or less complex, shaped what the test is able to measure. There are other theoretical understandings of literacy—for example, the view of reading as a process of constructing meaning in interaction with a text rather than just extracting meaning from a text. It is important to recognize that the particular theoretical stance that underpins NAAL will have implications for the development and analysis of test items.

Furthermore, the NAAL items were designed to measure literacy according to an information-processing model for a distinct set of purposes— for what might be called "functional" literacy or the everyday kinds of tasks that people may encounter in the course of their daily lives. Such tasks may include reading a bus schedule, deciphering an advertisement, or filling out a form. These are valuable and necessary types of literacy, but they exclude other purposes for literacy, such as reading literature for pleasure, engaging in literacy-related activities for religious purposes, or studying lengthy and complex texts in order to acquire new knowledge. Nor does NAAL ask respondents, in the context of functional literacy, to do very much writing. Many everyday literacy tasks do not, in fact, require as much writing as reading. Still, literacy has come to include, in many popular as well as academic usages, the production of text rather than only the reception of it. This understanding of literacy is not captured by NAAL.

Finally, it is important to remember that although the test simulates materials and activities that adults may encounter in their daily lives, it does not capture how they may actually engage with those materials in a real-world setting. A good example of this distinction is that NAAL requires participants to work alone, without help or assistance, whereas adults in real life can engage in literacy tasks jointly or in collaboration. Investigating how adults engage with literacy in everyday life would require different research methods.

Another limitation posed by the definition of literacy that guided test development has to do with the now ubiquitous presence of computers and information technology in the lives of most adults and children and the impact of these on literacy. NAAL is a paper-and-pencil test and therefore not designed to assess adults' performance on computer-mediated literacy tasks. This means, for example, that the kinds of reading required to navigate the Internet or interact with hypertextual or hypermedia reading and writing environments are not represented.

Moreover, the assessment measures only English literacy skills. Neither NALS nor NAAL was designed to yield information about individuals who are not literate in English but who are fully literate in another language. Literacy is not language specific, however, and English literacy is not the only literacy that matters. At the United States-Mexico border, for example, as well as in cities with a high percentage of immigrants (e.g., San Francisco, Los Angeles, Chicago, New York, Seattle, Miami), biliteracy, the ability to read and write in two languages, affords a number of social and economic benefits. In terms of the job opportunities available to them, individuals in California and Texas who are monolingual in English or in another language are at a distinct disadvantage compared with bilingual adults. When literacy assessments test only literacy in English, they ignore the literacy skills of immigrants and refugees who are able to read and write in their native language, skills that should be considered when a nation with the diversity of the United States paints a picture of the literacy abilities of its citizens.

COMMITTEE'S APPROACH TO THE CHARGE

The committee began its work with a review of empirical studies on the relationships between NALS literacy scores and data collected via the background questionnaire (see Smith, 2003). A draft of this paper was ready prior to the committee's first meeting and served as the starting place for much of our subsequent work.

Between December 2002 and October 2004, the committee held six full committee meetings. The first three meetings focused on gathering information about NALS and NAAL: how literacy is defined for the two assessments and the tasks used to measure these skills, how the performance levels were determined for NALS, who is included in the sample of respondents, how the assessment is administered, and what sorts of data are collected on the background questionnaire administered in conjunction with the assessment. The contractor responsible for identifying the sample, collecting the data, and determining the sampling weights for both assessments was Westat. The contractor responsible for developing the test and analyzing and reporting the results was the ETS in 1992 and the AIR in 2003. Our information gathering included a review of available written documentation about the 1992 procedures (primarily from Campbell, Kirsch, and Kolstad, 1992; Kirsch et al., 1993; Kirsch, Jungeblut, and Mosenthal, 2001) as well as conversations with those who worked on the 1992 NALS and the 2003 NAAL.

After the second meeting, the committee prepared and issued a letter report to address three areas of concern, two related to initial screening procedures for determining survey participants and whether they would take the low-level Adult Literacy Supplemental Assessment or not, and the other related to sampling procedures. The letter report can be found at http://www.nap.edu/catalog/10762.html.

To enhance our understanding of the assessment, the committee arranged to observe the training for NAAL interviewers, the individuals who would be visiting households to collect data. In addition, several committee members accompanied NAAL interviewers to sampled households to observe the actual administration of the assessment. The committee also gathered information about how literacy is defined for international assessments and about how policy strategies are implemented in other countries.

The committee's fourth meeting in February 2004 included a public forum to hear from stakeholders regarding the ways in which NALS results are used, the ways stakeholders anticipate using NAAL results, and the types of information that stakeholders would like to see included in reports of NAAL results. At this meeting, the committee provided samples of performance levels and their descriptions and asked for stakeholders' reactions. They also solicited feedback from directors of adult education in states that had subsidized additional sampling during the NAAL data collection process in order to obtain state-level NAAL results. The list of the stakeholders who were contacted and who participated in the committee's activities appears in Appendix A.

The committee also sponsored two standard-setting sessions, one with the 1992 data and test questions and one with the 2003 data and test questions, to obtain judgments about cut scores for new performance levels and to receive additional feedback about performance-level descriptions. Participants in these standard settings included adult educators (directors, coordinators, and teachers of adult education services), adult literacy researchers, middle and high school classroom teachers, industrial and organizational psychologists, and human resources specialists.

OVERVIEW OF THE REPORT

Background information about the measurement of adult literacy, about the two assessments (NALS and NAAL), and about adult education is presented in Chapter 2. In Chapter 3, we review the process and procedures for determining the five performance levels used to report the 1992 NALS results. Chapters 4 and 5 describe our processes for developing new performance-level descriptions and determining the scores that separate the performance levels (cut scores). In Chapter 6, we discuss strategies for reporting and communicating about results for NAAL and suggest ways for using the results. The final chapter contains our suggestions for improving future assessments of adults' literacy skills.

2

Adult Literacy Assessments and Adult Education

T his chapter begins with a discussion of the types of literacy demands adults encounter in their daily lives and the reasons for assessing their literacy skills. We then give a brief overview of the National Adult Literacy Survey (NALS) and its successor, the National Assessment of Adult Literacy (NAAL). One of the chief uses of the results of the earlier survey was to determine needed programmatic interventions, many of which are offered through adult education systems. The chapter concludes with information about adult education services in this country.

LITERACY DEMANDS AND THE NEED FOR ASSESSMENTS

In a rapidly changing world, literacy is an essential skill, one that helps people thrive individually, socially, and economically. Literacy is important for all aspects of an individual's life, from handling personal affairs, to raising children, to engaging in the workforce, to participating in a democratic society.

In the home, individuals use their literacy skills for a wide range of activities, such as reading mail, paying bills, handling contracts and leases, and helping children with school matters. Regardless of one's occupation, literacy skills are needed in a variety of work contexts—applying for a job, traveling to and from work, choosing a benefits package, and understanding and handling paychecks.

Adults also use their literacy skills to handle health and safety matters, such as reading and using product safety and nutrition labels, filling out insurance forms, using tools and measurement devices, and reading dosage directions on prescription and over-the-counter medicines. Literacy skills are essential to keep family members healthy and safe and to assist elders as they make life-enhancing or life-changing decisions.

Literacy skills are also needed for adults to participate in a democratic society. Such activities as keeping apprised of local and national issues, understanding one's rights and responsibilities, reading ballots, and voting all require literacy skills.

Although some of these tasks can be accomplished in languages other than English (e.g., newspapers in various languages provide information; bilingual ballots are available in most states), American society places a high priority on literacy skills in English. Literacy in English accrues significant benefits to individuals in this country, including the opportunity to attain U.S. citizenship, to work in a well-paying job, and to fully participate in the democratic process.

While literacy skills are important for individuals' functioning and well-being, they are also critical for the social good and for a well-functioning society. Literacy skills have an impact on a nation's economic status, the health and well-being of its citizens, the capabilities of its workforce and military, and its ability to compete in a global society. Deficiencies in literacy skills and mismatches between the skills of citizens and the needs of an economy can have serious repercussions.

Policy makers rely on assessments of literacy skills to evaluate both the extent of such mismatches and the need for services that provide basic literacy skills to adults. Such assessments can provide the foundation and impetus for policy interventions. The NALS, mandated by the Adult Education Amendments of 1988 (amendments to the Adult Education Act of 1966), was designed to provide such information. This legislation required the U.S. Department of Education to evaluate the nature and extent of literacy among adults.

In response, the National Center for Education Statistics (NCES) and the Office of Vocational and Adult Education planned a nationally representative household survey to assess the literacy skills of the adult population in the United States. The NALS was administered in 1992; it was revised and repeated in 2003 under a new name, the NAAL. A great deal of information is available about the two assessments on the NCES web site (http://www.nces.ed.gov). In this chapter, we briefly summarize the assessments to acquaint the reader with relevant background information, but interested readers are referred to the NCES web sites for further details about the assessments.

LITERACY ASSESSMENTS

At the time that NALS was being designed, two prior large-scale assessments of subsets of the adult population in the United States had been conducted: the Young Adult Literacy Survey (YALS),[1] conducted in 1985, and the Department of Labor Survey of Workplace Literacy,[2] conducted in 1990. The group appointed to guide the development of NALS, called the Literacy Definition Committee, recommended adopting the same conceptual framework for NALS as was used for these two prior surveys. One reason for this decision was to enable comparisons of trends between NALS and the prior surveys. As a result of this decision, the methodologies and approaches used for the prior surveys were applied to NALS, and about half of the literacy tasks developed for the earlier surveys were readministered. In addition, much of the Technical Manual for NALS (Kirsch et al., 2001) covers procedures used for the earlier surveys.

The stated goals of NALS and NAAL are to describe the status and progress of literacy in the nation. Both assessments were comprised of the following: an introductory screening interview, a background questionnaire, and a literacy assessment. The total time for the interview is about 90 minutes. Scores are reported for three types of literacy—prose, document, and quantitative.

Description of the Literacy Tasks

The definition of literacy that guided the development of NALS was the same as for the prior surveys (Kirsch et al., 2001, p. 70): "Literacy is the ability to use printed and written information to function in society, to achieve one's goals, and to develop one's knowledge and potential."

As noted earlier, NALS and NAAL are considered to be measures of functional literacy in English, in that they focus on how adults use printed and written information. The assessments are intended to evaluate literacy demands encountered in everyday settings at home, in the workplace, and in the community and to profile adults' literacy skills in these contexts.

Each assessment task includes a stimulus, which is designed to simulate

---

[1]Sponsored by the U.S. Department of Education, YALS assessed the literacy skills of a nationally representative household sample of 3,600 young adults between the ages of 21 and 25 living in the 48 contiguous states (http://www.nces.ed.gov/naal/design/about85.asp). The assessment evaluated literacy skills in the contexts of everyday life, including home, school, work, and social environments.

[2]The Department of Labor Survey of Workplace Literacy profiled the literacy skills of a national sample of nearly 20 million participants in two U.S. Department of Labor programs: job seekers in the Employment Service/Unemployment Insurance programs and eligible applicants for the Job Placement and Partnership Act training.

materials adults frequently encounter, and a series of questions about the stimulus. The questions are presented before the stimulus to represent the way adults often approach a task in real life, in which functional reading is often driven by a need to know. Questions are open-ended, not multiple choice, again out of a desire to mimic realistic tasks. The tasks are categorized into the three types of literacy:

> **Prose literacy:** the knowledge and skills needed to locate, understand, and use information contained in expository and narrative prose text, such as editorials, newspaper articles, poems, and stories.
>
> **Document literacy:** the knowledge and skills required to locate, understand, and use relevant information found in documents, such as job applications, bus schedules, maps, payroll forms, indexes, and tables.
>
> **Quantitative literacy:** the knowledge and skills needed to apply basic arithmetic operations, alone or sequentially, to numbers embedded in printed materials, such as entering cash and check amounts onto a bank deposit slip, balancing a checkbook, completing an order form, and determining the amount of interest from a loan advertisement.

The 1992 assessment consisted of a total of 165 tasks, of which 82 were newly developed and 83 were reused from the prior surveys. Development of the new tasks was guided by a test blueprint that specified the characteristics of the items according to the structure of the stimulus (exposition, narrative, tables, graphs, forms, maps, etc.), the cognitive process required to respond to the question (locate, integrate, generate, add, subtract, etc.), the difficulty of the item, and the context from which the stimulus was drawn. The materials were drawn from six contexts of everyday life: home and family, health and safety, community and citizenship, consumer economics, work, and leisure and recreation. Additional information about item development can be found in Chapter 4 of the Technical Manual (Kirsch et al., 2001).

Changes Implemented with NAAL

In 1992, there were some participants who had such limited literacy skills that they were able to complete only part of the assessment, and others who attempted to perform the literacy tasks they were given and were unsuccessful (Kirsch et al., 1993). In order to provide literacy tasks that even very low-literate adults could complete successfully, NAAL added a new component, the Adult Literacy Supplemental Assessment (ALSA), designed to assess skills in identifying numbers, letters, and comprehension of simple prose and documents. This component is interactive and uses a one-on-one format. The assessor presents each item to the respondent and then asks questions orally. This format is designed to minimize the chance that low-functioning respondents fail to respond correctly to an item because they misunderstand the written directions or have difficulty with texts appearing outside their everyday environments.

NAAL's literacy assessment begins with a relatively easy set of seven literacy tasks, referred to as the "core questions," that are used to decide whether test takers should take the main NAAL assessment or the supplemental ALSA. Individuals who performed well on the core questions were assessed using the main NAAL, and individuals who performed poorly on the core questions were assessed with ALSA. NAAL consisted of 152 tasks, 54 prose tasks, 52 document tasks, and 64 quantitative tasks.

ALSA was designed to use highly familiar stimulus materials that are real and contextualized. The materials offer respondents the opportunity to see items as part of the product in which they appear in real life. For example, rather than just reading recipe directions on a printed page (e.g., for making soup), the respondent is asked to read directions that appear on the actual package (e.g., on the soup can).[3] Similarly, respondents may be asked to point to letters or words on a product (e.g., point to the words "apple juice" on a juice can), identify the price of a food item on a grocery flyer, or interpret the directions on a medicine warning label. ALSA begins with simple word and letter identification tasks presented in context; proceeds to short, simple prose texts and documents (e.g., advertisements, road signs); and concludes with several tasks that involve location of information in documents that contain more distracting information, such as newspapers or more complicated advertisements. Oral directions and questions are provided in either English or Spanish by the interviewer. ALSA also allows participants to answer in either English or Spanish, although the stimulus materials themselves contain only English text.

Also new to the NAAL is a component designed to evaluate reading fluency. The fluency assessment uses speech recognition software to assess decoding, word recognition, and reading fluency. All participants in NAAL complete the fluency assessment after they have answered the background questionnaire, the core questions, and either the main NAAL or ALSA. Fluency tasks include lists of words and numbers as well as text passages to be read aloud by the respondent. Oral directions and questions are provided in English or Spanish, depending on the respondents' preference, but the text itself appears only in English, and answers must be given in English. Only a bilingual interviewer, fully proficient in English and Spanish, is allowed to give directions or ask questions in Spanish when such support is

---

[3]Because the test questions are secure, these examples are intended to represent the types of questions included on ALSA, but are not the actual questions.

desired. The fluency tasks are administered at the end of the assessment, in an attempt to preserve comparability of the main NAAL with the 1992 assessment.

The 2003 NAAL also includes tasks that require application of literacy skills to the understanding of health-related materials and forms. Some health-related tasks were included on NALS, but the number of such tasks was increased for NAAL to allow reporting of a "health literacy" score.[4] There are 28 health-related tasks as well as 10 health-related background questions.

Additional information about the new features included on NAAL can be found at http://www.nces.ed.gov/NAAL/design/about02.asp#C.

Administration of the Literacy Assessment

NALS and NAAL are designed to provide reliable group-level estimates of literacy skills. The assessment is not designed to provide reliable scores for individuals (although statistical estimates of individuals' performance on the assessment can be derived and used for research purposes). Because individual scores are not reported, the assessments can utilize a matrix sampling approach to the assignment of test questions to individuals. The approach involves splitting a large set of tasks into smaller sets, or blocks. A similar design has long been used for the National Assessment of Educational Progress; it provides a means to minimize the number of test questions an individual must take and is efficient when the goal of an assessment is to provide reliable estimates of group-level performance.

With this approach, literacy tasks are assigned to blocks that can be completed in about 15 minutes, and these blocks are compiled into booklets, so that each block appears in each position (first, middle, and last) and each block is paired with every other block. Blocks of simulation tasks are assembled into booklets, each of which could be completed in about 45 minutes, although there were no time constraints placed on the participants for completing the tasks. Additional information about this can be found at http://www.nces.ed.gov/naal/design/design92.asp#design.

Measuring Trends Between 1992 and 2003

One chief aim of the 2003 assessment is to measure the trend from the previous assessment. NAAL consists of 13 blocks of tasks, 6 that were

---

[4]Health literacy has been defined as the degree to which individuals have the capacity to obtain, process, and understand basic health information and services needed to make appropriate health decisions (Ratzan and Parker, 2000).

repeated from 1992 and 7 newly developed for the 2003 assessment. The new blocks were based on the 1992 frameworks and were designed to be similar to the replaced blocks of items with regard to skills measured, content, and item statistics. After collection of the 2003 data, statistical linking procedures were used to place NALS and NAAL scores on the same scale.

The Department of Education plans to make NAAL data publicly available to researchers and others interested in conducting studies on the results. The results can be grouped according to the score ranges used for the old 1992 performance levels or the new 2003 levels. Trend comparisons will be possible based either on the 1992 levels or on the new levels adopted for NAAL.

The Sample for NALS and NAAL

For both assessments, data were collected via a household survey of a stratified random sample of adults age 16 and older. Additional samples were obtained in specific states in order to provide state-level results; this portion of the assessment was referred to as the State Adult Literacy Survey. In 1992, 12 states participated (California, Florida, Illinois, Indiana, Iowa, Louisiana, New Jersey, New York, Ohio, Pennsylvania, Texas, and Washington); in 2003, 6 states participated (Kentucky, Maryland, Massachusetts, Missouri, New York, and Oklahoma). For both assessments, an additional sample was obtained of individuals incarcerated in federal and state prisons.

Approximately 26,000 individuals age 16 and older participated in the 1992 NALS. Of these, 9.8 percent reported speaking a language other than English at home. The overall number included 13,600 selected as part of the national sample as well as about 12,000 (1,000 per state) selected through the State Adult Literacy Survey. The survey also included 1,147 inmates from 87 state and federal prisons who were selected to represent the inmate population in the United States. Their participation helped to provide better estimates of the literacy levels of the total population and made it possible to report on the literacy proficiencies of this important segment of society. See http://www./nces.ed.gov/naal/design/about92.asp for additional details about the sampling.

Sampling procedures were similar for the 2003 NAAL. The nationally representative sample of 19,714 adults included 18,541 participants living in households, about 6,500 of whom were selected from six states (approximately 1,000 per state). An additional 1,173 participants were selected from adults living in state or federal prisons.

The Interview Process

The assessment is administered in the home by trained interviewers. The first step in the process is to administer the "screener," a set of questions used to determine the number of eligible respondents (e.g., age 16 or older) in the household. The screening process involves recording the names, relationships, sex, age, and race/ethnicity of all household members at the selected household. Some bilingual interviewers are trained to administer the screener in either English or Spanish. Interviewers can also ask a household member or a family friend to translate the screening questions into Spanish or other languages, although there is no check on the accuracy of the translation.

To select respondents, interviewers list the names and ages (in descending age order) of all eligible household members and then refer to a sampling table. In households with three or fewer eligible household members, one is randomly selected for the interview; in households with four or more eligible persons, two are selected. Selected participants receive an incentive payment for participating in the assessment ($20 in 1992, $30 in 2003). See http://www.nces.ed.gov/naal/design/data92.asp#collection for additional details about the data collection process.

After completion of the screener and selection of participants, the background questionnaire is administered. The background questionnaire can also be administered in Spanish or English. If the participant does not speak Spanish and is not proficient enough in English to understand and respond to the interviewer, the interaction is terminated and the person is classified as having a language problem. These procedures were changed slightly in 2003 in an effort to obtain literacy information from as many participants as possible. In 2003, participants who did not speak Spanish or who were not sufficiently proficient in English to respond to the entire background questionnaire, were allowed to skip one or more of the background questions that they were not able to answer and move to the literacy assessment. Interviewers recorded each skipped background question as "don't know" and documented the reason for skipping the question.

The background questionnaire collects general background information about language experience (e.g., language spoken at home), educational background and experiences, political and social participation, labor force participation, employment and earnings experiences, health, literacy activities and practices, and demographic information. The background questions are read to the respondent by an interviewer who then marks the answers on an answer sheet. The actual background questionnaire used in 1992 can be found in Appendix G of the *Technical Report and Data File Users Manual for the 1992 National Adult Literacy Survey* (http://www./ nces.ed.gov/pubsearch/pubsinfo.asp?pubid=2001457). The background questionnaire used in 2003 is available from NCES.

After administration of the background questionnaire, the interviewer proceeds to the literacy assessment. The literacy tasks (a stimulus and a set of questions) on the assessment are presented one at a time. There are no time limits for responding. Participants continue until they reach the final item or they choose to stop. When a participant stops before finishing the set of tasks, the reason for stopping is recorded.

USES OF RESULTS OF ADULT LITERACY ASSESSMENTS

There are many uses for the results of adult literacy assessments. Over the past decade, NALS results have been used by a wide variety of audiences, including those concerned about the status of the workforce in this country and for evaluating the need for training programs, officials in the public health sector who are concerned about the extent to which adults make wise and informed health and safety decisions, researchers studying the relationships between literacy and participation in civic activities and political processes, and experts in family literacy evaluating the extent to which parents are able to participate in their children's educational process. NALS results have been widely cited in the research literature and continue to be used to argue for needed resources for adult education services.

Although NALS results have been used in a variety of ways, one of the chief uses over the past decade has been to determine the extent to which adult basic education services are available to meet the needs of adults with low levels of literacy. In the next section, we provide a brief overview of the adult education system in this country to provide context for discussions that appear in later sections of the report and several of the decisions the committee made about performance levels for NAAL.

Adult Education in the United States

Ideally, literacy skills are acquired as people progress through the K-12 education system in this country. However, this system does not always work for all who pass through it, and many who have immigrated to the United States have never participated in it. In addition, increasing societal and workplace demands may exceed what is taught in school, creating situations in which the skills of the populace are not aligned with the needs of the nation.

The adult education system is intended to remedy basic skill deficiencies and mismatches between skill requirements and adults' proficiencies and to provide developmental English language and literacy services to immigrants and refugees not yet proficient in English. The adult education system is, for the most part, guided legislatively by the Adult Education Act of 1966 and the Workforce Investment Act of 1998, Title II, Adult

Education and Family Literacy Act. Through a combination of federal, state, and local funding, the adult education system sponsors adult basic education (ABE) programs through which individuals can improve their literacy skills and prepare for the general educational development (GED) assessment, the test taken to acquire the equivalent of a high school diploma. According to recent statistics available from the Office of Vocational and Adult Education, 2,891,895 individuals age 16 and older were enrolled in adult education in 2000 (http://www.ed.gov/about/offices/list/ovae/pi/AdultEd/2000age.html). In 2001, over 600,000 adults were issued GED credentials after passing the test (GED Testing Service, 2004).

The adult education system also provides courses in English for speakers of other languages (referred to as ESOL programs), designed to assist immigrants to learn and function in English. Of the close to 3 million adults enrolled in ABE programs in 1999, 1 million were enrolled as ESOL students (National Center for Education Statistics, 2003). ESOL programs serve people with a wide array of literacy skills in English and in their native language. For example, immigrants to the United States may not be literate in English, but they may have strong literacy skills in another language, skills that are likely to transfer to English literacy once their English skills improve.

Other immigrants may struggle with literacy both in the native language and in English, such as those who had only an elementary school education or less in their native country. Acquiring an education is a substantial challenge for this group as a consequence of their weak foundation in literacy (in any language) and lack of the background knowledge that others obtain through formal schooling. These individuals, most of whom are immigrants from Mexico and Central America and refugees from Haiti, Laos, and Africa, will need adult education services that are quite different from those offered to their more educated counterparts. Both groups, highly literate and low-literate English learners, may need services that focus on oral communication skills along with literacy. Newcomers may need skills and strategies associated with acculturation to the United States as well. In that respect, the services that adult language learners require are quite different from those provided for adult learners who grew up speaking English.

The relative literacy skills of a third group, often referred to as "generation 1.5," may need to be considered as well.[5] These individuals are generally bilingual young adults who were born elsewhere but partially educated in the United States or who were born and educated in the United States but

---

[5]See http://www.cal.org/resources/digest/0305harklau.html and http://www.american.edu/tesol/Roberge_article.pdf.

who grew up in linguistically isolated communities in which a language other than English was spoken at home. Their conversational skills in both the home language and in English may be quite strong, but some generation 1.5 adults are still learning formal, written English, while others have learned a nonstandard form of English that carries over to their writing.[6] The literacy education needs of these adults are varied. Some of them may benefit from traditional ESOL programs. Others may benefit more from mainstream education with an emphasis on identifying and correcting the errors associated with the use of nonstandard English. In many ways, this second group of generation 1.5 adults has similar characteristics to native-born young adults who grew up speaking English but are academically unprepared.

While most individuals enroll in adult education programs voluntarily, some are encouraged or required to do so by their employers. Still others are required to attend classes in order to receive funds or services that are contingent on participation in education or training, including ABE/ESOL programs. Some individuals receiving income support through Temporary Assistance to Needy Families (commonly known as welfare) and displaced workers receiving stipends under the North American Free Trade Agreement fall into this category.

Increasingly, adult education programs are offered in the nation's prisons. Recent statistics (1999) indicate that 25 percent of jail jurisdictions offer an ABE program (National Institute for Literacy, 2002). According to the Bureau of Justice Statistics (2000), 80 percent of state prisons, nearly all federal prisons, about 70 percent of private prisons, and over half of jails offered high school level classes, which generally focus on GED preparation. In some states, completion of the GED preparation program and passing the GED result in early release from prison (e.g., Nevada, personal communication with Sanford Marks; and Indiana, Lawrence et al., 2002). Studies of reincarceration rates for adults in Virginia, Ohio, Minnesota, and Maryland suggest that enrolling in literacy and ABE education programs lower the likelihood of recidivism (Wedgeworth, 2003). Research also indicates that only 7 to 10 percent of inmates who qualify for literacy education programs actually take advantage of the opportunity (Langley, 1999), despite the fact that 70 percent of incarcerated adults are estimated to read below the fourth-grade level (Haigler et al., 1994).

---

[6]See http://www.cal.org/resources/digest/0305harklau.html and http://www.american.edu/tesol/Roberge_article.pdf.

Legislative Oversight of Adult Education Programs

An important aspect of adult education programs is an accountability system, known as the National Reporting System (NRS), that was implemented through Title II of the Workforce Investment Act of 1998 (Public Law 105-220).[7] As part of the NRS, adult education participants are administered an assessment (state's choice) upon entry into an adult education program and take a posttest after a period of instruction as determined by each state. Results for the assessment are reported in terms of the NRS educational functioning levels, a set of six levels that include brief descriptions of the skills that students are expected to demonstrate in the areas of reading and writing, numeracy, and functional and workplace skills. There are separate level descriptions for ABE and ESOL (see Tables 2-1 and 2-2). States report the percentage of adult education participants who move from one level to the next as measured by pre-posttest gains in a program year. The Workforce Investment Act includes a system of incentives provided to states based on their students' test performance as well as on other criteria.

The lowest NRS level (i.e., beginning literacy) ranges from an individual having "no or minimal reading and writing skills" to being able to "recognize, read, and write letters and numbers, but has a limited understanding of connected prose." The second NRS level (i.e., beginning basic education) is described as equating to reading grade levels of 2.0-3.9 on standardized tests and includes individuals who can "read simple material on familiar subjects and comprehend simple compound sentences in single or linked paragraphs containing a familiar vocabulary." The third NRS level (i.e., low intermediate basic education) is described as equating to reading grade levels 4.0-5.9 on standardized reading tests and includes individuals who can "read text on familiar subjects that have a simple and clear underlying structure (e.g., clear main idea, chronological order)" and "can interpret actions required in specific written directions." The fourth NRS level (i.e., high intermediate basic education) is described as equating to reading grade levels 6.0-8.9 on standardized tests and including readers who can "read simple descriptions and narratives on familiar subjects or from which new vocabulary can be determined by context." They can also "make some minimal inferences about familiar texts and compare and contrast information from such texts, but not consistently."

The adult education field relies on information from assessments such as NALS/NAAL to project program needs. Most individuals served by adult education programs have skills in the ranges described by the current

---

[7]See http://www.thomas.loc.gov/cgi-bin/bdquery/z?d105:HR01385:|TOM:/bss/d105query. html [accessed Dec. 2004].

NALS Levels 1 and 2.[8] Knowing about the skill levels of those likely to enroll in adult education programs assists policy makers and program coordinators in determining where to focus funding initiatives and in designing instruction programs.[9] The greatest interest and concern among adult educators relates to information about potential students at the lowest four NRS levels: beginning literacy, beginning basic education, low intermediate basic education, and high intermediate basic education. Adult students at the very lowest level may need one-on-one instruction and a good deal of guidance. Adult students at the next two levels can function a bit more independently but still are not ready to take classes focusing on the GED high school equivalency diploma. Adult students at the fourth level read at levels comparable to middle school students and are likely to be ready to pursue GED instruction.

The committee was aware of the fact that the adult education community hoped to be able to map the performance levels adopted for NAAL onto the NRS levels. Although NAAL did not appear to have been designed for this purpose, we kept this desire in mind as we proceeded with our work and, as spelled out in the report, attempted to develop performance levels that would meet the needs of this community.

---

[8]A comparison of NALS assessments and GED examinees suggested that test takers who failed to pass the GED exams were likely to be included in the NALS Level 2 category (Baldwin et al., 1995).

[9]Individual states, for example Tennessee, often decide funding by using NALS Levels 1 and 2 to guide state appropriations for ABE programs. For Tennessee's state plan, see http://www.cls.coe.utk.edu/stateplan/ [accessed February 25, 2005].

TABLE 2-1 Educational Functioning Level Descriptors—Adult Basic Education Levels

Literacy Level	Basic Reading and Writing

Beginning ABE Literacy
Benchmarks:
TABE (5–6) scale scores
(grade level 0–1.9):
    Total Reading: 529 and below
    Total Math: 540 and below
    Total Language: 599 and below
TABE (7–8) scale scores
(grade level 0–1.9):
    Reading: 367 and below
    Total Math: 313 and below
    Language: 391 and below
CASAS: 200 and below
AMES (B, ABE) scale scores
(grade level 0–1.9):
    Reading: 500 and below
    Total Math: 476 and below
    Communication: 496 and below
ABLE scale scores (grade level 0–1.9):
    Reading: 523 and below
    Math: 521 and below
	• Individual has no or minimal reading and writing skills.
	• May have little or no comprehension of how print corresponds to spoken language and may have difficulty using a writing instrument.
	• At upper range of this level, individual can recognize, read and write letters and numbers, but has a limited understanding of connected prose and may need frequent re-reading.
	• Can write a number of basic sight words and familiar words and phrases.
	• May also be able to write simple sentences or phrase, including simple messages.
	• Can write basic personal information.
	• Narrative writing is disorganized and unclear, inconsistently uses simple punctuation (e.g., periods, commas, question marks).
	• Contains frequent spelling errors.

Beginning Basic Education
TABE (5–6) scale scores
(grade level 2–3.9):
    Total Reading: 530–679
    Total Math: 541–677
    Total Language: 600–977
TABE (7–8) scale scores
(grade level 2–3.9):
    Reading: 368–460
    Total Math: 314–441
    Language: 392–490
CASAS: 201–210
AMES (B, ABE) scale scores
(grade level 2–3.9):
    Total Math: 477–492
    Communication: 498–506
ABLE scale scores (grade level 2–3.9):
    Reading: 525–612
    Math: 530–591
	• Individual can read simple material on familiar subjects and comprehend simple compound sentences in single or linked paragraphs containing a familiar vocabulary.
	• Can write simple notes and messages on familiar situations, but lacks clarity and focus.
	• Sentence structure lacks variety, but shows some control of basic grammar (e.g., present and past tense), and consistent use of punctuation (e.g., periods, capitalization).

Numeracy Skills	Functional and Workplace Skills
• Individual has little or no recognition of numbers or simple counting skills or may have only minimal skills, such as the ability to add or subtract single digit numbers.	• Individual has little or no ability to read basic signs or maps, can provide limited personal information on simple forms. • The individual can handle routine entry-level jobs that require little or no basic written communication or computational skills and no knowledge of computers or other technology.
• Individual can count, add, and subtract three-digit numbers; can perform multiplication through 12. • Can identify simple fractions and perform other simple arithmetic operations.	• Individual is able to read simple directions, signs, and maps; fill out simple forms requiring basic personal information; write phone messages and make simple change. • There is minimal knowledge of, and experience with, using computers and related technology. • The individual can handle basic entry-level jobs that require minimal literacy skills. • Can recognize very short, explicit, pictorial texts, e.g., understands logos related to worker safety before using a piece of machinery. • Can read want ads and complete job applications.

continued

TABLE 2-1 Continued

Literacy Level	Basic Reading and Writing
Low Intermediate Basic Education Benchmarks: TABE (5–6) scale scores (grade level 6–8.9): Total Reading: 723–761 Total Math: 730–776 Total Language: 706–730 TABE (7–8) scale scores (grade level 6–8.9): Reading: 518–566 Total Math: 506–565 Language: 524–559 CASAS: 221–235 AMES (C and D, ABE) scale scores (grade level 6–8.9): Reading (C): 525–612 Reading (D): 522–543 Total Math (C): 510–627 Total Math (D): 509–532 Communication (C): 516–611 Communication (D): 516–523 ABLE scale scores (grade level 6–8.9): Reading: 646–680 Math: 643–693	• Individual can read text on familiar subjects that have a simple and clear underlying structure (e.g., clear main idea, chronological order). • Can use context to determine meaning. • Can interpret actions required in specific written directions, can write simple paragraphs with main idea and supporting detail on familiar topics (e.g., daily activities, personal issues) by recombining learned vocabulary and structures. • Can self- and peer edit for spelling and punctuation errors.
High Intermediate Basic Education Benchmarks: TABE (5–6) scale scores (grade level 6–8.9): Total Reading: 723–761 Total Math: 730–776 Total Language: 706–730 TABE (7–8) scale scores (grade level 6–8.9): Reading: 518–566 Total Math: 506–565 Language: 524–559 CASAS: 221–235 AMES (C and D, ABE) scale scores (grade level 6–8.9): Reading (C): 525–612 Reading (D): 522–543 Total Math (C): 510–627 Total Math (D): 509–532	• Individual is able to read simple descriptions and narratives on familiar subjects or from which new vocabulary can be determined by context. • Can make some minimal inferences about familiar texts and compare and contrast information from such texts, but not consistently. • The individual can write simple narrative descriptions and short essays on familiar topics. • Has consistent use of basic punctuation, but makes grammatical errors with complex structures.

Numeracy Skills	Functional and Workplace Skills
• Individual can perform with high accuracy all four basic math operations using whole numbers up to three digits. • Can identify and use all basic mathematical symbols.	• Individual is able to handle basic reading, writing, and computational tasks related to life roles, such as completing medical forms, order forms, or job applications. • Can read simple charts, graphs, labels, and payroll stubs and simple authentic material if familiar with the topic. • The individual can use simple computer programs and perform a sequence of routine tasks given direction using technology (e.g., fax machine, computer operation). • The individual can qualify for entry-level jobs that require following basic written instructions and diagrams with assistance, such as oral clarification. • Can write a short report or message to fellow workers. • Can read simple dials and scales and take routine measurements.
• Individual can perform all four basic math operations with whole numbers and fractions. • Can determine correct math operations for solving narrative math problems and can convert fractions to decimals and decimals to fractions. • Can perform basic operations on fractions.	• Individual is able to handle basic life skills tasks such as graphs, charts, and labels, and can follow multistep diagrams. • Can read authentic materials on familiar topics, such as simple employee handbooks and payroll stubs. • Can complete forms such as a job application and reconcile a bank statement. • Can handle jobs that involve following simple written instructions and diagrams. • Can read procedural texts, where the information is supported by diagrams, to remedy a problem, such as locating a problem with a machine or carrying out repairs using a repair manual.

continued

TABLE 2-1 Continued

Literacy Level	Basic Reading and Writing

Communication (C): 516–611
Communication (D): 516–523
ABLE scale scores (grade level 6–8.9):
    Reading: 646–680
    Math: 643–693

Low Adult Secondary Education
Benchmarks:
TABE (5–6) scale scores
(grade level 9–10.9):
    Total Reading: 762–775
    Total Math: 777–789
    Total Language: 731–743
TABE (7–8) scale scores
(grade level 9–10.9):
    Reading: 567–595
    Total Math: 566–594
    Language: 560–585
CASAS: 236–245
AMES (E, ABE) scale scores
(grade level 9–10.9):
    Reading: 544–561
    Total Math: 534–548
    Communication: 527–535
ABLE scale scores (grade level 9–10.9):
    Reading: 682–697
    Math: 643–716

- Individual can comprehend expository writing and identify spelling, punctuation, and grammatical errors.
- Can comprehend a variety of materials such as periodicals and notechnical journals on common topics.
- Can comprehend library reference materials and compose multiparagraph essays.
- Can listen to oral instructions and write an accurate synthesis of them.
- Can identify the main idea in reading selections and use a variety of context issues to determine meaning.
- Writing is organized and cohesive with few mechanical errors.
- Can write using a complex sentence structure.
- Can write personal notes and letters that accurately reflect thoughts.

High Adult Secondary Education
Benchmarks:
TABE (5–6) scale scores
(grade level 11–12):
    Total Reading: 776 and above
    Total Math: 790 and above
    Total Language: 744 and above
TABE (7–8) scale scores
(grade level 11–12):
    Reading: 596 and above
    Total Math: 595 and above
    Language: 586 and above
CASAS: 246 and above
AMES (E, ABE) scale score
(grade level 11–12):

- Individual can comprehend, explain, and analyze information from a variety of literacy works, including primary source materials and professional journals.
- Can use context cues and higher order processes to interpret meaning of written material.
- Writing is cohesive with clearly expressed ideas supported by relevant detail.
- Can use varied and complex sentence structures with few mechanical errors.

Numeracy Skills	Functional and Workplace Skills
	• The individual can learn or work with most basic computer software, such as using a word processor to produce own texts. • Can follow simple instructions for using technology.
• Individual can perform all basic math functions with whole numbers, decimals, and fractions. • Can interpret and solve simple algebraic equations, tables and graphs, and can develop own tables and graphs. • Can use math in business transactions.	• Individual is able or can learn to follow simple multistep directions and read common legal forms and manuals; • Can integrate information from texts, charts, and graphs. • Can create and use tables and graphs. • Can complete forms and applications and complete resumes. • Can perform jobs than require interpreting information from various sources and writing or explaining tasks to other workers. • Is proficient using computers and can use most common computer applications. • Can understand the impact of using different technologies. • Can interpret the appropriate use of new software and technology.
• Individual can make mathematical estimates of time and space and can apply principles of geometry to measure angles, lines and surfaces. • Can also apply trigonometric functions.	• Individuals are able to read technical information and complex manuals. can comprehend some college level books and apprenticeship manuals. • Can function in most job situations involving higher order thinking. • Can read text and explain a procedure about a complex and unfamiliar work procedure, such as operating a complex piece of machinery. • Can evaluate new work situations and processes, can work productively and collaboratively in groups and serve as facilitator and reporter of group work.

continued

TABLE 2-1 Continued

Literacy Level	Basic Reading and Writing

Reading: 565 and above
Total Math: 551 and above
Communication: 538 and above
ABLE scale scores (grade level 11–12):
  Reading: 699 and above
  Math: 717 and above

SOURCE: National Reporting System (2002).

Numeracy Skills	Functional and Workplace Skills
	• The individual is able to use common software and learn new software applications.
	• Can define the purpose of new technology and software and select appropriate technology.
	• Can adapt use of software or technology to new situations and can instruct others, in written or oral form, on software and technology use.

TABLE 2-2 National Reporting System Levels for Non-English Speakers

Literacy Level	Speaking and Listening
Beginning ESL Literacy Benchmarks: CASAS (Life Skills): 180 and below SPL (Speaking): 01 SPL (Reading and Writing): 01 Oral BEST: 015 Literacy BEST: 07	• Individual cannot speak or understand English, or understands only isolated words or phrases.
Beginning ESL Benchmarks: CASAS (Life Skills): 181–200 SPL (Speaking): 2–3 SPL (Reading and Writing): 2 Oral BEST: 16–41 Literacy BEST: 8–46	• Individual can understand frequently used words in context and very simple phrases spoken and slowly with some repetition. • There is little communicative output and only in the most routine situations. • Little or no control over basic grammar. • Survival needs can be communicated simply, and there is some understanding of simple questions.
Low Intermediate ESL Benchmarks: CASAS (Life Skills): 201–210 SPL (Speaking): 4 SPL (Reading and Writing): 5 Oral BEST: 42–50 Literacy BEST: 47–53	• Individual can understand simple learned phrases and limited new phrases containing familiar vocabulary spoken slowly with frequent repetition. • Can ask and respond to questions using such phrases. • Can express basic survival needs and participate in some routine social conversations, although with some difficulty. • Has some control of basic grammar.

Basic Reading and Writing	Functional and Workplace Skills
• Individual has no or minimal reading or writing skills in any language. • May have little or no comprehension of how print corresponds to spoken language and may have difficulty using a writing instrument.	• Individual functions minimally or not at all in English and can communicate only through gestures or a few isolated words, such as name and other personal information. • May recognize only common signs or symbols (e.g., stop sign, product logos). • Can handle only very routine entry-level jobs that do not require oral or written communication in English. • There is no knowledge or use of computers or technology.
• Individual can recognize, read, and write numbers and letters, but has a limited understanding of connected prose and may need frequent re-reading. • Can write a limited number of basic sight words and familiar words and phrases. • May also be able to write simple sentences or phrases, including very simple messages. • Can write basic personal information. • Narrative writing is disorganized and unclear. • Inconsistently uses simple punctuation (e.g., periods, commas, question marks). • Contains frequent errors in spelling.	• Individual functions with difficulty in situations related to immediate needs and in limited social situations. • Has some simple oral communication abilities using simple learned and repeated phrases. • May need frequent repetition. • Can provide personal information on simple forms. • Can recognize common forms of print found in the home and environment, such as labels and product names. • Can handle routine entry-level jobs that require only the most basic written or oral English communication and in which job tasks can be demonstrated. • There is minimal knowledge or experience using computers or technology.
• Individual can read simple material on familiar subjects and comprehend simple and compound sentences in single or linked paragraphs containing a familiar vocabulary. • Can write simple notes and messages on familiar situations, but lacks clarity and focus. • Sentence structure lacks variety, but shows some control of basic grammar (e.g., past and present tense) and consistent use of punctuation (e.g., periods and capitalization).	• Individual can interpret simple directions and schedules, signs and maps. • Can fill out simple forms, but needs support on some documents that are not simplified. • Can handle routine entry-level jobs that involve some written or oral English communication, but in which job tasks can be demonstrated. • Individual can use simple computer programs and can perform a sequence of routine tasks given directions using technology (e.g., fax machine, computer).

continued

TABLE 2-2 Continued

Literacy Level	Speaking and Listening
High Intermediate ESL Benchmarks: CASAS (Life Skills): 211–220 SPL (Speaking): 5 SPL (Reading and Writing): 6 Oral BEST: 51–57 Literacy BEST: 54–65	• Individual can understand learned phrases and short new phrases containing familiar vocabulary spoken slowly, with some repetition. • Can communicate basic survival needs with some help. • Can participate in conversation in limited social situations and use new phrases with hesitation. • Relies on description and concrete terms. • There is inconsistent control of more complex grammar.
Low Advanced ESL Benchmarks: CASAS (Life Skills): 221–235 SPL (Speaking): 6 SPL (Reading and Writing): 7 Oral BEST: 58–64 Literacy BEST: 65 and above	• Individual can converse on many everyday subjects and some subjects with unfamiliar vocabulary, but may need repetition, rewording, or slower speech. • Can speak creatively, but with hesitation. • Can clarify general meaning by rewording and has control of basic grammar. • Understands descriptive and spoken narrative and can comprehend abstract concepts in familiar contexts.

Basic Reading and Writing	Functional and Workplace Skills
• Individual can read text on familiar subjects that have a simple and clear underlying structure (e.g., clear main idea, chronological order). • Can use context to determine meaning. • Can interpret actions required in specific written directions. • Can write simple paragraphs with main idea and supporting detail on familiar topics (e.g., daily activities, personal issues) by recombining learned vocabulary and structures. • Can self- and peer edit for spelling and punctuation errors.	• Individual can meet basic survival and social needs. • Can follow simple oral and written instruction and has some ability to communicate on the telephone on familiar subjects. • Can write messages and notes related to basic needs; complete basic medical forms and job applications. • Can handle jobs that involve basic oral instructions and written communication in tasks that can be clarified orally. • The individual can work with or learn basic computer software, such as word processing. • Can follow simple instructions for using technology.
• Individual is able to read simple descriptions and narratives on familiar subjects or from which new vocabulary can be determined by context. • Can make some minimal inferences about familiar texts and compare and contrast information from such texts, but not consistently. • The individual can write simple narrative descriptions and short essays on familiar topics, such as customs in native country. • Has consistent use of basic punctuation, but makes grammatical errors with complex structures.	• Individual can function independently to meet most survival needs and can communicate on the telephone on familiar topics. • Can interpret simple charts and graphics. • Can handle jobs that require simple oral and written instructions, multi-step diagrams, and limited public interaction. • The individual can use all basic software applications, understand the impact of technology, and select the correct technology in a new situation.

continued

TABLE 2-2 Continued

Literacy Level	Speaking and Listening
High Advanced ESL Benchmarks: CASAS (Life Skills): 236–245 SPL (Speaking): 7 SPL (Reading and Writing): 8 Oral BEST: 65 and above	• Individual can understand and participate effectively in face-to-face conversations on everyday subjects spoken at normal speed. • Can converse and understand independently in survival, work, and social situations. • Can expand on basic ideas in conversation, but with some hesitation. • Can clarify general meaning and control basic grammar, although still lacks total control over complex structures.

SOURCE: National Reporting System (2002).

Basic Reading and Writing	Functional and Workplace Skills
• Individual can read authentic materials on everyday subjects and can handle most reading related to life roles. • Can consistently and fully interpret descriptive narratives on familiar topics and gain meaning from unfamiliar topics. • Uses increased control of language and meaning-making strategies to gain meaning of unfamiliar texts. • The individual can write multiparagraph essays with a clear introduction and development of ideas. • Writing contains well-formed sentences, appropriate mechanics and spelling, and few grammatical errors.	• Individual has a general ability to use English effectively to meet most routine social and work situations. • Can interpret routine charts, graphs and tables and complete forms. • Has high ability to communicate on the telephone and understand radio and television. • Can meet work demands that require reading and writing and can interact with the public. • The individual can use common software and learn new applications. • Can define the purpose of software and select new applications appropriately. • Can instruct others in use of software and technology.

3

Developing Performance Levels for the National Adult Literacy Survey

I n this chapter, we document our observations and findings about the procedures used to develop the performance levels for the 1992 National Adult Literacy Survey (NALS). The chapter begins with some background information on how performance levels and the associated cut scores are typically determined. We then provide a brief overview of the test development process used for NALS, as it relates to the procedures for determining performance levels, and describe how the performance levels were determined and the cut scores set. The chapter also includes a discussion of the role of response probabilities in setting cut scores and in identifying assessment tasks to exemplify performance levels; the technical notes at the end of the chapter provides additional details about this topic.

BACKGROUND ON DEVELOPING PERFORMANCE LEVELS

When the objective of a test is to report results using performance levels, the number of levels and the descriptions of the levels are usually articulated early in the test development process and serve as the foundation for test development. The process of determining the number of levels and their descriptions usually involves consideration of the content and skills evaluated on the test as well as discussions with stakeholders about the inferences to be based on the test results and the ways the test results will be used. When the number of levels and the descriptions of the levels are laid out in advance, development efforts can focus on constructing items that measure the content and skills described by the levels. It is important to develop a sufficient number of items that measure the skills described by each of the levels. This allows for more reliable estimates of test-takers' skills and more accurate classification of individuals into the various performance levels.

While determination of the performance-level descriptions is usually completed early in the test development process, determination of the cut scores between the performance levels is usually made after the test has been administered and examinees' answers are available. Typically, the process of setting cut scores involves convening a group of panelists with expertise in areas relevant to the subject matter covered on the test and familiarity with the test-taking population, who are instructed to make judgments about what test takers need to know and be able to do (e.g., which test items individuals should be expected to answer correctly) in order to be classified into a given performance level. These judgments are used to determine the cut scores that separate the performance levels.

Methods for setting cut scores are used in a wide array of assessment contexts, from the National Assessment of Educational Progress (NAEP) and state-sponsored achievement tests, in which procedures are used to determine the level of performance required to classify students into one of several performance levels (e.g., basic, proficient, or advanced), to licensing and certification tests, in which procedures are used to determine the level of performance required to pass such tests in order to be licensed or certified.

There is a broad literature on procedures for setting cut scores on tests. In 1986, Berk documented 38 methods and variations on these methods, and the literature has grown substantially since. All of the methods rely on panels of judges, but the tasks posed to the panelists and the procedures for arriving at the cut scores differ. The methods can be classified as test-centered, examinee-centered, and standards-centered.

The *modified Angoff* and *bookmark* procedures are two examples of test-centered methods. In the modified Angoff procedure, the task posed to the panelists is to imagine a typical minimally competent examinee and to decide on the probability that this hypothetical examinee would answer each item correctly (Kane, 2001). The bookmark method requires placing all of the items in a test in order by difficulty; panelists are asked to place a "bookmark" at the point between the most difficult item borderline test takers would be likely to answer correctly and the easiest item borderline test takers would be likely to answer incorrectly (Zeiky, 2001).

The *borderline group* and *contrasting group* methods are two examples of examinee-centered procedures. In the borderline group method, the panelists are tasked with identifying examinees who just meet the performance standard; the cut score is set equal to the median score for these examinees (Kane, 2001). In the contrasting group method, the panelists are asked to categorize examinees into two groups—an upper group that has clearly met the standard and a lower group that has not met the standard. The cut score is the score that best discriminates between the two groups.

The *Jaeger-Mills integrated judgment procedure* and the *body of work* procedure are examples of standards-centered methods. With these methods, panelists examine full sets of examinees' responses and match the full set of responses to a performance level (Jaeger and Mills, 2001; Kingston et al., 2001). Texts such as Jaeger (1989) and Cizek (2001a) provide full descriptions of these and the other available methods.

Although the methods differ in their approaches to setting cut scores, all ultimately rely on judgments. The psychometric literature documents procedures for systematizing the process of obtaining judgments about cut scores (e.g., see Jaeger, 1989; Cizek, 2001a). Use of systematic and careful procedures can increase the likelihood of obtaining fair and reasoned judgments, thus improving the reliability and validity of the results. Nevertheless, the psychometric field acknowledges that there are no "correct" standards, and the ultimate judgments depend on the method used, the way it is carried out, and the panelists themselves (Brennan, 1998; Green, Trimble, and Lewis, 2003; Jaeger, 1989; Zieky, 2001).

The literature on setting cut scores includes critiques of the various methods that document their strengths and weaknesses. As might be expected, methods that have been used widely and for some time, such as the modified Angoff procedure, have been the subject of more scrutiny than recently developed methods like the bookmark procedure. A review of these critiques quickly reveals that there are no perfect or correct methods. Like the cut-score-setting process itself, choice of a specific procedure requires making an informed judgment about the most appropriate method for a given assessment situation. Additional information about methods for setting cut scores appears in Chapter 5, where we describe the procedures we used.

DEVELOPMENT OF NALS TASKS

The NALS tasks were drawn from the contexts that adults encounter on a daily basis. As mentioned in Chapter 2, these contexts include work, home and family, health and safety, community and citizenship, consumer economics, and leisure and recreation. Some of the tasks had been used on the earlier adult literacy assessments (the Young Adult Literacy Survey in 1985 and the survey of job seekers in 1990), to allow comparison with the earlier results, and some were newly developed for NALS.

The tasks that were included on NALS were intended to profile and describe performance in each of the specified contexts. However, NALS was not designed to support inferences about the level of literacy adults need in order to function in the various contexts. That is, there was no attempt to systematically define the critical literacy demands in each of the contexts. The test designers specifically emphasize this, saying: "[The literacy levels] do not reveal the types of literacy demands that are associated with particular contexts. . . . They do not enable us to say what specific level of prose, document, or quantitative skill is required to obtain, hold, or advance in a particular occupation, to manage a household, or to obtain legal or community services" (Kirsch et al., 1993, p. 9). This is an important point, because it demonstrates that some of the inferences made by policy makers and the media about the 1992 results were clearly not supported by the test development process and the intent of the assessment.

The approach toward test development used for NALS does not reflect typical procedures used when the objective of an assessment is to distinguish individuals with adequate levels of skills from those whose skills are inadequate. We point this out, not to criticize the process, but to clarify the limitations placed on the inferences that can be drawn about the results. To explain, it is useful to contrast the test development procedures used for NALS with procedures used in other assessment contexts, such as licensing and credentialing or state achievement testing.

Licensing and credentialing assessments are generally designed to distinguish between performance that demonstrates sufficient competence in the targeted knowledge, skills, and capabilities to be judged as passing and performance that is inadequate and judged as failing. Typically, licensing and certification tests are intentionally developed to distinguish between adequate and inadequate performance. The test development process involves specification of the skills critical to adequate performance generally determined by systematically collecting judgments from experts in the specific field (e.g., via surveys) about what a licensed practitioner needs to know and be able to do. The process for setting cut scores relies on expert judgments about just how much of the specific knowledge, skills, and capabilities is needed for a candidate to be placed in the passing category.

The process for test development and determining performance levels for state K-12 achievement tests is similar. Under ideal circumstances, the performance-level categories and their descriptions are determined in advance of or concurrent with item development, and items are developed to measure skills described by the performance levels. The process of setting the cut scores then focuses on determining the level of performance considered to be adequate mastery of the content and skills (often called "proficient"). Categories of performance below and above the proficient level are also often described to characterize the score distribution of the group of test takers.

The process for developing NALS and determining the performance levels was different. This approach toward test development does not—and was not intended to—provide the necessary foundation for setting standards for what adults need in order to adequately function in society, and there is no way to compensate for this after the fact. That is, there is no way to set a specific cut score that would separate adults who have sufficient literacy skills to function in society from those who do not. This does not mean that performance levels should not be used for reporting NALS results or that cut scores should not be set. But it does mean that users need to be careful about the inferences about the test results that can be supported and the inferences that cannot.

DEVELOPMENT OF PERFORMANCE-LEVEL DESCRIPTIONS AND CUT SCORES

Overview of the Process Used for the 1992 NALS

The process of determining performance levels for the 1992 NALS was based partially on analyses conducted on data from the two earlier assessments of adults' literacy skills. The analyses focused on identifying the features of the assessment tasks and stimulus materials that contributed to the difficulty of the test questions. These analyses had been used to determine performance levels for the Survey of Workplace Literacy, the survey of job seekers conducted in 1990.[1] The analyses conducted on the prior surveys were not entirely replicated for NALS. Instead, new analyses were conducted to evaluate the appropriateness of the performance levels and associated cut scores that had been used for the survey of job seekers. Based on these analyses, slight adjustments were made in the existing performance levels before adopting them for NALS. This process is described more fully below.

The first step in the process that ultimately led to the formulation of NALS performance levels was an in-depth examination of the items included on the Young Adult Literacy Survey and the Survey of Workplace Literacy, to identify the features judged to contribute to their complexity.[2]

For the prose literacy items, four features were judged to contribute to their complexity:

- **Type of match:** whether finding the information needed to answer

---

[1]The analyses were conducted on the Young Adult Literacy Survey but performance levels were not used in reporting its results. The analyses were partly replicated and extended to yield performance levels for the Survey of Workplace Literacy.

[2]See Chapter 13 of the NALS Technical Manual for additional details about the process (http://www.nces.ed.gov/pubsearch/pubsinfo.asp?pubid=2001457).

the question involved simply locating the answer in the text, cycling through the text iteratively, integrating multiple pieces of information, or generating new information based on prior knowledge.

- **Abstractness** of the information requested.
- **Plausibility of distractors**: the extent of and location of information related to the question, other than the correct answer, that appears in the stimulus.
- **Readability index** as estimated using Fry's (1977) readability index.

The features judged to contribute to the complexity of document literacy items were the same as for prose, with the exception that an index of the structural complexity of the display was substituted for the readability index. For the quantitative literacy items, the identified features included type of match and plausibility of the distractors, as with the prose items, and structural complexity, as with the document items, along with two other features:

- **Operation specificity**: the process required for identifying the operation to perform and the numbers to manipulate.
- **Type of calculation**: the type and number of arithmetic operations.

A detailed schema was developed for use in "scoring" items according to these features, and the scores were referred to as complexity ratings.

The next step in the process involved determination of the cut scores for the performance levels used for reporting results of the 1990 Survey of Workplace Literacy. The process involved rank-ordering the items according to a statistical estimate of their difficulty, which was calculated using data from the actual survey respondents. The items were listed in order from least to most difficult, and the judgment-based ratings of complexity were displayed on the listing. Tables 3-1 through 3-3, respectively, present the lists of prose, document, and quantitative items rank-ordered by difficulty level.

This display was visually examined for natural groupings or break points. According to Kirsch, Jungeblut, and Mosenthal (2001, p. 332), "visual inspection of the distribution of [the ratings] along each of the literacy scales revealed several major [break] points occurring at roughly 50 point intervals beginning with a difficulty score of 225 on each scale."

The process of determining the break points was characterized as containing "some noise" and not accounting for all the score variance associated with performance on the literacy scales. It was noted that the shifts in complexity ratings did not necessarily occur at exactly 50 point intervals on the scales, but that assigning the exact range of scores to each level (e.g.,

TABLE 3-1 List of *Prose* Literacy Tasks, Along with RP80 Task
Difficulty, IRT Item Parameters, and Values of Variables Associated with
Task Difficulty: 1990 Survey of the Literacy of Job-Seekers

	Identifier	Task Description	Scaled RP80
Level 1	A111301	Toyota, Acura, Nissan	189
	AB21101	Swimmer: Underline sentence telling what Ms. Chanin ate	208
	A120501	Blood donor pamphlet	216
	A130601	Summons for jury service	237
Level 2	A120301	Blood donor pamphlet	245
	A100201	PHP subscriber letter	249
	A111401	Toyota, Acura, Nissan	250
	A121401	Dr. Spock column: Alterntv to phys punish	251
	AB21201	Swimmer: Age Ms. Chanin began to swim competitively	250
	A131001	Shadows Columbus saw	280
	AB80801	Illegal questions	265
	AB41001	Declaration: Describe what poem is about	263
	AB81101	New methods for capital gains	277
	AB71001	Instruction to return appliance: Indicate best note	275
	AB90501	Questions for new jurors	281
	AB90701	Financial security tips	262
	A130901	Shadows Columbus saw	282
Level 3	AB60201	Make out check: Write letter explaining bill error	280
	AB90601	Financial security tips	299
	A121201	Dr. Spock column: Why phys punish accptd	285
	AB70401	Almanac vitamins: List correct info from almanac	289
	A100301	PHP subscriber letter	294
	A130701	Shadows Columbus saw	298
	A130801	Shadows Columbus saw	303
	AB60601	Economic index: Underline sentence explaining action	305
	A121301	Dr. Spock column: 2 cons against phys punish	312
	AB90401	Questions for new jurors	300
	AB80901	Illegal questions	316
	A111101	Toyota, Acura, Nissan	319

IRT Parameters				Type of	Distractor	Information
a	b	c	Readability	Match	Plausibility	Type
0.868	−2.488	0.000	8	1	1	1
1.125	−1.901	0.000	8	1	1	1
0.945	−1.896	0.000	7	1	1	2
1.213	−1.295	0.000	7	3	2	2
0.956	−1.322	0.000	7	1	2	3
1.005	−1.195	0.000	10	3	1	3
1.144	−1.088	0.000	8	3	2	4
1.035	−1.146	0.000	8	2	2	3
1.070	−1.125	0.000	8	3	4	2
1.578	−0.312	0.000	9	3	1	2
1.141	−0.788	0.000	6	3	2	2
0.622	−1.433	0.000	4	3	1	3
1.025	−0.638	0.000	7	4	1	3
1.378	−0.306	0.266	5	3	2	3
1.118	−0.493	0.000	6	4	2	1
1.563	−0.667	0.000	8	3	2	4
1.633	−0.255	0.000	9	3	4	1
1.241	−0.440	0.000	7	3	2	4
1.295	−0.050	0.000	8	2	2	4
1.167	−0.390	0.000	8	3	2	4
0.706	−0.765	0.000	7	3	4	1
0.853	−0.479	0.000	10	4	3	2
1.070	−0.203	0.000	9	3	2	3
0.515	−0.929	0.000	9	3	2	2
0.809	−0.320	0.000	10	3	2	4
0.836	−0.139	0.000	8	3	3	4
1.230	−0.072	0.000	6	4	2	3
0.905	−0.003	0.000	6	4	3	3
0.772	−0.084	0.000	8	4	3	2

continued

TABLE 3-1 Continued

	Identifier	Task Description	Scaled RP80
Level 4	AB40901	Korean Jet: Give argument made in article	329
	A131101	Shadows Columbus saw	332
	AB90801	Financial security tips	331
	AB30601	Technology: Orally explain info from article	333
	AB50201	Panel: Determine surprising future headline	343
	A101101	AmerExp: 2 similarities in handling receipts	346
	AB71101	Explain difference between 2 types of benefits	348
	AB81301	New methods for capital gains	355
	A120401	Blood donor pamphlet	358
	AB31201	Dickinson: Describe what is expessed in poem	363
	AB30501	Technology: Underline sentence explaining action	371
Level 5	AB81201	New methods for capital gains	384
	A111201	Toyota, Acura, Nissan	404
	A101201	AmExp: 2 diffs in handling receipts	441
	AB50101	Panel: Find information from article	469

TABLE 3-2 List of *Document* Literacy Tasks, Along with RP80 Task Difficulty Score, IRT Item Parameters, and Values of Variables Associated with Task Difficulty (structural complexity, type of match, plausibility of distractor, type of information): 1990 Survey of the Literacy of Job-Seekers

	Identifier	Task Description	RP80
Level 1	SCOR100	Social Security card: Sign name on line	70
	SCOR300	Driver's license: Locate expiration date	152
	SCOR200	Traffic signs	176
	AB60803	Nurses' convention: What is time of program?	181
	AB60802	Nurses' convention: What is date of program?	187
	SCOR400	Medicine dosage	186
	AB71201	Mark correct movie from given information	189
	A110501	Registration & tuition info	189
	AB70104	Job application: Complete personal information	193
	AB60801	Nurses' convention: Write correct day of program	199
	SCOR500	Theatre trip information	197

IRT Parameters

a	b	c	Readability	Type of Match	Distractor Plausibility	Information Type
0.826	0.166	0.000	10	4	4	4
0.849	0.258	0.000	9	5	4	1
0.851	0.236	0.000	8	5	5	2
0.915	0.347	0.000	8	4	4	4
1.161	0.861	0.196	13	4	4	4
0.763	0.416	0.000	8	4	2	4
0.783	0.482	0.000	9	6	2	5
0.803	0.652	0.000	7	5	5	3
0.458	−0.056	0.000	7	4	5	2
0.725	0.691	0.000	6	6	2	4
0.591	0.593	0.000	8	6	4	4
0.295	−0.546	0.000	7	2	4	2
0.578	1.192	0.000	8	8	4	5
0.630	2.034	0.000	8	7	5	5
0.466	2.112	0.000	13	6	5	4

IRT Parameters

a	b	c	Complexity	Type of Match	Distractor Plausibility	Information Type
0.505	−4.804	0.000	1	1	1	1
0.918	−2.525	0.000	2	1	2	1
0.566	−2.567	0.000	1	1	1	1
1.439	−1.650	0.000	1	1	1	1
1.232	−1.620	0.000	1	1	1	1
0.442	−2.779	0.000	2	1	2	2
0.940	−1.802	0.000	8	2	2	1
0.763	−1.960	0.000	3	1	2	2
0.543	−2.337	0.000	1	2	1	2
1.017	−1.539	0.000	1	1	2	1
0.671	−1.952	0.000	2	1	2	2

continued

TABLE 3-2 Continued

	Identifier	Task Description	RP80
	AB60301	Phone message: Write correct name of caller	200
	AB60302	Phone message: Write correct number of caller	202
	AB80301	How companies share market	203
	AB60401	Food coupons	204
	AB60701	Nurses' convention: Who would be asked questions	206
	A120601	MasterCard/Visa statement	211
	AB61001	Nurses' convention: Write correct place for tables	217
	A110301	Dessert recipes	216
	AB70903	Checking deposit: Enter correct amount of check	223
	AB70901	Checking deposit: Enter correct date	224
	AB50801	Wage & tax statement: What is current net pay?	224
	A130201	El Paso Gas & Electric bill	223
Level 2	AB70801	Classified: Match list with coupons	229
	AB30101	Street map: Locate intersection	232
	AB30201	Sign out sheet: Respond to call about resident	232
	AB40101	School registration: Mark correct age information	234
	A131201	Tempra dosage chart	233
	AB31301	Facts about fire: Mark information in article	235
	AB80401	How companies share market	236
	AB60306	Phone message: Write whom message is for	237
	AB60104	Make out check: Enter correct amount written out	238
	AB21301	Bus schedule	238
	A110201	Dessert recipes	239
	AB30301	Sign out sheet: Respond to call about resident	240
	AB30701	Major medical: Locate eligibility from table	245
	AB60103	Make out check: Enter correct amount in numbers	245
	AB60101	Make out check: Enter correct date on check	246
	AB60102	Make out check: Paid to the correct place	246
	AB50401	Catalog order: Order product one	247
	AB60303	Phone message: Mark "please call" box	249
	AB50701	Almanac football: Explain why an award is given	254
	AB20101	Energy graph: Find answer for given conditions (1)	255
	A120901	MasterCard/Visa statement	257
	A130101	El Paso Gas & Electric bill	257
	AB91101	Minimum wage power	260
	AB81001	Consumer Reports books	261
	AB90101	Pest control warning	261
	AB21501	With graph, predict sales for spring 1985	261
	AB20601	Yellow pages: Find place open Saturday	266
	A130401	El Paso Gas & Electric bill	270
	AB70902	Checking deposit: Enter correct cash amount	271

| IRT Parameters | | | | Type of | Distractor | Information |
a	b	c	Complexity	Match	Plausibility	Type
1.454	−1.283	0.000	1	1	2	1
1.069	−1.434	0.000	1	1	1	1
1.292	−1.250	0.000	7	2	2	2
0.633	−1.898	0.000	3	2	2	1
1.179	−1.296	0.000	1	2	2	1
0.997	−1.296	0.000	6	1	2	2
0.766	−1.454	0.000	1	1	2	2
1.029	−1.173	0.000	5	3	2	1
1.266	−0.922	0.000	3	2	2	1
0.990	−1.089	0.000	3	1	1	1
0.734	−1.366	0.000	5	2	2	2
1.317	−0.868	0.000	8	1	2	2
1.143	−0.881	0.000	8	2	3	1
0.954	−0.956	0.000	4	2	2	2
0.615	−1.408	0.000	2	3	2	1
0.821	−1.063	0.000	6	2	2	3
1.005	−0.872	0.000	5	2	3	3
0.721	−1.170	0.000	1	2	3	2
1.014	−0.815	0.000	7	3	2	2
0.948	−0.868	0.000	1	2	3	1
1.538	−0.525	0.000	6	3	2	1
0.593	−1.345	0.000	2	2	3	2
0.821	−0.947	0.000	5	3	2	1
0.904	−0.845	0.000	2	2	2	3
0.961	−0.703	0.000	4	2	2	2
0.993	−0.674	0.000	6	3	2	1
1.254	−0.497	0.000	6	3	2	1
1.408	−0.425	0.000	6	3	2	1
0.773	−0.883	0.000	8	3	2	1
0.904	−0.680	0.000	1	2	2	2
1.182	−0.373	0.000	6	2	2	3
1.154	−0.193	0.228	4	3	2	1
0.610	−0.974	0.000	6	1	2	2
0.953	−0.483	0.000	8	2	2	2
0.921	−0.447	0.000	4	3	3	2
1.093	−0.304	0.000	4	3	2	1
0.889	−0.471	0.000	2	3	3	2
0.799	−0.572	0.000	5	3	2	2
1.078	−0.143	0.106	7	3	2	1
0.635	−0.663	0.000	8	3	3	2
0.858	−0.303	0.000	3	3	3	2

continued

TABLE 3-2 Continued

	Identifier	Task Description	RP80
Level 3	AB50601	Almanac football: Locate page of info in almanac	276
	A110701	Registration & tuition info	277
	AB20201	Energy graph: Find answer for given conditions (2)	278
	AB31101	Abrasive gd: Can product be used in given case?	280
	AB80101	Burning out of control	281
	AB70701	Follow directions on map: Give correct location	284
	A110801	Washington/Boston schedule	284
	AB70301	Almanac vitamins: Locate list of info in almanac	287
	AB20401	Yellow pages: Find a list of stores	289
	AB20501	Yellow pages: Find phone number of given place	291
	AB60305	Phone message: Write who took the message	293
	AB30401	Sign out sheet: Respond to call about resident (2)	297
	AB31001	Abrasive guide: Type of sandpaper for sealing	304
	AB20301	Energy: Yr 2000 source prcnt power larger than 71	307
	AB90901	U.S. Savings Bonds	308
	AB60304	Phone message: Write out correct message	310
	AB81002	Consumer Reports books	311
	AB20801	Bus schd: Take correct bus for given condition (2)	313
	AB50402	Catalog order: Order product two	314
	AB40401	Almanac: Find page containing chart for given info	314
	AB21001	Bus schd: Take correct bus for given condition (4)	315
	AB60502	Petroleum graph: Complete graph including axes	318
	A120701	MasterCard/Visa statement	320
	AB20701	Bus schd: Take correct bus for given condition (1)	324
Level 4	A131301	Tempra dosage chart	326
	AB50501	Telephone bill: Mark information on bill	330
	AB91401	Consumer Reports index	330
	AB30801	Almanac: Find page containing chart for given info	347
	AB20901	Bus schd: After 2:35, how long til Flint&Acad bus	348
	A130301	El Paso Gas & Electric bill	362
	A120801	MasterCard/Visa statement	363
	AB91301	Consumer Reports index	367
Level 5	AB60501	Petroleum graph: Label axes of graph	378
	AB30901	Almanac: Determine pattern in exports across years	380
	A100701	Spotlight economy	381
	A100501	Spotlight economy	386
	A100401	Spotlight economy	406
	AB51001	Income tax table	421
	A100601	Spotlight economy	465

| IRT Parameters | | | | Type of | Distractor | Information |
a	b	c	Complexity	Match	Plausibility	Type
1.001	−0.083	0.000	5	3	2	2
0.820	−0.246	0.000	3	2	5	2
0.936	−0.023	0.097	4	4	2	1
0.762	−0.257	0.000	10	5	2	3
0.550	−0.656	0.000	2	3	2	2
0.799	−0.126	0.000	4	4	2	2
0.491	−0.766	0.000	9	2	4	2
0.754	−0.134	0.000	5	3	4	2
0.479	−0.468	0.144	7	2	5	1
0.415	−0.772	0.088	7	2	4	2
0.640	−0.221	0.000	1	5	2	1
0.666	−0.089	0.000	2	2	1	4
0.831	0.285	0.000	10	4	2	2
1.090	0.684	0.142	4	4	2	1
0.932	0.479	0.000	6	4	4	2
0.895	0.462	0.000	1	5	2	3
0.975	0.570	0.000	4	3	5	2
1.282	0.902	0.144	10	3	5	2
1.108	0.717	0.000	8	4	4	3
0.771	0.397	0.000	5	4	3	2
0.730	0.521	0.144	10	3	4	2
1.082	0.783	0.000	10	6	2	2
0.513	−0.015	0.000	6	2	4	2
0.522	0.293	0.131	10	3	4	2
0.624	0.386	0.000	5	4	4	2
0.360	−0.512	0.000	7	4	4	2
0.852	0.801	0.000	7	3	5	3
0.704	0.929	0.000	5	4	5	2
1.169	1.521	0.163	10	5	4	2
0.980	1.539	0.000	8	5	4	5
0.727	1.266	0.000	6	5	4	2
0.620	1.158	0.000	7	4	5	3
1.103	1.938	0.000	11	7	2	5
0.299	0.000	0.000	7	5	5	3
0.746	1.636	0.000	10	5	5	2
0.982	1.993	0.000	10	5	5	5
0.489	1.545	0.000	10	5	5	2
0.257	0.328	0.000	9	4	5	2
0.510	2.737	0.000	10	7	5	2

TABLE 3-3 List of *Quantitative* Literacy Tasks, Along with RP80 Task Difficulty, IRT Item Parameters, and Values of Variables Associated with Task Difficulty (structural complexity, type of match, plausibility of distractors, type of calculation, and specificity of operation): 1990 Survey of the Literacy of Job-Seekers

	Identifier	Quantitative Literacy Items	RP80
Level 1	AB70904	Enter total amount of both checks being deposited	221
Level 2	AB50404	Catalog order: Shipping, handling, and total	271
	AB91201	Tempra coupon	271
	AB40701	Check ledger: Complete ledger (1)	277
	A121001	Insurance protection workform	275
Level 3	AB90102	Pest control warning	279
	AB40702	Check ledger: Complete ledger (2)	281
	AB40703	Check ledger: Complete ledger (3)	282
	A131601	Money rates: Thursday vs. one year ago	281
	AB40704	Check ledger: Complete ledger (4)	283
	AB80201	Burning out of control	286
	A110101	Dessert recipes	289
	AB90201	LPGA money leaders	294
	A120101	Businessland printer stand	300
	AB81003	Consumer Reports books	301
	AB80601	Valet airport parking discount	307
	AB40301	Unit price: Mark economical brand	311
	A131701	Money rates: Compare S&L w/mutual funds	312
	AB80701	Valet airport parking discount	315
	A100101	Pizza coupons	316
	AB90301	LPGA money leaders	320
	A110401	Dessert recipes	323
	A131401	Tempra dosage chart	322
Level 4	AB40501	Airline schedule: Plan travel arrangements (1)	326
	AB70501	Lunch: Determine correct change using info in menu	331
	A120201	Businessland printer stand	340
	A110901	Washington/Boston train schedule	340
	AB60901	Nurses' convention: Write number of seats needed	346
	AB70601	Lunch: Determine 10% tip using given info	349
	A111001	Washington/Boston train schedule	355
	A130501	El Paso Gas & Electric bill	352
	A100801	Spotlight economy	356

IRT Parameters				Type of Match	Distractor Plausibility	Calculation Type	Op Specfy
a	b	c	Complexity				
0.869	−1.970	0.000	2	1	1	1	1
0.968	−0.952	0.000	6	3	2	1	3
0.947	−0.977	0.000	1	2	1	5	4
1.597	−0.501	0.000	3	2	2	1	4
0.936	−0.898	0.000	2	3	2	3	2
0.883	−0.881	0.000	2	3	3	1	4
1.936	−0.345	0.000	3	2	2	2	4
1.874	−0.332	0.000	3	1	2	2	4
1.073	−0.679	0.000	4	3	2	2	4
1.970	−0.295	0.000	3	2	2	2	4
0.848	−0.790	0.000	2	3	2	2	4
0.813	−0.775	0.000	5	3	2	2	4
0.896	−0.588	0.000	5	2	2	2	4
1.022	−0.369	0.000	2	3	3	2	4
0.769	−0.609	0.000	7	2	3	1	4
0.567	−0.886	0.000	2	3	3	2	4
0.816	0.217	0.448	2	2	3	4	6
1.001	−0.169	0.000	4	3	3	2	2
0.705	−0.450	0.000	2	2	3	3	4
0.690	−0.472	0.000	2	3	3	1	4
1.044	0.017	0.000	5	1	2	4	3
1.180	0.157	0.000	5	3	2	3	6
1.038	0.046	0.000	5	3	3	2	4
0.910	0.006	0.000	3	3	3	5	3
0.894	0.091	0.000	2	2	2	5	4
0.871	0.232	0.000	2	3	4	3	5
1.038	0.371	0.000	7	4	4	2	5
0.504	−0.355	0.000	3	4	4	1	5
0.873	0.384	0.000	2	1	2	5	7
0.815	0.434	0.000	7	4	4	2	5
0.772	0.323	0.000	8	3	4	2	2
0.874	0.520	0.000	8	5	4	2	2

continued

TABLE 3-3 Continued

	Identifier	Quantitative Literacy Items	RP80
	AB40201	Unit price: Estimate cost/oz of peanut butter	356
	A121101	Insurance protection workform	356
	A100901	Camp advertisement	366
	A101001	Camp advertisement	366
	AB80501	How companies share market	371
Level 5	A131501	Tempra dosage chart	381
	AB50403	Catalog order: Order product three	382
	AB91001	U.S. Savings Bonds	385
	A110601	Registration & tuition info	407
	AB50301	Interest charges: Orally explain computation	433

277-319 for Level 3 of document literacy; and 331-370 for Level 4 of quantitative literacy) would imply a level of precision of measurement that the test designers believed was inappropriate for the methodology adopted. Thus, identical score intervals were adopted for each of the three literacy scales as shown below:

- Level 1: 0–225
- Level 2: 226–275
- Level 3: 276–325
- Level 4: 326–375
- Level 5: 376–500

Performance-level descriptions were developed by summarizing the features of the items that had difficulty values that fell within each of the score ranges.

  These procedures were not entirely replicated to determine the performance levels for NALS, in part because NALS used some of the items from the two earlier assessments. Instead, statistical estimates of test question difficulty levels were carried out for the newly developed NALS items (the items that had not been used on the earlier assessments), and the correlation between these difficulty levels and the item complexity ratings was determined. The test designers judged the correlations to be sufficiently similar to those from the earlier assessments and chose to use the same score scale breakpoints for NALS as had been used for the performance levels for the Survey of Workplace Literacy. Minor adjustments were made to the lan-

IRT Parameters				Type of Match	Distractor Plausibility	Calculation Type	Op Specfy
a	b	c	Complexity				
0.818	0.455	0.000	2	1	2	4	5
0.860	0.513	0.000	2	1	2	5	4
0.683	0.447	0.000	2	2	4	5	4
0.974	0.795	0.000	2	3	4	5	4
1.163	1.027	0.000	6	3	2	3	6
0.916	1.031	0.000	5	3	5	3	5
0.609	0.601	0.000	6	4	5	5	5
0.908	1.083	0.000	6	4	5	2	4
0.624	1.078	0.000	8	2	5	5	5
0.602	1.523	0.000	2	5	5	5	7

guage describing the existing performance levels. The resulting performance-level descriptions appear in Table 3-4.

Findings About the Process Used for the 1992 NALS

The available written documentation about the procedures used for determining performance levels for NALS does not specify some of the more important details about the process (see Kirsch, Jungeblut, and Mosenthal, 2001, Chapter 13). For instance, it is not clear who participated in producing the complexity ratings or exactly how this task was handled. Determination of the cut scores involved examination of the listing of items for break points, but the break points are not entirely obvious. It is not clear that other people looking at this list would make the same choices for break points. In addition, it is not always clear whether the procedures described in the technical manual pertain to NALS or to one of the earlier assessments. A more open and public process combined with more explicit, transparent documentation is likely to lead to better understanding of how the levels were determined and what conclusions can be drawn about the results.

The performance levels produced by this approach were score ranges based on the cognitive processes required to respond to the items. While the 1992 score levels were used to inform a variety of programmatic decisions, there is a benefit to developing performance levels through open discussions with stakeholders. Such a process would result in levels that would be more readily understood.

The process for determining the cut scores for the performance levels

TABLE 3-4 National Adult Literacy Survey (NALS) Performance-Level Descriptions

	Prose	Document	Quantitative
Level 1 *0-225*	Most of the tasks in this level require the reader to read relatively short text to locate a single piece of information which is identical to or synonymous with the information given in the question or directive. If plausible but incorrect information is present in the text, it tends not to be located near the correct information.	Tasks in this level tend to require the reader either to locate a piece of information based on a literal match or to enter information from personal knowledge onto a document. Little, if any, distracting information is present.	Tasks in this level require readers to perform single, relatively simple arithmetic operations, such as addition. The numbers to be used are provided and the arithmetic operation to be performed is specified.
Level 2 *226-275*	Some tasks in this level require readers to locate a single piece of information in the text; however, several distractors or plausible but incorrect pieces of information may be present, or low-level inferences may be required. Other tasks require the reader to integrate two or more pieces of information or to compare and contrast easily identifiable information based on a criterion provided in the question or directive.	Tasks in this level are more varied than those in Level 1. Some require the readers to match a single piece of information; however, several distractors may be present, or the match may require low-level inferences. Tasks in this level may also ask the reader to cycle through information in a document or to integrate information from various parts of a document.	Tasks in this level typically require readers to perform a single operation using numbers that are either stated in the task or easily located in the material. The operation to be performed may be stated in the question or easily determined from the format of the material (for example, an order form).
Level 3 *276-325*	Tasks in this level tend to require readers to make literal or synonymous matches between the text and information given in the task, or to make matches that require low-level inferences. Other tasks ask readers to integrate information from dense or lengthy text that contains no organizational aids such as headings. Readers may also be asked to generate a response based on information that can be easily identified in the text. Distracting information is present, but is not located near the correct information.	Some tasks in this level require the reader to integrate multiple pieces of information from one or more documents. Others ask readers to cycle through rather complex tables or graphs which contain information that is irrelevant or inappropriate to the task.	In tasks in this level, two or more numbers are typically needed to solve the problem, and these must be found in the material. The operation(s) needed can be determined from the arithmetic relation terms used in the question or directive.
Level 4 *326-375*	These tasks require readers to perform multiple-feature matches and to integrate or synthesize information from complex or lengthy passages. More complex inferences are needed to perform successfully. Conditional information is frequently present in tasks at this level and must be taken into consideration by the reader.	Tasks in this level, like those at the previous levels, ask readers to perform multiple-feature matches, cycle through documents, and integrate information; however, they require a greater degree of inferencing. Many of these tasks require readers to provide numerous responses but do not designate how many responses are needed. Conditional information is also present in the document tasks at this level and must be taken into account by the reader.	These tasks tend to require readers to perform two or more sequential operations or a single operation in which the quantities are found in different types of displays, or the operations must be inferred from semantic information given or drawn from prior knowledge.
Level 5 *376-500*	Some tasks in this level require the reader to search for information in dense text which contains a number of plausible distractors. Others ask readers to make high-level inferences or use specialized background knowledge. Some tasks ask readers to contrast complex information.	Tasks in this level require the reader to search through complex displays that contain multiple distractors, to make high-level text-based inferences, and to use specialized knowledge.	These tasks require readers to perform multiple operations sequentially. They must disembed the features of the problem from text or rely on background knowledge to determine the quantities or operations needed.

Source: U.S. Department of Education, National Center for Education Statistics, National Adult Literacy Survey, 1992.

used for reporting NALS in 1992 did not involve one of the typical methods documented in the psychometric literature. This is not to criticize the test designers' choice of procedures, as it appears that they were not asked to set standards for NALS, and hence one would not expect them to use one of these methods. It is our view, however, that there are benefits to using one or more of these documented methods. Use of established procedures for setting cut scores allows one to draw from the existing research and experiential base to gather information about the method, such as prescribed ways to implement the method, variations on the method, research on its advantages and disadvantages, and so on. In addition, use of established procedures facilitates communication with others about the general process. For example, if the technical manual for an assessment program indicates that the *body of work method* was used to set the cut scores, people can refer to the research literature for further details about what this typically entails.

CHOICE OF RESPONSE PROBABILITY VALUES

The Effects of Response Probability Values on the Performance Levels

The difficulty level of test questions can be estimated using a statistical procedure called item response theory (IRT). With IRT, a curve is estimated that gives the probability of a correct response from individuals across the range of proficiency. The curve is described in terms of parameters in a mathematical model. One of the parameter estimates, the difficulty parameter, typically corresponds to the score (or proficiency level) at which an individual has a 50 percent chance of answering the question correctly. Under this approach, it is also possible to designate, for the purposes of interpreting an item's response curve, the proficiency at which the probability is any particular value that users find helpful. In 1992 the test developers chose to calculate test question difficulty values representing the proficiency level at which an individual had an 80 percent chance of answering an item correctly. The items were rank-ordered according to this estimate of their difficulty levels. Thus, the scaled scores used in determining the score ranges associated with the five performance levels were the scaled scores associated with an 80 percent probability of responding correctly.

The choice of the specific response probability value (e.g., 50, 65, or 80 percent) does not affect either the estimates of item response curves or distributions of proficiency. It is nevertheless an important decision because it affects users' interpretations of the value of the scale scores used to separate the performance levels. Furthermore, due to the imprecision of the connection between the mathematical definitions of response probability values and the linguistic descriptions of their implications for performance that judges use to set standards, the cut scores could be higher or lower simply as a consequence of the response probability selected. As mentioned earlier, the decision to use a response probability of 80 percent for the 1992 NALS has been the subject of subsequent debate, which has centered on whether the use of a response probability of 80 percent may have misrepresented the literacy levels of adults in the United States by producing cut scores that were too high (Baron, 2002; Kirsch, 2002; Kirsch et al., 2001, Ch. 14; Matthews, 2001; Sticht, 2004), to the extent that having a probability lower than 80 percent was misinterpreted as "not being able to do" the task required by an item.

In the final chapter of the technical manual (see Kirsch et al., 2001, Chapter 14), Kolstad demonstrated how the choice of a response probability value affects the value of the cut scores, under the presumption that response probability values might change considerably, while the everyday interpretation of the resulting numbers did not. He conducted a reanalysis of NALS data using a response probability value of 50 percent; that is, he calculated the difficulty of the items based on a 50 percent probability of responding correctly. This reanalysis demonstrated that use of a response probability value of 50 percent rather than 80 percent, with both interpreted by the same everyday language interpretation (e.g., that an individual at that level was likely to get an item correct), would have lowered the cut scores associated with the performance levels in such a way that a much smaller percentage of adults would have been classified at the lowest level. For example, the cut score based on a response probability of 80 placed slightly more than 20 percent of respondents in the lowest performance level; the cut score based on a response probability of 50 classified only 9 percent at this level.

It is important to point out here that the underlying distribution of scores did not change (and clearly could not change) with this reanalysis. There were no differences in the percentages of individuals scoring at each scale score. The only changes were the response probability criteria and interpretation of the cut scores. Using 80 percent as the response probability criterion, we would say that 20 percent of the population could perform the skills described by the first performance level with 80 percent accuracy. If the accuracy level was set at 50 percent and the same everyday language interpretation was applied, a larger share of the population could be said to perform these skills.

Findings About the Choice of Response Probability Values

Like many decisions made in connection with developing a test, the choice of a specific response probability value requires both technical and nontechnical considerations. For example, a high response probability may be adopted when the primary objective of the test is to certify, with a high degree of certainty, that test takers have mastered the content and skills. In licensing decisions, one would want to have a high degree of confidence that a potential license recipient has truly mastered the requisite subject matter and skills. When there are no high-stakes decisions associated with test results, a lower response probability value may be more appropriate.

Choice of a response probability value requires making a judgment, and reasonable people may disagree about which of several options is most appropriate. For this reason, it is important to lay out the logic behind the decision. It is not clear from the NALS Technical Manual (Kirsch et al., 2001) that the consequences associated with the choice of a response probability of 80 percent were fully explored or that other options were considered. Furthermore, the technical manual (Kirsch et al., 2001) contains contradictory information—one chapter that specifies the response probability value used and another chapter that demonstrates how alternate choices would have affected the resulting cut scores. Including contradictory information like this in a technical manual is very disconcerting to those who must interpret and use the assessment results.

It is our opinion that the choice of a response probability value to use in setting cut scores should be based on a thorough consideration of technical and nontechnical factors, such as the difficulty level of the test in relation to the proficiency level of the examinees, the objectives of the assessment, the ways the test results are used, and the consequences associated with these uses of test results. The logic and rationale for the choice should be clearly documented. Additional discussion of response probabilities appears in the technical note to this chapter, and we revisit the topic in Chapter 5.

MAPPING ITEMS TO PERFORMANCE LEVELS

Response probabilities are calculated for purposes other than determining cut scores. One of the most common uses of response probability values is to "map" items to specific score levels in order to more tangibly describe what it means to score at the specific level. For NALS, as described in the preceding section, the scale score associated with an 80 percent probability of responding correctly—abbreviated in the measurement literature as rp80—was calculated for each NALS item. Selected items were then mapped to the performance level whose associated score range encompassed the rp80 difficulty value. The choice of rp80 (as opposed to rp65, or some other value) appears to have been made both to conform to conventional item mapping practices at the time (e.g., NAEP used rp80 at the time, although it has since changed to rp67) and because it represents the concept of "mastery" as it is generally conceptualized in the field of education (Kirsch et al., 2001; personal communication, August 2004).

Item mapping is a useful tool for communicating about test performance. A common misperception occurs with its use, however: namely, that individuals who score at the specific level will respond correctly and those at lower levels will respond incorrectly. Much of the NALS results that were publicly reported displayed items mapped to only a single performance level, the level associated with a response probability of 80 percent. This all-or-nothing interpretation ignores the continuous nature of response probabilities. That is, for any given item, individuals at every score point have some probability of responding correctly.

Table 3-5, which originally appeared in Chapter 14 of the technical manual as Figure 14-4 (Kirsch et al., 2001), demonstrates this point using four sample NALS prose tasks. Each task is mapped to four different scale scores according to four different probabilities of a correct response (rp80, rp65, rp50, and rp35). Consider the first mapped prose task, "identify country in short article." According to the figure, individuals who achieved a scaled score of 149 had an 80 percent chance of responding correctly; those who scored 123 had a 65 percent change of responding correctly; those with a score of 102 had a 50 percent chance of responding correctly; and those who scored 81 had a 35 percent chance of responding correctly.

Although those who worked on NALS had a rationale for selecting an rp80 criterion for use in mapping exemplary items to the performance levels, other response probability values might have been used and displays such as in Table 3-5 might have been prepared. If item mapping procedures are to be used in describing performance on NAAL, we encourage use of display more like that in Table 3-5. Additional information about item mapping appears in the technical note to this chapter. We also revisit this issue in Chapter 6, where we discuss methods of communicating about NAAL results.

Recommendation 3-1: If the Department of Education decides to use an item mapping procedure to exemplify performance on the National Assessment of Adult Literacy (NAAL), displays should demonstrate that individuals who score at all of the performance levels have some likelihood of responding correctly to the items.

CONCLUSION

As clearly stated by the test designers, the decision to collapse the NALS score distribution into five categories or ranges of performance was not done with the intent or desire to establish standards reflecting the extent of literacy skills that adults in the United States need or should have. Creating such levels was a means to convey the summary of performance on NALS.

Some of the more important details about the process were not specified in the NALS Technical Manual (Kirsch et al., 2001). Determination of the cut scores involved examination of the listing of items for break points, but the actual break points were not entirely obvious. It is not clear who participated in this process or how decisions were made. In addition, the choice of the response probability value of 80 percent is not fully documented. All of this suggests that one should not automatically accept the five NALS performance categories as the representation of defensible or justified levels of performance expectations.

The performance levels produced by the 1992 approach were groupings based on judgments about the complexity of the thinking processes required to respond to the items. While these levels might be useful for characterizing adults' literacy skills, the process through which they were determined is not one that would typically be used to derive performance levels expected to inform policy interventions or to identify needed programs. It is the committee's view that a more open, transparent process that relies on and utilizes stakeholder feedback is more likely to result in performance levels informative for the sorts of decisions expected to be based on the results.

Such a process is more in line with currently accepted practices for setting cut scores. The *Standards for Educational and Psychological Testing* (American Educational Research Association, American Psychological Association, and National Council on Measurement in Education, 1999) specifically call for (1) clear documentation of the rationale and procedures used for establishing cut scores (Standard 4.19), (2) investigation of the relations between test scores and relevant criteria (Standard 4.20), and (3) designing the judgmental process so that judges can bring their knowledge and experience to bear in a reasonable way (Standard 4.21). We relied on this guidance offered by the *Standards* in designing our approach to developing performance levels and setting cut scores, which is the subject of the remainder of this report.

TECHNICAL NOTE

Item Response Theory and Response Probabilities: A More Technical Explanation

This technical note provides additional details about item response theory and response probabilities. The section begins with a brief introduction to the two-parameter item response model. This is followed by a discussion of how some of the features of item response models can be exploited to devise ways to map test items to scale score levels and further exemplify the skills associated with specified proficiency levels. The section

TABLE 3-5 Difficulty Values of Selected Tasks Along the Prose Literacy Scale, Mapped at Four Response Probability Criteria: The 1992 National Adult Literacy Survey

	RP 80	RP 65	RP 50	RP 35
75				<81> Identify country in short article[a]
			<102> Identify country in short article[a]	
		<123> Identify country in short article[a]		
125				
				<145> Underline sentence explaining action stated in short article
	<149> Identify country in short article[a]			
			<169> Underline sentence explaining action stated in short article	
175				
		<194> Underline sentence explaining action stated in short article		
	<224> Underline sentence explaining action stated in short article			
225				
				<255> State in writing an argument made in a long newspaper story

TABLE 3-5 Continued

	RP 80	RP 65	RP 50	RP 35
275			<278> State in writing an argument made in a long newspaper story	
		<300> State in writing an argument made in a long newspaper story		
325	<329> State in writing an argument made in a long newspaper story			
				<358> Interpret a brief phrase from a lengthy news article
375			<378> Interpret a brief phrase from a lengthy news article	
		<398> Interpret a brief phrase from a lengthy news article		
	<424> Interpret abrief phrase from a lengthy news article			
425				

*a*At a scale score of 149, an individual has an 80 percent chance of a correct response to this item. At a scale score of 123, an individual has a 65 percent chance of a correct response. At a scale score of 102 and 81, individuals have, respectively, a 50 percent chance of responding correctly to the item.

concludes with a discussion of factors to consider when selecting response probability values.

Overview of the Two-Parameter Item Response Model

As mentioned above, IRT methodology was used for scaling the 1992 NALS items. While some of the equations and computations required by IRT are complicated, the underlying theoretical concept is actually quite straightforward, and the methodology provides some statistics very useful for interpreting assessment results. The IRT equation (referred to as the two-parameter logistic model, or 2-PL for short) used for scaling the 1992 NALS data appears below:

$$P\left(x_i = 1 \mid \theta_j\right) = \frac{1}{1 + e^{a_i(\theta - b_i)}} \tag{3-1}$$

The left-hand side of the equation symbolizes the probability (P) of responding correctly to an item (e.g., item i) given a specified ability level (referred to as theta or θ). The right-hand side of the equation gives the mechanism for calculating the probability of responding correctly, where a_i and b_i are referred to as "item parameters,"[3] and θ is the specified ability level. In IRT, this equation is typically used to estimate the probability that an individual, with a specified ability level θ, will correctly respond to an item. Alternatively, the probability P of a correct response can be specified along with the item parameters (a_i and b_i), and the equation can be solved for the value of theta associated with the specified probability value.

Exemplifying Assessment Results

A hallmark of IRT is the way it describes the relation of the probability of an item response to scores on the scale reflecting the level of performance on the construct measured by the test. That description has two parts, as illustrated in Figure 3-1. The first part describes the population density, or distribution of persons over the variable being measured. For the illustration in Figure 3-1, the variable being measured is prose literacy as defined by the 1992 NALS. A hypothetical population distribution is shown in the upper panel of Figure 3-1, simulated as a normal distribution.[4]

---

[3]Item discrimination is denoted by a_i; item location (difficulty) is denoted by b_i.

[4]A normal distribution is used for simplicity. The actual NALS distribution was skewed (see page N-3 of the NALS Technical Manual).

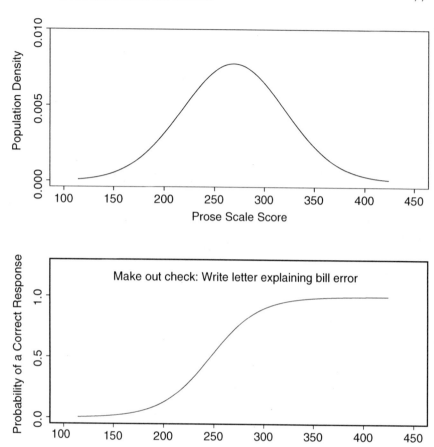

FIGURE 3-1 Upper panel: Distribution of proficiency in the population for the prose literacy scale. Lower panel: The trace line, or item characteristic curve, for a sample prose item.

The second part of an IRT description of item performance is the trace line, or item characteristic curve. A trace line shows the probability of a correct response to an item as a function of proficiency (in this case, prose literacy). Such a curve is shown in the lower panel of Figure 3-1 for an item that is described as requiring "the reader to write a brief letter explaining that an error has been made on a credit card bill" (Kirsch et al., 1993, p. 78). For this item, the trace line in Figure 3-1 shows that people with prose literacy scale scores higher than 300 are nearly certain to respond correctly, while those with scores lower than 200 are nearly certain to fail. The probability of a correct response rises relatively quickly as scores increase from 200 to 300.

Making Use of Trace Lines

Trace lines can be determined for each item on the assessment. The trace lines are estimated from the assessment data in a process called item calibration. Trace lines for the 39 open-ended items on the prose scale for the 1992 NALS are shown in Figure 3-2. The trace line shown in Figure 3-1 is one of those in the center of Figure 3-2. The variation in the trace lines for the different items in Figure 3-2 shows how the items vary in difficulty. Some trace lines are shifted to the left, indicating that lower scoring individuals have a high probability of responding correctly. Some trace lines are shifted to right, which means the items are more difficult and only very high-scoring individuals are likely to respond correctly.

As Figure 3-2 shows, some trace lines are steeper than others. The steeper the trace line, the more discriminating the item. That is, items with

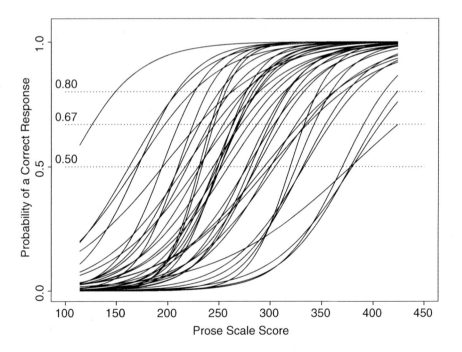

FIGURE 3-2 Trace lines for the 39 open-ended items on the prose scale for the 1992 NALS.

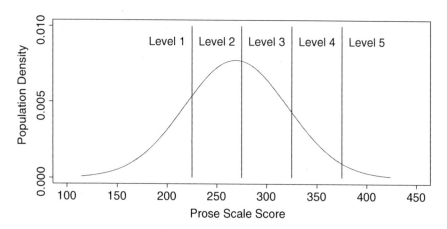

FIGURE 3-3 Division of the 1992 NALS prose literacy scale into five levels.

higher discrimination values are better at distinguishing among test takers' proficiency levels.

The collection of trace lines is used for several purposes. One purpose is the computation of scores for persons with particular patterns of item responses. Another purpose is to link the scales from repeated assessments. Such trace lines for items repeated between assessments were used to link the scale of the 1992 NALS to the 1985 Young Adult Literacy Survey. A similar linkage was constructed between the 1992 NALS and the 2003 NAAL.

In addition, the trace lines for each item may be used to describe how responses to the items are related to alternate reporting schemes for the literacy scale. For reporting purposes, the prose literacy scale for the 1992 NALS was divided into five levels using cut scores that are shown embedded in the population distribution in Figure 3-3. Using these levels for reporting, the proportion of the population scoring 225 or lower was said to be in Level 1, with the proportions in Levels 2, 3, and 4 representing score ranges of 50 points, and finally Level 5 included scores exceeding 375.

Mapping Items to Specific Scale Score Values

With a response probability (rp) criterion specified, it is possible to use the IRT model to "place" the items at some specific level on the scale. Placing an item at a specific level allows one to make statements or predictions about the likelihood that a person who scores at the level will answer the question correctly. For the 1992 NALS, items were placed at a specific

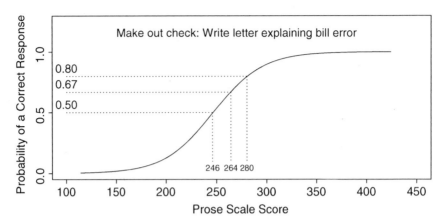

FIGURE 3-4 Scale scores associated with rp values of .50, .67, and .80 for a sample item from the NALS prose scale.

level as part of the process that was used to decide on the cut scores among the five levels and for use in reporting examples of items. For the 1992 NALS, an rp value of .80 was used. This means that each item was said to be "at" the value of the prose score scale for which the probability of a correct response was .80. For example, for the "write letter" item, it was said "this task is at 280 on the prose scale" (Kirsch et al., 1993, p. 78), as shown by the dotted lines in Figure 3-4.

Using these placements, items were said to be representative of what persons scoring in each level could do. Depending on where the item was placed within the level, it was noted whether an item was one of the easier or more difficult items in the level. For example, the "write letter" item was described as "one of the easier Level 3 tasks" (Kirsch, 1993, p. 78). These placements of items were also shown on item maps, such as the one that appeared on page 10 of Kirsch, 1993 (see Table 3-6); the purpose of the item maps is to aid in the interpretation of the meaning of scores on the scale and in the levels.

Some procedures, such as the bookmark standard-setting procedures, require the specification of an rp value to place the items on the scale. However, even when it is necessary to place an item at a specific point on the scale, it is important to remember that an item can be placed *anywhere* on the scale, with *some* rp value. For example, as illustrated in Figure 3-4, the "write letter" item is "at" 280 (and "in" Level 3, because that location is above 275) for an rp value of .80. However, this item is at 246, which places it in the lower middle of Level 2 (between 226 and 275) for an rp value of .50, and it is at 264, which is in the upper middle of Level 2 for an rp value of .67.

TABLE 3-6 National Adult Literacy Survey (NALS) Item Map

	Prose		Document		Quantitative
149	Identify country in short article	69	Sign your name	191	Total a bank deposit entry
210	Locate one piece of information in sports article	151	Locate expiration date on driver's license		
224	Underline sentence explaining action stated in short article	180	Locate time of meeting on a form		
		214	Using pie graph, locate type of vehicle having specific sales		
225					
226	Underline meaning of a term given in government brochure on supplemental security income	232	Locate intersection on a street map	238	Calculate postage and fees for certified mail
250	Locate two features of information in sports article	245	Locate eligibility from table of employee benefits	246	Determine difference in price between tickets for two shows
		259	Identify and enter background information on application for social security card	270	Calculate total costs of purchase from an order form
275 275	Interpret instructions from an appliance warranty	277	Identify information from bar graph depicting source of energy and year	278	Using calculator, calculate difference between regular and sale price from an advertisement
280	Write a brief letter explaining error made on a credit card bill	296	Use sign out sheet to respond to call about resident	308	Using calculator, determine the discount from an oil bill if paid within 10 days
304	Read a news article and identify a sentence that provides interpretation of a situation	314	Use bus schedule to determine appropriate bus for given set of conditions		
316	Read lengthy article to identify two behaviors that meet a stated condition	323	Enter information given into an automobile maintenance record form		
325					
328	State in writing an argument made in lengthy newspaper article	342	Identify the correct percentage meeting specified conditions from a table of such information	325	Plan travel arrangements for meeting using flight schedule
347	Explain difference between two types of employee benefits	348	Use bus schedule to determine appropriate bus for given set of conditions	331	Determine correct change using information in a menu
359	Contrast views expressed in two editorials on technologies available to make fuel-efficient cars			350	Using information stated in news article, calculate amount of money that should go to raising a child
362	Generate unfamiliar theme from short poems			368	Using eligibility pamphlet, calculate the yearly amount a couple would receive for basic supplemental security income
374	Compare two metaphors used in poem				
375					
382	Compare approaches stated in narrative on growing up	379	Use table of information to determine pattern in oil exports across years	375	Calculate miles per gallon using information given on mileage record chart
410	Summarize two ways lawyers may challenge prospective jurors	387	Using table comparing credit cards, identify the two categories used and write two differences between them	382	Determine individual and total costs on an order form for items in a catalog
423	Interpret a brief phrase from a lengthy news article	396	Use a table depicting information about parental involvement in school survey to write a paragraph summarizing extent to which parents and teachers agree	405	Using information in news article, calculate difference in times for completing a race
500				421	Using calculator, determine the total cost of carpet to cover a room

Source: U.S. Department of Education, National Center for Education Statistics, National Adult Literacy Survey, 1992.

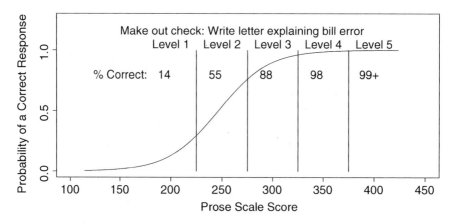

FIGURE 3-5 Percentage expected to answer the sample item correctly within each of the five levels of the 1992 NALS scale.

It should be emphasized that it is not necessary to place items at a single score location. For example, in reporting the results of the assessment, it is not necessary to say that an item is "at" some value (such as 280 for the "write letter" item).

Futhermore, there are more informative alternatives to placing items at a single score location. If an item is said to be "at" some scale value or "in" some level (as the "write letter" item is at 280 and in Level 3), it suggests that people scoring lower, or in lower levels, do not respond correctly. That is not the case. The trace line itself, as shown in Figure 3-4, reminds us that many people scoring in Level 2 (more than the upper half of those in Level 2) have a better than 50-50 chance of responding correctly to this item. A more accurate depiction of the likelihood of a correct response was presented in Appendix D of the 1992 technical manual (Kirsch et al., 2001). That appendix includes a representation of the trace line for each item at seven equally spaced scale scores between 150 and 450 (along with the rp80 value). This type of representation would allow readers to make inferences about this item much like those suggested by Figure 3-4.

Figure 3-5 shows the percentage expected to answer the "write letter" item in each of the five levels. These values can be computed from the IRT model (represented by equation 3-1), in combination with the population distribution.[5] With access to the data, one can alternatively simply tabulate

---

[5]They are the weighted average of the probabilities correct given by the trace line for each score within the level, weighted by the population density of persons at that score (in the upper panel of Figure 3-1). Using the Gaussian population distribution, those values are not extremely accurate for 1992 NALS; however, they are used here for illustrative purposes.

the observed proportion of examinees who responded correctly at each reporting level. The latter has been done often in recent NAEP reports (e.g., *The Nation's Report Card: Reading 2002*, http://www.nces.ed.gov/pubsearch/pubsinfo.asp?pubid=2003521, Chapter 4, pp. 102ff).

The values in Figure 3-5 show clearly how misconceptions can arise from statements such as "this item is 'in' Level 3" (using an rp value of .80). While the item may be "in" Level 3, 55 percent of people in Level 2 responded correctly. So statements such as "because the item is in Level 3, people scoring in Level 2 would respond incorrectly" are wrong. For reporting results using sets of levels, a graphical or numerical summary of the probability of a correct response at multiple points on the scale score, such as shown in Figure 3-5, is likely to be more informative and lead to more accurate interpretations.

Use of Response Probabilities in Standard Setting

As previously mentioned, for some purposes, such as the bookmark method of standard setting, it is essential that items be placed at a single location on the score scale. An rp value must be selected to accomplish that. The bookmark method of standard setting requires an "ordered item booklet" in which the items are placed in increasing order of difficulty. With the kinds of IRT models that are used for NALS and NAAL, different rp values place the items in different orders. For example, Figure 3-2 includes dotted lines that denote three rp values: rp80, rp67, and rp50. The item trace lines cross the dotted line representing an rp value of 80 percent in one sequence, while they cross the dotted line representing an rp value of 67 percent in another sequence, and they cross the dotted line representing an rp value of 50 percent in yet another sequence. There are a number of factors to consider in selecting an rp criterion.

Factors to Consider in Selecting a Response Probability Value

One source of information on which to base the selection of an rp value involves empirical studies of the effects of different rp values on the standard-setting process (e.g., Williams and Schultz, 2005). Another source of information relevant to the selection of an rp value is purely statistical in nature, having to do with the relative precision of estimates of the scale scores associated with various rp values. To illustrate, Figure 3-6 shows the trace line for the "write letter" item as it passes through the middle of the prose score scale. The trace line is enclosed in dashed lines that represent the boundaries of a 95 percent *confidence envelope* for the curve. The confidence envelope for a curve is a region that includes the curves corresponding to the central 95 percent confidence interval for the (item) param-

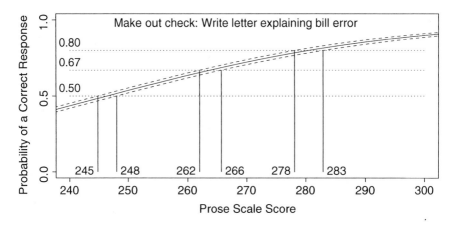

FIGURE 3-6 A 95 percent confidence envelope for the trace line for the sample item on the NALS prose scale.

eters that produce the curve. That is, the confidence envelope translates statistical uncertainty (due to random sampling) in the estimation of the item parameters into a graphical display of the consequent uncertainty in the location of the trace line itself.[6]

A striking feature of the confidence envelope in Figure 3-6 is that it is relatively narrow. This is because the standard errors for the item parameters (reported in Appendix A of the 1992 NALS Technical Manual) are very small. Because the confidence envelope is very narrow, it is difficult to see in Figure 3-6 that it is actually narrower (either vertically or horizontally) around rp50 than it is around rp80. This means that there is less uncertainty associated with proficiency estimates based on rp50 than on rp80. While this finding is not evident in the visual display (Figure 3-6), it has been previously documented (see Thissen and Wainer, 1990, for illustrations of confidence envelopes that are not so narrow and show their characteristic asymmetries more clearly).

Nonetheless, the confidence envelope may be used to translate the uncertainty in the item parameter estimates into descriptions of the uncertainty of the scale scores corresponding to particular rp values. Using the "write letter" NALS item as an illustration, at rp50 the confidence envelope

---

[6]For a more detailed description of confidence envelopes in the context of IRT, see Thissen and Wainer (1990), who use results obtained by Thissen and Wainer (1982) and an algorithm described by Hauck (1983) to produce confidence envelopes like the dashed lines in Figure 3-6.

encloses trace lines that would place the corresponding scale score anywhere between 245 and 248 (as shown by the solid lines connected to the dotted line for 0.50 in Figure 3-6). That range of three points is smaller than the four-point range for rp67 (from 262 to 266), which is, in turn, smaller than the range for the rp80 scale score (278-283).[7]

The rp80 values, as used for reporting the 1992 NALS results, have statistical uncertainty that is almost twice as large (5 points, from 278 to 283, around the reported value of 280 for the "write letter" item) as the rp50 values (3 points, from 245 to 248, for this item). The rp50 values are always most precisely estimated. So a purely statistical answer to the question, "What rp value is most precisely estimated, given the data?" would be rp50 for the item response model used for the binary-scored open-ended items in NALS and NAAL. The statistical uncertainty in the scale scores associated with rp values simply increases as the rp value increases above 0.50. It actually becomes very large for rp values of 90, 95, or 99 percent (which is no doubt the reason such rp values are never considered in practice).

Nevertheless, the use of rp50 has been reported to be very difficult for judges in standard-setting processes, as well as other consumers, to interpret usefully (Williams and Schulz, 2004). What does it mean to say "the score at which the person has a 50-50 chance of responding correctly"? While that value may be useful (and interpretable) for a data analyst developing models for item response data, it is not so useful for consumers of test results who are more interested in ideas like "mastery." An rp value of 67 percent, now commonly used in bookmark procedures (Mitzel et al., 2001), represents a useful compromise for some purposes. That is, the idea that there is a 2 in 3 chance that the examinee will respond correctly is readily interpretable as "more likely than not." Furthermore, the statistical uncertainty of the estimate of the scale score associated with rp67 is larger than for rp50 but not as large as for rp80.

Figure 3-4 illustrates another statistical property of the trace lines used for NALS and NAAL that provides motivation for choosing an rp value closer to 50 percent. Note in Figure 3-2 that not only are the trace lines in a different (horizontal) *order* for rp values of 50, 67, and 80 percent, but they are also considerably more variable (more widely spread) at rp80 than

---

[7]Some explanation is needed. First, the rp50 interval is actually symmetrical. Earlier (Figure 3-4), the rp50 value was claimed to be 246. The actual value, before rounding, is very close to 246.5, so the interval from 245 to 248 (which is rounded very little) is both correct and symmetrical. The intervals for the higher rp values are *supposed* to be asymmetrical.

they are at rp50. These greater variations at rp80, and the previously described wider confidence envelope, are simply due to the inherent shape of the trace line. As it approaches a value of 1.0, it must flatten out and so it must develop a "shoulder" that has very uncertain location (in the left-right direction) for any particular value of the probability of a correct response (in the vertical direction). Figure 3-2 shows that variation in the discrimination of the items greatly accentuates the variation in the scale score location of high and low rp values.

Again, these kinds of purely statistical considerations would lead to a choice of rp50. Considerations of mastery for the presentation and description of the results to many audiences suggests higher rp values. A compromise value of rp67, combined with a reminder that the rp values are arbitrary values used in the standard-setting process, and reporting of the results can describe the likelihood or correct responses for *any* level or scale score, are what we suggest.

4

Determining Performance Levels for the National Assessment of Adult Literacy

The committee began its work by reviewing the processes for developing the National Adult Literacy Survey (NALS) and determining the 1992 performance levels in order to gain a comprehensive understanding of the assessment and to evaluate whether new performance levels were needed. Our review revealed that the 1992 levels were essentially groupings based on the cognitive processes required to respond to the items. The committee decided that a more open and transparent procedure could be used to develop performance levels that would be defensible and informative with regard to the policy and programmatic decisions likely to be based on them. It was clear from the press coverage of the release of 1992 results that people wanted information about the extent of literacy problems in the country as well as an indication of the portion of adults whose literacy skills were adequate to function in society. Although the test development process was not designed to support inferences like this, we decided that new performance levels could be developed that would be more informative to stakeholders and the public about adults' literacy skills.

On the basis of our review, the committee decided to embark on a process for defining a new set of performance levels for the National Assessment of Adult Literacy (NAAL). This decision meant that we needed to address five main questions:

1. How many performance levels should be used?
2. Should performance levels be developed for each of the literacy scales (prose, document, and quantitative) or should one set of levels be developed?

3. What should the levels be called?
4. How should the levels be described?
5. What score ranges should be associated with each of the levels?

In this chapter, we take up the first three questions and describe our process for determining the number of performance levels and their purposes. In Chapter 5, we discuss our procedures for determining the descriptions of the levels and the associated cut scores.

Our process for determining the performance levels combined feedback from stakeholders regarding the ways they used the 1992 results and anticipated using the 2003 results with information from analyses of the relationships between NALS literacy scores and background data. We began our work by using two documents prepared prior to our first meeting: *Developing the National Assessment of Adult Literacy: Recommendations from Stakeholders* (U.S. Department of Education, 1998), which reported on a series of discussion sessions conducted by the National Center for Education Statistics (NCES) in 1998, and *The National Adult Literacy Survey: A Review of Primary and Secondary Analyses of the NALS* (Smith, 2002), a literature review prepared for the committee that summarizes the empirical research on the relationships between NALS literacy scores and background characteristics.

These documents served as the starting place for the committee's work. The report on the discussion sessions indicated ways in which NALS results were used, the problems users had in interpreting and using the results, and the information stakeholders would like to obtain from reports of NAAL results. The literature review assisted us in designing analyses to explore whether alternative versions of performance levels would permit such uses and interpretations.

This chapter begins with a summary of key points stakeholders made during the NCES discussion sessions and the public forum convened by the committee. This is followed by a description of analyses we carried out and the performance levels we recommend.

STAKEHOLDER VIEWS

Discussion Sessions Sponsored by NCES

When NCES began planning for the NAAL, it commissioned the American Institutes for Research (AIR) to convene a series of discussion sessions to gather feedback from stakeholders that would guide development efforts. Three discussion groups were held in January and February 1998 at AIR's offices in Washington, DC, and included federal and state policy makers and program directors as well as representatives from the general and educational media. AIR facilitators posed questions to stakeholders to hear their comments about the ways the 1992 data had been used and interpreted, the problems associated with using and interpreting the data, and issues to consider in designing the new assessment. A summary of these discussion sessions and a listing of the participants has been published (see U.S. Department of Education, 1998).

Stakeholders indicated that the 1992 survey results were used to describe the status of literacy to policy makers at the federal and state levels; to argue for increased funding and support for adult literacy programs; to support requests for studies of special populations such as non-English speakers, welfare recipients, incarcerated individuals, and elderly populations; to document needed reforms in education and welfare policy; and to enable international comparisons.

Participants described a number of problems associated with interpreting the results, including the following:

- Stakeholders need data that can be used to make programmatic decisions. They had trouble using the 1992 NALS results for such purposes because the levels were difficult to understand, there was no definition of "how much literacy was enough," and the results were not connected to workplace requirements or measures of employability.
- The lowest level was so broad that it made it difficult to identify the truly nonliterate population.
- Having three literacy scales crossed with five performance levels produced so much information that it was difficult to present the results to policy makers and others. It was hard to distill the information into easily interpreted messages.
- Some participants said they used only one scale when reporting information to the public and suggested that a composite literacy score be developed. They believed this was justified because the three scales were so highly correlated with each other.
- The five performance levels were difficult to understand, in part because there were no concrete meanings associated with them. That is, there was no definition of which people "needed help" and which people had "enough" literacy. Some tried to equate the levels to high school graduation and beyond.
- There was a lack of congruence between self-perception of literacy skills and NALS literacy scores. Some cited the work of Berliner (1996), whose research showed that individuals who scored in the bottom two NALS levels reported reading the newspaper on a daily basis.

- Some suggested that the NALS levels be cross-walked with those used by the National Reporting System (NRS)[1] and by other adult literacy assessments.
- The scores for non-English speakers were not reported separately, making it difficult to distinguish between literacy problems and lack of fluency in English.

Stakeholders also indicated that there was interest in conducting studies of special populations (e.g., those living in rural areas, immigrants, non-English speakers), but the sampling design used for NALS did not support such studies. They encouraged oversampling participants in NAAL to allow such studies and adding background questions to clearly identify those in the categories of interest.

Discussion Sessions Sponsored by the Committee

The committee arranged for several opportunities to obtain feedback from various stakeholders regarding the ways NALS results were used, the ways stakeholders anticipate using NAAL results, and the types of information that stakeholders would like to see included in reports of NAAL results. We collected information about the types of inferences that might be based on NAAL results, the policy and program decisions that might be made, the number of performance levels needed to support these inferences and uses, and the types of performance-level descriptions that would communicate appropriately to the various audiences for NAAL results.

The committee's fourth meeting, on February 27, 2004, included a public forum to hear feedback from stakeholders. Participating stakeholders included representatives from organizations likely to be involved in policy and programmatic decisions based on NAAL results, some of whom were individuals who had participated in the earlier discussion sessions sponsored by NCES. The committee also solicited feedback from directors of adult education in states that subsidized additional sampling during NAAL in order to obtain state-level NAAL results (see Appendix A for a list of individuals who provided feedback, their affiliations, and the materials they were asked to react to).

The stakeholders were helpful in delineating the types of uses that would be made of the results. Overall, their comments tended to concur with those made by participants in the NCES-sponsored discussion sessions. In general, it appeared that NAAL results would be used to advocate

---

[1]See Chapter 2 for an explanation of the levels used by the NRS.

for needed policy and to shape and design programs. Forum participants indicated that they expected to use NAAL results to evaluate preparedness for work and the need for job training programs, adults' ability to understand health- and safety-related reading matter and physicians' instructions, parents' readiness to help their children with their schooling, and the need for adult education and literacy services. Most also emphasized that having scores for the three literacy scales was useful, and that the scores were used for different purposes (e.g., the tasks used to evaluate document literacy were most relevant to work skills).

The feedback from stakeholders indicated considerable diversity of opinions about the number of performance levels needed for reporting assessment results, what the levels should be called, and the type of description needed to best communicate with the various audiences. For example, reporters and journalists present at the forum argued for straightforward approaches that could be easily communicated to the public (e.g., two performance levels described with nontechnical terminology). They maintained that the public is most interested in simply knowing how many people in the country are literate and how many are not. Others argued for more than two levels—some thought there should be three levels, while others thought there should be six or seven, with finer distinctions made at the lower levels.

Some stakeholders, particularly those from the health literacy field, preferred that the 1992 levels be used for NAAL, commenting that consistency was needed so as not to disrupt on-going longitudinal research or interfere with programs and interventions already in place. NCES staff members present at the forum pointed out that the data files would be made available and score data provided so that users could group the scores based on the score ranges used for the 1992 performance levels or any other grouping that fit their particular needs.

With regard to qualitative names for the levels, some favored labels for the levels, noting that this can provide a means for succinctly and accurately communicating the meaning of the levels (e.g., satisfactory literacy skills, deficient literacy skills). Reporters present at the forum suggested two labels, literate and not literate. They warned that if the labels did not clearly indicate which adults were not literate, they would derive a means to figure this out on their own. Some participants recommended the labels used by state achievement testing programs and by the National Assessment of Educational Progress (i.e., below basic, basic, proficient, and advanced) since the public is well acquainted with these terms.

Others argued against labeling the levels (e.g., proficient, fully functional), especially labels that place a stigma on the lowest levels of literacy (e.g., minimally literate). They urged that if labels had to be used that they be descriptive, not imply normative standards, and not be connected with educational level. The question of the type of information to include in the performance-level descriptions solicited equally diverse perspectives. Some thought more detailed descriptions were better, while others argued for more succinct descriptions. It seemed clear that different levels of detail would be important for different uses of the performance levels.

Stakeholders representing adult education were most interested in having more detailed information about adults at the lowest levels. Several participants commented that adults who receive adult education services tend to have skills described by the bottom two levels used for reporting NALS 1992. Knowing more about the skills of those who fall in these two levels would be useful in identifying target clientele and making planning decisions.

RELATIONSHIPS BETWEEN LITERACY SCORES AND BACKGROUND CHARACTERISTICS

Although the NALS literacy assessments were not designed to distinguish between adequate and inadequate literacy skills, the committee thought that analyses of the background questionnaire might provide insight into ways to identify adults who were experiencing significant difficulties in life. We hypothesized that such analyses might reveal break points in the distribution of literacy scores at which individuals were at an unacceptably high risk for encountering social and economic hardships. This type of information might lead to obvious choices in performance levels, standards, or both.

The committee therefore focused its analytic work on the relationships between NALS literacy scores and relevant information collected on the background questionnaire. Our literature review (Smith, 2002) gave us a sense of the type of research that had been conducted with NALS over the past decade and the sorts of relationships found. The research findings generally indicated that individuals with lower literacy scores were more likely to experience difficulties, such as being in poverty, on welfare, or unemployed; working in a low-paying job; not having a high school diploma; or being unable to pass the general education development (GED) exam. Low literacy skills were also associated with being less likely to participate in such important aspects of life as voting and reading the newspaper.

With this literature review in mind, we tried to identify the levels of literacy at which the risk of encountering such difficulties differed, focusing specifically at the points where the risk would be unacceptably high. We thought that examining relationships with important socioeconomic factors might suggest categories of performance that would be useful in determining new policy-relevant performance levels. For these analyses, we used the following information from the NALS background questionnaire:[2] employment status; income; occupation; voting history over the past five years; receiving food stamps or other public assistance; receiving income from stocks, mutual funds, or other sources of interest income; and level of formal education. We also considered responses to questions about participation in reading-related activities, such as how often the participant reads a newspaper, reads or uses written information for personal use or for work, uses math for personal use or for work, and receives reading assistance from family and friends.

We had hoped to explore the relationships between literacy scores and the variables described above to develop performance levels that were not just descriptions of skills but were descriptions of the functional consequences of adults' literacy skills, such as education level, family income, and job status. In the end, however, we came to realize that the background questions did not provide the information needed for the analyses we had hoped to conduct.

Overall, the relationships between literacy scores and the background variables did not suggest obvious break points that could be used in defining performance levels. In part, this may have been because the background questions did not probe deeply enough into a particular area, or the answer choices did not allow for fine enough distinctions. For example, participants were asked to characterize their newspaper reading habits by indicating the frequency with which they read the newspaper and the sections of the newspaper that they read (news section, editorial, comics, etc.); however, they were not asked questions that could help evaluate the difficulty or complexity of the newspapers they read, such as *which* newspapers they read. Clearly, the news section of the *Wall Street Journal* requires different literacy skills than the news section of a local newspaper. Similar questions inquire about magazine and book reading but do not collect information that could be used to make inferences about the complexity of the books or magazines read. Thus, the information may be useful for making rough distinctions between those who do not read magazines, books, or newspapers at all and those who do—but not useful for making finer distinctions required to sort people into incremental levels of literacy.

Similar observations can be made about the information collected about voting behavior. The 1992 questionnaire included only a single question on this topic, asking participants if they had voted in a national or state

---

[2]See Appendix G of the technical manual for NALS (Kirsch et al., 2001) for the exact wording of the questions.

election in the past five years. This provides only a rough glimpse into voting behavior. A more in-depth query might have asked about voting in national and state elections separately and added questions about voting in local elections and other forms of civic participation (e.g., running for office, communicating with elected officials). Again, the information available from the background questionnaire can be used to make rough distinctions, such as between those who do and do not vote, but it is not useful for making more nuanced distinctions.

In the end, we concluded that the background information could not be used by itself to identify categories of literacy skills but could be used to evaluate the reasonableness of cut scores resulting from a more typical standard-setting procedure. In Chapter 5, we therefore use the results of our analyses as a complement to a standard- setting procedure using the test items themselves, rather than as an alternative to such a standard setting procedure.

The analyses discussed in this report are all univariate analyses. The committee also explored the use of multivariate regression techniques to look at the relationship between literacy scores and the various background questions. These multivariate analyses built on work by Sum (1999) related to employment and earnings and by Venezky (Venezky and Kaplan, 1998; Venezky, Kaplan, and Yu, 1998) on voting behavior. Not surprisingly, the independent explanatory power of literacy scores in such analyses is severely reduced by the inclusion of other variables, such as education, because these variables themselves have a complex bidirectional relationship with literacy. Upon reflection, the committee decided that it was beyond the scope of its charge and beyond the quality of the data to attempt to resolve the causal relationships of literacy with the various characteristics indicated in the background questions that might be entered as additional controls in multivariate regressions. Therefore, only the univariate analyses were used to suggest possible conclusions about performance levels.

To demonstrate the committee's exploratory analyses, the next sections provide information on the relationships between literacy scores and two variables: income and occupational status. These examples are illustrative of a larger set of findings that demonstrate that there are strong gradients across an array of literacy outcomes but no clear break points that would, *prima facie*, lead one to set cut points in the literacy distribution. For each variable, we show several approaches that highlight the continuous nature of the relationship and contrast those with an approach that can be used to suggest a contrast in functional level. The latter approach is then further developed in Chapter 5, when we present the procedures we used for setting the cut scores and discuss the complementary role played by the statistical analyses. Because the 2003 data were not available to us until the final months of our work, the analyses discussed in this chapter are based on the 1992 data alone. The complementary statistical analyses presented in the next chapter are carried out with both the 1992 and 2003 data sets.

Literacy Scores and Annual Income

It seems intuitively sensible that literacy should be related to how one functions in other critical aspects of life, and that income and occupation should serve as indicators of how well one is functioning. Furthermore, one would expect that low literacy skills should be associated with restricted opportunities, such as not pursuing postsecondary education or specialized training and working in lower paying jobs with no formal training requirements. With these assumptions in mind, we examined the relationships between literacy skills and income and occupation.

Three figures present information on the relationships between literacy skills and income. Figure 4-1, adapted from Kirsch et al. (1993), shows the percentages of adults who, according to federal guidelines, were poor or near poor or who had received food stamps in the year prior to the assessment at each of the five 1992 performance levels for prose literacy. This graph shows that the risk of being in poverty or being on food stamps increases as literacy scores decrease.

Because some stakeholders have reported that Level 1 was "too broad" to be informative about individuals with the lowest level of literacy skills, we adapted this figure and examined the relationships between poverty and prose literacy scores for specific groupings within the 0 to 225 score range

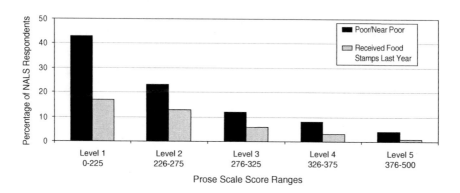

FIGURE 4-1 Percentage of NALS respondents who are poor or near poor or who received food stamps in the past year by prose literacy level.

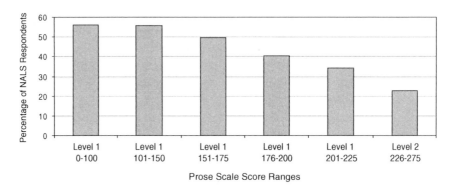

FIGURE 4-2 Percentage of NALS respondents who are poor or near poor for six groupings of NALS Level 1 prose scores and NALS Level 2 prose scores.

encompassed by Level 1. Figure 4-2 presents a comparison of the percentages of adults who were poor or near poor at six groupings of Level 1 scores and at the Level 2 score range (226-275). Clearly, the risk of being poor is not even across the Level 1 groupings; risk of being poor increases steadily as scores decrease with what appears to be substantial risk at scores of 175 or lower.

To see if this relationship between literacy and income suggested clear break points, we plotted the distribution of literacy scores for the 12 groupings of income levels used on the background questionnaire. Figure 4-3 presents this information in boxplots: each box shows the range of scores from the 25th percentile (bottom of the box) to the 75th percentile (top of box). The 50th percentile (median) score is marked within the box. Also displayed is the full range of scores for each income group, denoted by horizontal lines below the box (minimum score) and above the box (maximum score). Comparison of these boxplots shows that prose literacy scores tend to increase as annual income increases. But there is considerable overlap in the range of literacy scores across adjacent income levels, and no break points between adjacent income levels that would clearly signify a heightened risk of encountering difficulties in life associated with having a low income level.

Whereas there were no break points between adjacent income groups, there did appear to be differences between the more extreme groups, those with incomes of $15,000 or less and those with incomes of $75,000 or more. That is, 75 percent of those earning $75,000 or more achieved a prose score of 312 or higher, while 75 percent of those earning $15,000 or less scored 308 or lower on prose.

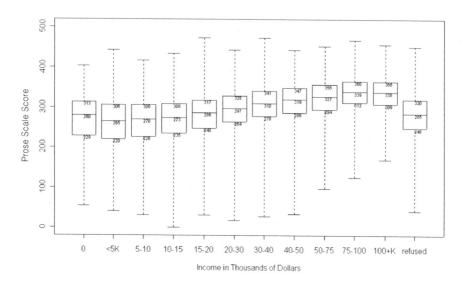

FIGURE 4-3 Boxplots illustrating the distribution of prose literacy scores for groupings of income levels, as indicated on the background questionnaire.

To follow up on this observation, we compared the responses to two background questions indirectly related to income. The first set of responses included whether or not the individual or household received Aid to Families with Dependent Children (AFDC, replaced in 1996 by Temporary Assistance for Needy Families) or food stamps; and the second set identified whether or not the individual or household received interest or dividend income. These questions identify respondents who are experiencing difficulty or success at a functional level associated with income that is not indicated by the income figures alone.

Figure 4-4 shows the boxplots of the prose literacy scores for respondents who answered "yes" to one or the other of the two questions. The boxplots indicate that approximately three-quarters of the people receiving AFDC or food stamps scored below 380, and three-quarters of the people receiving interest or dividend income scored above 275. To the extent that it is appropriate to link literacy level in a causal way to the set of behaviors that ultimately influence an individual's financial success, this figure suggests that a cut score somewhere in the 273 to 380 range might be a rough dividing line between individuals who are experiencing functional difficulties and individuals who are experiencing financial success.

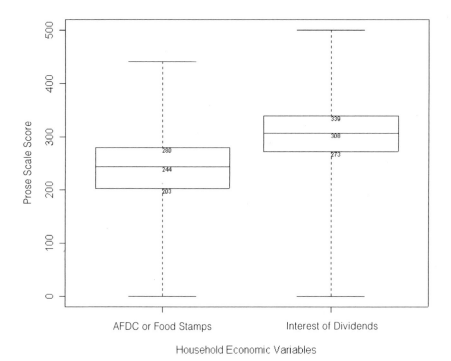

FIGURE 4-4 Boxplots that illustrate the distribution of prose literacy scores for respondents who indicated that they/their household received either (a) Aid to Families with Dependent Children or food stamps or (b) interest or dividend income.

Literacy Scores and Occupational Information

To examine the relationships between literacy scores and occupation, we drew on analyses conducted by Sum (1999), Rock, Latham, and Jeanneret (1996), and Barton (1999).[3] First, using information derived by Rock et al. (1996), we examined the mean quantitative score for occupa-

---

[3]The method of identifying the occupations of NAAL respondents, obviously crucial to examining the relationships between literacy scores and occupational classification, depends on accurate classification of a respondent's narrative description of their occupation into a

tional categories that contained at least 30 respondents in 1992. Table 4-1 displays this information with occupations rank-ordered according to their mean quantitative score and grouped by performance level. Second, we examined mean prose scores for a sample of occupations selected to be representative of Barton's (1999) nine broad categories identified through an analyses of job requirements. These categories are: (1) executive, administrative, and managerial; (2) professional specialty; (3) technicians and related support occupations; (4) marketing and sales; (5) administrative support; (6) service occupations; (7) agriculture, forestry, and fishing; (8) precision production, craft, and repair; and (9) operators, fabricators, and laborers. Figure 4-5 displays, for the selected occupations, the means (noted with a shaded diamond) as well as the range of scores bounded by the mean plus or minus one standard deviation (noted by the horizontal lines above and below the shaded diamond).

The data in these figures seem reasonable in that the general trend of the mean literacy scores required for the different occupations seems intuitively sensible—occupations that one would expect to require more literacy do indeed have higher mean scores. None of the occupations had mean scores that fell in the score range for Level 1 or Level 5, however; the preponderance of occupations had mean scores that fell in Level 3 (see Table 4-1). Only the mean for those who had never worked fell into Level 1 (see Figure 4-5). Most importantly, the variability of literacy scores within occupations showed considerable overlap between occupational groups (see Figure 4-5). Clearly, there are no obvious break points in the distribution of literacy scores; that is, there are no points on the scale at which there is a distinctly higher risk of being unemployed or working in a low-paying job.

Nonetheless, while the information does not seem to be useful in determining specific performance levels or identifying cut scores, it does demonstrate how opportunities to enter into white-collar, higher paying occupations increase as literacy skills increase. That is, for those at higher literacy levels, opportunities are readily accessible; for those at lower levels of literacy, the opportunities to obtain higher paying jobs are more limited.

As an alternate approach that could indicate a possible contrast in performance levels, the committee formed three clusters based on Barton's classifications. We included the occupations in Barton's groups 7, 8, and

---

standard occupational classification system. Currently the U.S. Department of Labor's Standard Occupational Classification is used. That is, two respondents who describe their occupations in the same or similar words during the collection of the NALS/NAAL data actually are in the same occupation and are classified in the same way by those making the classifications into occupational categories with that narrative description.

TABLE 4-1 Occupation with at Least 30 Respondents in NALS, 1992

	JOB	Quantity
Level 1	None	
Level 2	Janitor	234
	Sewing-machine operator, semiautomatic	243
	Orderly	251
	Construction worker II	253
	Bus driver	257
	Cook	261
	Physical therapy aide	264
	Cashier II	273
Level 3	Teacher aide II	276
	Farmworker, livestock	277
	Truck driver, heavy	278
	Clerk, general	278
	Mail-distribution-scheme examiner	285
	Sales clerk	285
	Waiter/waitress, formal	285
	Nurse, licensed practical	286
	Carpenter	289
	Chef	289
	Correction officer	291
	Automobile mechanic	292
	Manager, retail store	296
	Assistant construction superintendent	297
	Manager, property	297
	Manger, food service	298
	Teller	299
	Secretary	303
	Legal secretary	306
	Nurse, office	306
	Poultry farmer	307
	Disbursement clerk	307
	Superintendent, construction	311
	Police officer I	311
	Manager, department	315
	Sales agent, insurance	316
	Caseworker	319
	Sales agent, real estate	322
	Director, educational program	323
	Teacher, physically impaired	324

TABLE 4-1 Continued

	JOB	Quantity
Level 4	Teacher, elementary school	329
	Operations officer	332
	Public health physician	348
	Manager, financial institution	349
	Lawyer	350
	Accountant	351
	Systems analyst	352
Level 5	None	

9 in a low category, the occupations in Barton's groups 1 and 2 in a high category, and the remainder of the occupations in a medium category. We then contrasted the literacy score distribution in the low and high categories.

Clustered in this way, the categories may be considered to indicate a contrast between occupations that have minimal formal education and training requirements and those that require formal education and training. Figure 4-6 shows the boxplots of the prose literacy scores for the employed respondents whose stated occupation fell into either the low or the high category. The boxplots indicate that these two groups of people can be roughly separated by drawing a cut score somewhere in the range 291-301. Three-quarters of the people who are in the low category are below this literacy range, and three-quarters of the people who are in the high category are above this literacy level. To the extent that it is appropriate to link literacy level in a causal way to the set of behaviors that ultimately influences an individual's occupational choice, Figure 4-6 suggests that a cut score somewhere in the range 291-301 might be a rough dividing line between individuals who work in occupations that require minimal formal education and training (and hence are lower paying) and individuals who work in occupations that require formal education and training (and hence are higher paying).

Assessing the Dimensionality of NALS

In *Adult Literacy in America*, Kirsch et al. (1993) presented a number of graphs that portrayed the relationships between background information and literacy scores, with separate graphs for each of the literacy scales (prose, document, and quantitative). One observation that can be made about such graphs is that, regardless of the background variable, the relationships are always similar for the three literacy scales (e.g., see Kirsch et

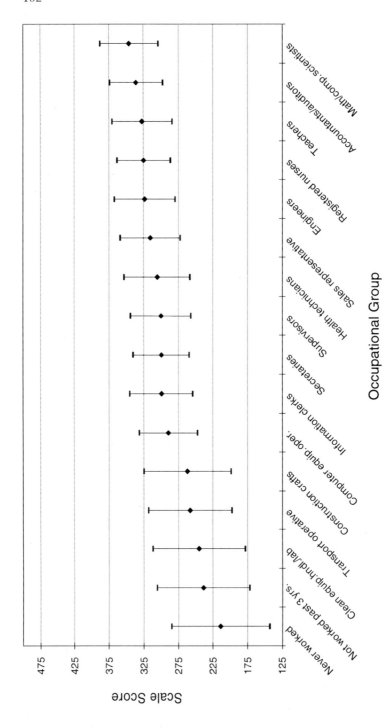

FIGURE 4-5 Distribution of the mean prose literacy scaled scores, within one standard deviation, for various occupational groups.

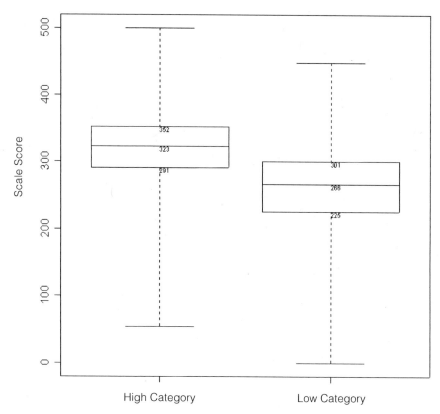

FIGURE 4-6 Boxplots that illustrate the distribution of prose literacy scores for respondents who were in either the low or high occupation category.

al., 1993, Figures 1.4, 1.5, and 1.6, p. 29, 31, 33). This observation led the committee to question the need for reporting three separate literacy scores. Questions about the extent to which the items included on an assessment support the number of scores reported are addressed through a statistical procedure called factor analysis, which is commonly used to examine the cognitive dimensions that underlie a set of test data.

Several investigations of the factor structure of NALS have been conducted (see, for example, Reder, 1998a, 1998b; Rock and Yamamoto, 1994). These analyses have repeatedly shown high intercorrelations among prose, document, and quantitative scores, suggesting that NALS tasks measure a single dimension of literacy rather than three. The committee chose to conduct its own dimensionality analyses using two different procedures. The first was exploratory in nature and generally replicated procedures used by Rock and Yamamoto (1994) but based the analyses on different blocks of items. The results revealed that a three-factor model (reporting scores for prose, document, and quantitative literacy) provided an acceptable fit to the data, although the intercorrelations among the three literacy scales tended to be quite high (mostly above .85). Additional details about this dimensionality analysis appear in Appendix B.

The second analysis addressed questions about the relationships between performance in the prose, document, and quantitative areas and an array of literacy outcomes (e.g., years of formal education, being in the labor force, occupation type, self-report about reading activities). Here, using a statistical procedure called structural equation modeling, we investigated the extent to which performance in the three literacy areas was differentially associated with the outcome measures (e.g., that one literacy area was more strongly associated with certain outcomes than another). If differential associations were found, there would be empirical support for using the separate dimensions to guide decision making about adult literacy policy and programs. If the associations were found to be similar across the three literacy areas, one would conclude that either the assessment does not measure the dimensions independently or there is little practical significance to the distinctions among them. In addition, we sought to determine if a single weighted combination of the prose, document, and quantitative scores adequately described the relationship of measured literacy to the outcome measures.

The results indicated that all three types of literacy had statistically significant associations with the outcome measures. The relationship of document literacy to the outcomes was much weaker than that observed for prose or quantitative literacy. In addition, the relationship between prose literacy and the outcomes was slightly stronger than that observed for quantitative literacy. Statistical tests, however, indicated that the relationships decreased if either document or quantitative literacy was excluded from the analysis (in statistical terminology, model fit deteriorated if document or quantitative literacy was ignored).

These results highlight the apparently prime importance of prose literacy but also point out that the other dimensions should not be ignored. For the most part, the three types of literacy have similar relationships with each of the outcome measures. That is, if an outcome was strongly related to prose literacy, its relationships with document and quantitative literacy were also relatively strong, and vice versa. There were a few notable exceptions. For example, quantitative literacy was more highly correlated with earnings and the use of mathematics on the job than one would expect from the relationships of the three types of literacy with the other outcomes. The findings suggest that for some purposes it may be useful to construct a composite of the three literacy scores. Additional details about these analyses are presented in Appendix B, and we revisit these findings again in Chapter 6.

DEVELOPING POLICY-RELEVANT PERFORMANCE LEVELS

Although the above-described factor analyses and the analyses of relationships with background data did not lead us to specific performance-level categories, we used the results to guide our decision making about performance levels and their descriptions. We designed a process for determining the performance levels that was iterative and that integrated information obtained from several sources: our analyses of NALS literacy and background data, feedback from stakeholders, and a review of the test items. This process is described below.

The feedback from stakeholders suggested the importance of performance levels that could be linked to meaningful policy choices and levels of proficiency understood by the public. Our information gathering suggested that stakeholders seek answers to four policy-related questions from NAAL results. They want to know what percentage of adults in the United States:

- Have very low literacy skills and are in need of basic adult literacy services, including services for adult English language learners.
- Are ready for GED preparation services.
- Qualify for a GED certificate or a high school diploma.
- Have attained a sufficient level of English literacy that they can be successful in postsecondary education and gain entry into professional, managerial, or technical occupations.

Based on the information obtained from data analyses, stakeholder feedback, and review of test items, we initially developed a basic framework for the performance-level descriptions that conformed to the policy-related contrasts suggested by the above questions. These contrasts indicate points at which public policy effectively draws a line delineating the literacy level adults need or should have by making available extra educational services to those adults below that level. We then developed draft performance-level descriptions corresponding to these groupings to reflect the types of literacy skills generally needed at each level and that were evaluated on the assessment, as determined by a review of the assessment frameworks and test items. The descriptions were revised and finalized by obtaining feedback on various versions of the performance-level descriptions from standard-setting panelists on three occasions.

The factor analyses revealed high intercorrelations among the three literacy scales, which suggested that a single literacy score would be adequate for reporting the assessment results (e.g., an average of prose, document, and quantitative scores). It is quite likely that these dimensions are more independent than they appear to be in NALS, but that they are confounded due to the nature of the NALS tasks. That is, often multiple questions are based on a single stimulus (e.g., a bus schedule) presented to the test taker; the tasks may include questions from all three literacy areas. In addition, stakeholder feedback indicated that the three literacy scores are used for different purposes. We therefore developed a set of performance-level descriptions that includes both an overall description of each performance-level and subject-specific descriptions for prose, document, and quantitative literacy scales.

Based on this process, we recommend the use of five performance levels. We remind the reader that these performance levels are not intended to represent standards for what is required to perform adequately in society, since the assessment was not designed to support such inferences. To reinforce this, we have intentionally avoided the use of the term "proficient" in the labels for the performance levels.

RECOMMENDATION 4-1: The 2003 NAAL results should be reported using five performance levels for each of the three types of English literacy: nonliterate in English, below basic literacy, basic literacy, intermediate literacy, and advanced literacy.

These levels are described in Box 4-1. The recommended levels roughly correspond to the four policy questions posed earlier, with the exception that two levels describe the skills of individuals likely to be in need of basic adult literacy services. That is, the nonliterate in English group includes those whose literacy levels were too low to take NAAL and were administered the Adult Literacy Supplemental Assessment, and the below basic literacy group includes those who scored low on NAAL. The basic category is intended to represent the skills of individuals likely to be ready for GED preparation services. Likewise, the intermediate category generally describes the skills of individuals likely to have a GED certificate or a high school diploma. The advanced category is meant to portray the literacy skills of individuals who would be generally likely to succeed in college or postsecondary education. (We caution the reader that, in the end, we had some reservations about the adequacy of NALS and NAAL to measure skills at the advanced level and refer the reader to the discussion in Chapter 5.) The various versions of these descriptions and the process for revising them are described in the next chapter and in Appendix C.

In identifying these levels, we were conscious of the fact that one of the chief audiences for NAAL results is adult education programs, which are guided legislatively by the Workforce Investment Act of 1998. Title II of this act mandates an accountability system for adult education programs,

---

BOX 4-1
Performance-Level Descriptions Developed for 2003 NAAL

Nonliterate in English: May recognize some letters, numbers, and/or common sight words in frequently encountered contexts.

Below Basic: May sometimes be able to locate and make use of simple words, phrases, numbers, and quantities in short texts drawn from commonplace contexts and situations; may sometimes be able to perform simple one-step arithmetic operations.

Basic: Is able to read and understand simple words, phrases, numbers, and quantities in English when the information is easily identifiable; able to locate information in short texts drawn from commonplace contexts and situations; able to solve simple one-step problems in which the operation is stated or easily inferred.

Intermediate: Is able to read, understand, and use written material sufficiently well to locate information in denser, less commonplace texts, construct straightforward summaries, and draw simple inferences; able to make use of quantitative information when the arithmetic operation or mathematical relationship is not specified or easily inferred.

Advanced: Is able to read, understand, and use more complex written material sufficiently well to locate and integrate multiple pieces of information, perform more sophisticated analytical tasks such as making systematic comparisons, draw more sophisticated inferences, and can make use of quantitative information when multiple operations or more complex relationships are involved.

---

known as the NRS, that specifies a set of education functioning levels used in tracking the progress of enrollees. Feedback from stakeholders emphasized the usefulness of creating levels for NAAL aligned with the NRS levels. Although it was not possible to establish a clear one-to-one correspondence between NAAL performance levels and the NRS levels, there appears to be a rough parallel between nonliterate in English and the NRS beginning literacy level; between below basic and the NRS beginning basic and low intermediate levels; and between basic and the NRS high intermediate level.

In the next chapter, we detail the process we used for developing descriptions for the performance levels, obtaining feedback on them, and revising them to arrive at the final version.

5

Developing Performance-Level
Descriptions and Setting Cut Scores

In this chapter, we detail the processes we used for developing descriptions of the performance levels as well as the methods we used to determine the cut scores to be associated with each of the performance levels. The performance-level descriptions were developed through an iterative process in which the descriptions evolved as we drafted wording, solicited feedback, reviewed the assessment frameworks and tasks, and made revisions. The process of determining the cut scores involved using procedures referred to as "standard setting," which were introduced in Chapter 3.

As we noted in Chapter 3, standard setting is intrinsically judgmental. Science enters the process only as a way of ensuring the internal and external validity of informed judgments (e.g., that the instructions are clear and understood by the panelists; that the standards are statistically reliable and reasonably consistent with external data, such as levels of completed schooling). Given the judgmental nature of the task, it is not easy to develop methods and procedures that are scientifically defensible; indeed, standard-setting procedures have provoked considerable controversy (e.g., National Research Council [NRC], 1998; Hambleton et al., 2001). In developing our procedures, we have familiarized ourselves with these controversies and have relied on the substantial research base on standard setting[1] and, in

---

[1]While we familiarized ourselves with a good deal of this research, we do not provide an exhaustive listing of these articles and cite only the studies that are most relevant for the present project. There are several works that provide overviews of methods, their variations,

particular, on the research on setting achievement levels for the National Assessment of Educational Progress (NAEP).

NAEP's standard-setting procedures are perhaps the most intensely scrutinized procedures in existence today, having been designed, guided, and evaluated by some of the most prominent measurement experts in the county. The discussions about NAEP's procedures, both the favorable comments and the criticisms, provide guidance for those designing a standard-setting procedure. We attempted to implement procedures that reflected the best of what NAEP does and that addressed the criticisms that have been leveled against NAEP's procedures. Below we highlight the major criticisms and describe how we addressed them. We raise these issues, not to take sides on the various controversies, but to explain how we used this information to design our standard-setting methods.

NAEP has for sometime utilized the modified Angoff method for setting cut scores, a procedure that some consider to yield defensible standards (Hambleton and Bourque, 1991; Hambleton et al., 2000; Cizek, 1993, 2001a; Kane, 1993, 1995; Mehrens, 1995; Mullins and Green, 1994) and some believe to pose an overly complex cognitive task for judges (National Research Council, 1999; Shepard, Glaser, and Linn, 1993). While the modified Angoff method is still widely used, especially for licensing and certification tests, many other methods are available. In fact, although the method is still used for setting the cut scores for NAEP's achievement levels, other methods are being explored with the assessment (Williams and Schulz, 2005). Given the unresolved controversies about the modified Angoff method, we chose not to use it. Instead, we selected a relatively new method, the bookmark standard-setting method, that appears to be growing in popularity. The bookmark method was designed specifically to reduce the cognitive complexity of the task posed to panelists (Mitzel et al., 2001). The procedure was endorsed as a promising method for use on NAEP (National Research Council, 1999) and, based on recent estimates, is used by more than half of the states in their K-12 achievement tests (Egan, 2001).

Another issue that has been raised in relation to NAEP's standard-setting procedures is that different standard-setting methods were required for NAEP's multiple-choice and open-ended items. The use of different methods led to widely disparate cut scores, and there has been disagreement

---

and advantages and disadvantages, such as Jaegar's article in *Educational Measurement* (1989) and the collection of writings in Cizek's (2001b) *Setting Performance Standards*. We frequently refer readers to these writings because they provide a convenient and concise means for learning more about standard setting; however, we do not intend to imply that these were the only documents consulted.

about how to resolve these differences (Hambleton et al., 2000; National Research Council, 1999; Shepard, Glaser, and Linn, 1993). An advantage of the bookmark procedure is that it is appropriate for both item types. While neither the National Adult Literacy Survey (NALS) nor the National Assessment of Adult Literacy (NAAL) use multiple-choice items, both include open-ended items, some of which were scored as right or wrong and some of which were scored according to a partial credit scoring scheme (e.g., wrong, partially correct, fully correct). The bookmark procedure is suitable for both types of scoring schemes.

Another issue discussed in relation to NAEP's achievement-level setting was the collection of evidence used to evaluate the reasonableness of the cut scores. Concerns were expressed about the discordance between cut scores that resulted from different standard-setting methods (e.g., the modified Angoff method and the contrasting groups method yielded different cut scores for the assessment) and the effect of these differences on the percentages of students categorized into each of the achievement levels. Concerns were also expressed about whether the percentages of students in each achievement level were reasonable given other indicators of students' academic achievement in the United States (e.g., performance on the SAT, percentage of students enrolled in Advanced Placement programs), although there was considerable disagreement about the appropriateness of such comparisons. While we do not consider that our charge required us to resolve these disagreements about NAEP's cut scores, we did try to address the criticisms.

As a first step to address these concerns, we used the background data available from the assessment as a means for evaluating the reasonableness of the bookmark cut scores. To accomplish this, we developed an adapted version of the contrasting groups method, which utilizes information about examinees apart from their actual test scores. This *quasi-contrasting groups* (QCG) approach was not used as a strict standard-setting technique but as a means for considering adjustments to the bookmark cut scores. While validation of the recommended cut scores should be the subject of a thorough research endeavor that would be beyond the scope of the committee's charge, comparison of the cut scores to pertinent background data provides initial evidence.

We begin our discussion with an overview of the bookmark standard-setting method and the way we implemented it. Participants in the standard settings provided feedback on the performance-level descriptions, and we present the different versions of the descriptions and explain why they were revised. The results of the standard settings appear at the end of this chapter, where we also provide a description of the adapted version of the contrasting groups procedure that we used and make our recommendations for cut scores. The material in this chapter provides an overview of the bookmark procedures and highlights the most crucial results from the standard setting; additional details about the standard setting are presented in Appendixes C and D.

THE BOOKMARK STANDARD-SETTING METHOD

Relatively new, the bookmark procedure was designed to simplify the judgmental task by asking panelists to directly set the cut scores, rather than asking them to make judgments about test questions in isolation, as in the modified Angoff method (Mitzel et al., 2001). The method has the advantage of allowing participants to focus on the content and skills assessed by the test questions rather than just on the difficulty of the questions, as panelists are given "item maps" that detail item content (Zieky, 2001). The method also provides an opportunity to revise performance-level descriptions at the completion of the standard-setting process so they are better aligned with the cut scores.

In a bookmark standard-setting procedure, test questions are presented in a booklet arranged in order from easiest to hardest according to their estimated level of difficulty, which is derived from examinees' answers to the test questions. Panelists receive a set of performance-level descriptions to use while making their judgments. They review the test questions in these booklets, called "ordered item booklets," and place a "bookmark" to demark the set of questions that examinees who have the skills described by a given performance level will be required to answer correctly with a given level of accuracy. To explain, using the committee's performance-level categories, panelists would consider the description of skills associated with the basic literacy category and, for each test question, make a judgment about whether an examinee with these skills would be likely to answer the question correctly or incorrectly. Once the bookmark is placed for the first performance-level category, the panelists would proceed to consider the skills associated with the second performance-level category (intermediate) and place a second bookmark to denote the set of items that individuals who score in this category would be expected to answer correctly with a specified level of accuracy. The procedure is repeated for each of the performance-level categories.

The bookmark method requires specification of what it means to be "likely" to answer a question correctly. The designers of the method suggest that "likely" be defined as "67 percent of the time" (Mitzel et al., 2001, p. 260). This concept of "likely" is important because it is the response probability value used in calculating the difficulty of each test question (that is, the scale score associated with the item). Although a response probability of 67 percent (referred to as rp67) is common with the bookmark procedure, other values could be used, and we address this issue in more detail later in this chapter.

To demonstrate how the response probability value is used in making bookmark judgments, we rely on the performance levels that we recommended in Chapter 4. Panelists first consider the description of the basic literacy performance level and the content and skills assessed by the first question in the ordered item booklet, the easiest question in the booklet. Each panelist considers whether an individual with the skills described in the basic category would have a 67 percent chance of answering this question correctly (or stated another way, if an individual with the skills described in the basic category would be likely to correctly answer a question measuring these specific skills *two out of three* times). If a panelist judges this to be true, he or she proceeds to the next question in the booklet. This continues until the panelist comes to a question that he or she judges a basic-level examinee does *not* have a 67 percent chance of answering correctly (or would not be likely to answer correctly *two out of three* times). The panelist places his or her bookmark for the basic level on this question. The panelist then moves to the description of the intermediate level and proceeds through the ordered item booklet until reaching an item that he or she judges an individual with intermediate-level skills would not be likely to answer correctly 67 percent of the time. The intermediate-level bookmark would be placed on this item. Determination of the placement of the bookmark for the advanced level proceeds in a similar fashion.

Panelists sit at a table with four or five other individuals who are all working with the same set of items, and the bookmark standard-setting procedure is implemented in an iterative fashion. There are three opportunities, or rounds, for panelists to decide where to place their bookmarks. Panelists make their individual decisions about bookmark placements during Round 1, with no input from other panelists. Afterward, panelists seated at the same table compare and discuss their ratings and then make a second set of judgments as part of Round 2. As part of the bookmark process, panelists discuss their bookmark placements, and agreement about the placements is encouraged. Panelists are not required to come to consensus about the placement of bookmarks, however.

After Round 2, bookmark placements are transformed to test scale scores, and the median scale score is determined for each performance level. At this stage, the medians are calculated by considering the bookmark placements for all panelists who are working on a given test booklet (e.g., all panelists at all tables who are working on the prose ordered item booklet).

Panelists are usually provided with information about the percentage of test takers whose scores would fall into each performance-level category based on these medians. This feedback is referred to as "impact data" and serves as a reality check to allow panelists to adjust and fine-tune their judgments. Usually, all the panelists working on a given ordered item booklet assemble and review the bookmark placements, the resulting median scale scores, and the impact data together. Panelists then make a final set of judgments during Round 3, working individually at their respective tables.

The median scale scores are recalculated after the Round 3 judgments are made. Usually, mean scale scores are also calculated, and the variability in panelists' judgments is examined to evaluate the extent to which they disagree about bookmark placements. At the conclusion of the standard setting, it is customary to allot time for panelists to discuss and write performance-level descriptions for the items reviewed during the standard setting.

Committee's Approach with the Bookmark Method

The committee conducted two bookmark standard-setting sessions, one in July 2004 with data from the 1992 NALS and one in September 2004 with data from the 2003 NAAL. This allowed us to use two different groups of panelists, to try out our procedures with the 1992 data and then make corrections (as needed) before the standard setting with the 2003 data was conducted, and to develop performance-level descriptions that would generalize to both versions of the assessment. Richard Patz, one of the developers of the bookmark method, served as consultant to the committee and led the standard-setting sessions. Three additional consultants and National Research Council project staff assisted with the sessions, and several committee members observed the sessions. The agendas for the two standard-setting sessions appear in Appendixes C and D.

Because the issue of response probability had received so much attention in relation to NALS results (see Chapter 3), we arranged to collect data from panelists about the impact of using different instructions about response probabilities. This data collection was conducted during the July standard setting with the 1992 data and is described in the section of this chapter called "Bookmark Standard Setting with 1992 Data."

The standard-setting sessions were organized to provide opportunity to obtain feedback on the performance-level descriptions. During the July session, time was provided for the panelists to suggest changes in the descriptions based on the placement of their bookmarks after the Round 3 judgments had been made. The committee reviewed their feedback, refined the descriptions, and in August invited several of the July panelists to review the revised descriptions. The descriptions were again refined, and a revised version was prepared for the September standard setting. An extended feedback session was held at the conclusion of the September standard setting to finalize the descriptions.

The July and September bookmark procedures were implemented in relation to the top four performance levels only—below basic, basic, intermediate, and advanced. This was a consequence of a decision made by the Department of Education during the development of NAAL. As mentioned in Chapter 2, in 1992, a significant number of people were unable to complete any of the NALS items and therefore produced test results that were clearly low but essentially unscorable. Rather than expanding the coverage of NAAL into low levels of literacy at the letter, word, and simple sentence level, the National Center for Education Statistics (NCES) chose to develop a separate low-level assessment, the Adult Literacy Supplemental Assessment (ALSA). ALSA items were not put on the same scale as the NAAL items or classified into the three literacy areas. As a result, we could not use the ALSA questions in the bookmark procedure. This created a de facto cut score between the nonliterate in English and below basic performance levels. Consequently, all test takers who performed poorly on the initial screening questions (the core questions) and were administered ALSA are classified into the nonliterate in English category.[2]

As a result, the performance-level descriptions used for the bookmark procedures included only the top four levels, and the skills evaluated on ALSA were incorporated into the below basic description. After the standard settings, each of the performance-level descriptions for the below basic category were revised, and the nonliterate in English category was formulated. The below basic description was split to separate the skills that individuals who took ALSA would be likely to have from the skills that individuals who were administered NAAL, but who were not able to answer enough questions correctly to reach the basic level, would be likely to have.

Initially, the committee hoped to consolidate prose, document, and quantitative items into a singled ordered item booklet for the bookmark standard setting, which would have produced cut scores for an overall, combined literacy scale. This was not possible, however, because of an operational decision made by NCES and its contractors to scale the test

---

[2]Some potential test takers were not able to participate due to various literacy-related reasons, as determined by the interviewer, and are also classified as nonliterate in English. These nonparticipants include individuals who have difficulty with reading or writing or who are not able to communicate in English or Spanish. Another group of individuals who were not able to participate are those with a mental disability, such as retardation, a learning disability, or other mental or emotional conditions. Given the likely wide variation in literacy skills of individuals in this group, these individuals are treated as nonparticipants and are not included in the nonliterate in English category. Since some of these individuals are likely to have low literacy skills, however, an upper bound on the size of the nonliterate in English category could be obtained by including these individuals in the nonliterate in English category.

items separately by literacy area. That is, the difficulty level of each item was determined separately for prose, document, and quantitative items. This means that it was impossible to determine, for example, if a given prose item was harder or easier than a given document item. This decision appears to have been based on the assumption that the three scales measure different dimensions of literacy and that it would be inappropriate to combine them into a single scale. Regardless of the rationale for the decision, it precluded our setting an overall cut score.

Participants in the Bookmark Standard Settings

Selecting Panelists

Research and experience suggest that the background and expertise the panelists bring to the standard-setting activity are factors that influence the cut score decisions (Cizek, 2001a; Hambleton, 2001; Jaeger, 1989, 1991; Raymond and Reid, 2001). Furthermore, the *Standards for Educational and Psychological Testing* (American Educational Research Association, American Psychological Association, and National Council on Measurement in Education, 1999) specify that panelists should be highly knowledgeable about the domain in which judgments are required and familiar with the population of test takers. We therefore set up a procedure to solicit recommendations for potential panelists for both standard-setting sessions, review their credentials, and invite those with appropriate expertise to participate. Our goal was to assemble a group of panelists who were knowledgeable about acquisition of literacy skills, had an understanding of the literacy demands placed on adults in this country and the strategies adults use when presented with a literacy task, had some background in standardized testing, and would be expected to understand and correctly implement the standard-setting tasks.

Solicitations for panelists were sent to a variety of individuals: stakeholders who participated in the committee's public forum, state directors of adult education programs, directors of boards of adult education organizations, directors of boards of professional organizations for curriculum and instruction of adult education programs, and officials with the Council for Applied Linguistics, the National Council of Teachers of English, and the National Council of Teachers of Mathematics. The committee also solicited recommendations from state and federal correctional institutions as well as from the university community for researchers in the areas of workplace, family, and health literacy. Careful attention was paid to including representatives from as many states as possible, including representatives from the six states that subsidized additional testing of adults in 2003 (Kentucky, Maryland, Massachusetts, Missouri, New York, and Oklahoma).

The result of this extensive networking process produced a panel of professionals who represented adult education programs in urban, suburban, and rural geographic areas and a mix of practitioners, including teachers, tutors, coordinators, and directors. Almost all of the panelists had participated at some point in a range-finding or standard-setting activity, which helped them understand the connection between the performance-level descriptions and the task of determining an appropriate cut score.

Panelists' Areas of Expertise

Because NALS and NAAL are assessments of adult literacy, we first selected panelists with expertise in the fields of adult education and adult literacy. Adult educators may specialize in curriculum and instruction of adult basic education (ABE) skills, preparation of students for the general educational development (GED) certificate, or English for speakers of other languages. In addition, adult education and adult literacy professionals put forth significant curricular, instructional, and research efforts in the areas of workplace literacy, family literacy, and heath literacy. Expertise in all of these areas was represented among the panelists.[3]

For the July standard setting, only individuals working in adult education and adult literacy were selected to participate. Based on panelist feedback following this standard setting, we decided to broaden the areas of expertise for the September standard setting. Specifically, panelists indicated they would have valued additional perspectives from individuals in areas affected by adult education services, such as human resource management, as well as from teachers who work with middle school and high school students. Therefore, for the second session, we selected panelists from two additional fields: (1) middle or high school language arts teachers and (2) industrial and organizational psychologists who specialize in skill profiling or employee assessment for job placement.

The language arts classroom teachers broadened the standard-setting discussions by providing input on literacy instruction for adolescents who were progressing through the grades in a relatively typical manner, whereas teachers of ABE or GED had experience working with adults who, for

---

[3]We note that we considered including college faculty as panelists, as they would have brought a different perspective to the standard setting. In the end, we were somewhat concerned about their familiarity with adults with lower literacy skills and thought that it would be difficult for those who primarily work in college settings to make judgments about the skills of adults who would be classified at the levels below intermediate. There was a limit to the number of panelists we could include, and we tried to include those with experience working with adults whose skills fell at the levels primarily assessed on NALS and NAAL.

whatever reason, did not acquire the literacy skills attained by most students who complete the U.S. school system. The industrial and organizational psychologists who participated came from academia and corporate environments and brought a research focus and a practitioner perspective to the discussion that complemented those of the other panelists, who were primarily immersed in the adult education field. Table 5-1 gives a profile of the panelists who participated in the two standard-setting sessions.

BOOKMARK STANDARD SETTING WITH 1992 DATA

The first standard-setting session was held to obtain panelists' judgments about cut scores for the 1992 NALS and to collect their feedback about the performance-level descriptions. A total of 42 panelists participated in the session. Panelists were assigned to groups, and each group was randomly assigned to two of the three literacy areas (prose, document, or quantitative). Group 1 worked with the prose and document items; Group 2 worked with the prose and quantitative items; and Group 3 worked with the document and quantitative items. The sequence in which they worked on the different literacy scales was alternated in an attempt to balance any potential order effects.

For each literacy area, an ordered item booklet was prepared that rank-ordered the test questions from least to most difficult according to NALS examinees' responses. The ordered item booklets consisted of all the available NALS tasks for a given literacy area, even though with the balanced incomplete block spiraling (see Chapter 2), no individual actually responded to all test questions. The number of items in each NALS ordered item booklet was 39 for prose literacy, 71 for document literacy, and 42 for quantitative literacy.

Two training sessions were held, one for the "table leaders," the individuals assigned to be discussion facilitators for the tables of panelists, and one for all panelists. The role of the table leader was to serve as a discussion facilitator but not to dominate the discussion or to try to bring the tablemates to consensus about cut scores.

The bookmark process began by having each panelist respond to all the questions in the NALS test booklet for their assigned literacy scale. For this task, the test booklets contained the full complement of NALS items for each literacy scale, arranged in the order test takers would see them but not ranked-ordered as in the ordered item booklets. Afterward, the table leader facilitated discussion of differences among items with respect to knowledge, skills, and competencies required and what was measured by the scoring rubrics.

Panelists then received the ordered item booklets. They discussed each item and noted characteristics they thought made one item more difficult

TABLE 5-1 Profile of Panelists Involved in the Committee's Standard Settings

Participant Characteristics	July Standard Setting N = 42	September Standard Setting N = 30
Gender		
Female	83[a]	77
Male	17	23
Ethnicity		
Black	2	7
Caucasian	69	83
Hispanic	0	3
Native American	2	0
Not reported	26	7
Geographic Region[b]		
Midwest	26	37
Northeast	33	23
South	7	13
Southeast	19	7
West	14	20
Occupation[c]		
University instructors	7	10
Middle school, high school, or adult education instructors	19	30
Program coordinators or directors	38	40
Researchers	12	7
State office of adult education representative	24	13

than another. Each table member then individually placed their Round 1 bookmarks representing cut points for basic, intermediate, and advanced literacy.

In preparation for Round 2, each table received a summary of the Round 1 bookmark placements made by each table member and were provided the medians of the bookmark placements (calculated for each table). Table leaders facilitated discussion among table members about their respective bookmark placements, and panelists were then asked to independently make their Round 2 judgments.

In preparation for Round 3, each table received a summary of the Round 2 bookmark placements made by each table member as well as the medians for the table. In addition, each table received information about the proportion of the 1992 population who would have been categorized as having below basic, basic, intermediate, or advanced literacy based on the

TABLE 5-1 Continued

Participant Characteristics	July Standard Setting N = 42	September Standard Setting N = 30
Area of Expertise		
Adult education	100	70
Classroom teacher	0	17
Human resources or industrial and organizational psychology	0	13
Work Setting	NA[d]	
Rural		3
Suburban		33
Urban		43
Combination of all three settings		10
Other or not reported		10

[a]Percentage.

[b]The geographic regions were grouped in the following way: Midwest (IA, IL, IN, KY, MI, MN, MO, ND, OH, WI), Northeast (CT, DE, MA, ME, MD, NH, NJ, NY, PA, VT), South (AL, LA, MS, OK, TN, TX), Southeast (FL, GA, NC, SC, VA), and West (AZ, CA, CO, MT, NM, NV, OR, UT, WA, WY).

[c]Many panelists reported working in a variety of adult education settings where their work entailed aspects of instruction, curriculum development, program management, and research. For the purposes of constructing this table, the primary duties and/or job title of each panelist, as specified on the panelist's resume, was used to determine which of the five categories of occupation were appropriate for each panelist.

[d]Data not collected in July.

table's median cut points. After discussion, each panelist made his or her final, Round 3, judgments about bookmark placements for the basic, intermediate, and advanced literacy levels. At the conclusion of Round 3, panelists were asked to provide feedback about the performance-level descriptions by reviewing the items that fell between each of their bookmarks and editing the descriptions accordingly.

The processes described above were repeated for the second literacy area. The bookmark session concluded with a group session to obtain feedback from the panelists, both orally and through a written survey.

Using Different Response Probability Instructions

In conjunction with the July standard setting, the committee collected information about the impact of varying the instructions given to panelists with regard to the criteria used to judge the probability that an examinee would answer a question correctly (the response probability). The developers of the bookmark method recommend that a response probability of 67 (or two out of three times) be used and have offered both technical and nontechnical reasons for their recommendation. Their technical rationale stems from an analysis by Huynh (2000) in which the author demonstrated mathematically that the item information provided by a correct response to an open-ended item is maximized at the score point associated with a response probability of 67.[4] From a less technical standpoint, the developers of the bookmark method argue that a response probability of 67 percent is easier for panelists to conceive of than less familiar probabilities, such as 57.3 percent (Mitzel et al., 2001). They do not entirely rule out use of other response probabilities, such as 65 or 80, but argue that a response probability of 50 would seem to be conceptually difficult for panelists. They note, however, that research is needed to further understand the ways in which panelists apply response probability instructions and pose three questions that they believe remain to be answered: (1) Do panelists understand, internalize, and use the response probability criterion? (2) Are panelists sensitive to the response probability criterion such that scaling with different levels will systematically affect cut score placements? (3) Do panelists have a native or baseline conception of mastery that corresponds to a response probability?

Given these questions about the ways in which panelists apply response probability instructions, and the controversies surrounding the use of a response probability of 80 in 1992, the committee chose to investigate this issue further. We wanted to find out more about (1) the extent to which panelists understand and can make sense of the concept of response probability level when making judgments about cut scores and (2) the extent to which panelists make different choices when faced with different response probability levels. The committee decided to explore panelists' use and understanding of three response probability values—67, since it is commonly used with the bookmark procedures, as well as 80 and 50, since these values were discussed in relation to NALS in 1992.

The panelists were grouped into nine tables of five panelists each. Each group was given different instructions and worked with different ordered item booklets. Three tables (approximately 15 panelists) worked with booklets in which the items were ordered with a response probability of 80 percent and received instructions to use 80 percent as the likelihood that the examinee would answer an item correctly. Similarly, three tables used or-

---

[4]We refer the reader to the original article or to Mitzel et al. (2001) for more detailed information.

dered item booklets and instructions consistent with a response probability of 67 percent, and three tables used ordered item booklets and instructions consistent with a response probability of 50 percent.

Panelists received training in small groups about their assigned response probability instructions (see Appendix C for the exact wording). Each group was asked not to discuss the instructions about response probability level with anyone other than their tablemates so as not to cause confusion among panelists working with different response probability levels. Each table of panelists used the same response probability level for the second content area as they did for the first.

Refining the Performance-Level Descriptions

The performance-level descriptions used at the July standard setting consisted of overall and subject-specific descriptors for the top four performance levels (see Table 5-2). Panelists' written comments about and edits of the performance levels were reviewed. This feedback was invaluable in helping the committee rethink and reword the level descriptions in ways that better addressed the prose, document, and quantitative literacy demands suggested by the assessment items. Four panelists who had participated in the July standard-setting session were invited to review the revised performance-level descriptions prior to the September standard setting, and their feedback was used to further refine the descriptions. The performance-level descriptions used in the September standard setting are shown in Table 5-3.

BOOKMARK STANDARD SETTING WITH 2003 DATA

A total of 30 panelists from the fields of adult education, middle and high school English language arts, industrial and organizational psychology, and state offices of adult education participated in the second standard setting. Similar procedures were followed as in July with the exception that all panelists used the 67 percent response probability instructions.

Panelists were assigned to groups and the groups were then randomly assigned to literacy area with the subject area assignments balanced as they had been in July. Two tables worked on prose literacy first; one of these tables then worked on document literacy and the other on quantitative literacy. Two tables worked on document literacy first; one of these tables was assigned to work on quantitative literacy and the other to work on prose literacy. The remaining two tables that worked on quantitative literacy first were similarly divided for the second content area: one table was assigned to work on prose literacy while the other was assigned to work on document literacy.

TABLE 5-2 Performance-Level Descriptions Used During the July 2004 NALS Standard Setting

A. Overall Descriptions

Level	Description
An individual who scores at this level:	
I. Below Basic Literacy	May be able to recognize some letters, common sight words, or digits in English; has difficulty reading and understanding simple words, phrases, numbers, or quantities.
II. Basic Literacy	Can read and understand simple words, phrases, numbers, and quantities in English and locate information in short texts about commonplace events and situations; has some difficulty with drawing inferences and making use of quantitative information in such texts.
III. Intermediate Literacy	Can read and understand written material in English sufficiently well to locate information in denser, less commonplace texts, construct straightforward summaries, and draw simple inferences; has difficulty with drawing inferences from complex, multipart written material and with making use of quantitative information when multiple operations are involved.
IV. Advanced Literacy	Can read and understand complex written material in English sufficiently well to locate and integrate multiple pieces of information, perform sophisticated analytical tasks such as making systematic comparisons, draw sophisticated inferences from that material, and can make use of quantitative information when multiple operations are involved.

The National Adult Literacy Survey measures competence across a broad range of literacy development. Nonetheless, there exist meaningful distinctions in literacy outside of this range, including degrees of competence well above those described as required for "Advanced Literacy" and below what is required for "Basic Literacy." The "Below Basic Literacy" and "Advanced Literacy" levels by definition encompass all degrees of literacy below or above, respectively, those levels described in the above performance-level descriptors.

B. Subject-Area Descriptions

Level	Prose	Document	Quantitative
An individual who scores at this level:			
I. **Below Basic Literacy**	May be able to recognize letters but not able to consistently match sounds with letters; may be able to recognize a few common sight words.	May be able to recognize letters, numbers, and/or common sight words in familiar contexts such as on labels or signs; is not able to follow written instructions on simple documents.	May be able to recognize numbers and/or locate numbers in brief familiar contexts; is not able to perform simple arithmetic operations.
II. **Basic Literacy**	Is able to read and locate information in brief, commonplace text, but has difficulty drawing appropriate conclusions from the text, distinguishing fact from opinion or identifying an implied theme or idea in a selection.	Is able to understand or follow instructions on simple documents; able to locate and/or enter information based on a literal match of information in the question to information called for in the document itself.	Is able to locate easily identified numeric information in simple texts, graphs, tables, or charts; able to perform simple arithmetic operations or solve simple word problems when the operation is specified or easily inferred.
III. **Intermediate Literacy**	Is able to read and understand moderately dense, less commonplace text that contains long paragraphs; able to summarize, make inferences, determine cause and effect, and recognize author's purpose.	Is able to locate information in dense, complex documents in which repeated reviewing of the document is involved.	Is able to locate numeric information that is not easily identified in texts, graphs, tables, or charts; able to perform routine arithmetic operations when the operation is not specified or easily inferred.

continued

TABLE 5-2 Continued

B. Subject-Area Descriptions

Level	Prose	Document	Quantitative
IV. Advanced Literacy	Is able to read lengthy, complex, abstract texts; able to handle conditional text; able to synthesize information and perform complex inferences.	Is able to integrate multiple pieces of information in documents that contain complex displays; able to compare and contrast information; able to analyze and synthesize information from multiple sources.	Is able to locate and integrate numeric information in complex texts, graphs, tables, or charts; able to perform multiple and/or fairly complex arithmetic operations when the operation(s) is not specified or easily inferred.

TABLE 5-3 Performance-Level Descriptions Used During September 2004 NAAL Standard Setting

A. Overall Descriptions

Level	Description
An individual who scores at this level independently and in English:	
I. Below Basic Literacy	May independently be able to recognize some letters, common sight words, or digits in English; may sometimes be able to locate and make use of simple words, phrases, numbers, and quantities in short texts or displays (e.g., charts, figures, or forms) in English that are based on commonplace contexts and situations; may sometimes be able to perform simple one-step arithmetic operations; has some difficulty with reading and understanding information in sentences and short texts.
II. Basic Literacy	Is independently able to read and understand simple words, phrases, numbers, and quantities in English; able to locate information in short texts based on commonplace contexts and situations and enter such information into simple forms; is able to solve simple one-step problems in which the operation is stated or easily inferred; has some difficulty with drawing inferences from texts and making use of more complicated quantitative information.
III. Intermediate Literacy	Is independently able to read, understand, and use written material in English sufficiently well to locate information in denser, less commonplace texts, construct straightforward summaries, and draw simple inferences; able to make use of quantitative information when the arithmetic operation or mathematical relationship is not specified or easily inferred; able to generate written responses that demonstrate these skills; has difficulty with drawing inferences from more complex, multipart written material and with making use of quantitative information when multiple operations or complex relationships are involved.

continued

TABLE 5-3 Continued

A. Overall Descriptions

Level	Description
IV. Advanced Literacy	Is independently able to read, understand, and use more complex written material in English sufficiently well to locate and integrate multiple pieces of information, perform sophisticated analytical tasks such as making systematic comparisons, draw more sophisticated inferences from that material, and can make use of quantitative information when multiple operations or more complex relationships are involved; able to generate written responses that demonstrate these skills.

The National Assessment of Adult Literacy measures competence across a broad range of literacy development. Nonetheless, there exist meaningful distinctions in literacy outside of this range, including degrees of competence well above those described as required for "Advanced Literacy" and below what is required for "Basic Literacy." The "Below Basic Literacy" and "Advanced Literacy" levels by definition encompass all degrees of literacy below or above, respectively, those levels described in the above performance-level descriptors.

B. Subject-Area Descriptions

Level	Prose	Document	Quantitative
An individual who scores at this level independently and in English:			
I. Below Basic Literacy	May be able to recognize letters but not able to consistently match sounds with letters; may be able to recognize a few common sight words; may sometimes be able to locate information in short texts when the information is easily identifiable; has difficulty reading and understanding sentences.	May be able to recognize letters, numbers, and/or common sight words in frequently encountered contexts such as on labels or signs; may sometimes be able to follow written instructions on simple displays (e.g., charts, figures, or forms); may sometimes be able to locate	May be able to recognize numbers and/or locate numbers in frequently encountered contexts; may sometimes be able to perform simple arithmetic operations in commonly used formats or in simple problems when the

	Prose	Document	Quantitative
		easily identified information or to enter basic personal information in simple forms.	mathematical information is very concrete and mathematical relationships are primarily additive.
II. Basic Literacy	Is able to read, understand, and locate information in short, commonplace texts when the information is easily identifiable; has difficulty using text to draw appropriate conclusions, distinguish fact from opinion or identify an implied theme or idea in a selection.	Is able to read, understand, and follow instructions on simple displays; able to locate and/or enter easily identifiable information that primarily involves making a literal match of information in the question to information in the display.	Is able to locate and use easily identified numeric information in simple texts or displays; able to solve simple one-step problems when the arithmetic operation is specified or easily inferred, the mathematical information is familiar and relatively easy to manipulate, and mathematical relationships are primarily additive.
III. Intermediate Literacy	Is able to read and understand moderately dense, less commonplace text that may contain long paragraphs; able to summarize, make simple inferences, determine cause and effect, and recognize author's purpose; able to generate written responses that demonstrate these skills.	Is able to locate information in dense, complex displays in which repeated cycling through the display is involved; able to make simple inferences about the information in the display; able to generate written responses that demonstrate these skills.	Is able to locate and use numeric information that is not easily identified in texts or displays; able to solve problems when the arithmetic operation is not specified or easily inferred, and mathematical information is less familiar and more difficult to manipulate.

continued

TABLE 5-3 Continued

B. Subject-Area Descriptions

Level	Prose	Document	Quantitative
IV. **Advanced Literacy**	Is able to read lengthy, complex, abstract texts that are less commonplace and may include figurative language, to synthesize information and make complex inferences; able to generate written responses that demonstrate these skills.	Is able to integrate multiple pieces of information located in complex displays; able to compare and contrast information, and to analyze and synthesize information from multiple sources; able to generate written responses that demonstrate these skills.	Is able to locate and use numeric information in complex texts and displays; able to solve problems that involve multiple steps and multiple comparisons of displays when the operation(s) is not specified or easily inferred, the mathematical relationships are more complex, and the mathematical information is more abstract and requires more complex manipulations.

The ordered item booklets used for the second standard setting were organized in the same way as for the first standard setting, with the exception that some of the NAAL test questions were scored according to a partial credit scheme. When a partial credit scoring scheme is used, a difficulty value is estimated for both the partially correct score and the fully correct score. As a result, the test questions have to appear multiple times in the ordered item booklet, once for the difficulty value associated with partially correct and a second time for the difficulty value associated with fully correct. The ordered item booklets included the scoring rubric for determining partial credit and full credit scores.

Training procedures in September were similar to those used in July. Table leader training was held the day before the standard setting, and panelist training was held on the first day of the standard setting.

The procedures used in September were similar to those used in July, with the exception that the committee decided that all panelists in September should use the instructions for a response probability of 67 (the rationale for this decision is documented in the results section of this chapter). This meant that more typical bookmark procedures could be used for the Round 3 discussions. That is, groups of panelists usually work on the same ordered item booklet at different tables during Rounds 1 and 2 but join each other for Round 3 discussions. Therefore, in September, both tables working on the same literacy scale were merged for the Round 3 discussion.

During Round 3, panelists received data summarizing bookmark placements for the two tables combined. This included a listing of each panelist's bookmark placements and the median bookmark placements by table. In addition, the combined median scale score (based on the data from both tables) was calculated for each level, and impact data provided about the percentages of adults who would fall into the below basic, basic, intermediate, and advanced categories if the combined median values were used as cut scores.[5] Panelists from both tables discussed their reasons for choosing different bookmark placements, after which each panelist independently made a final judgment of items that separated the test among basic, intermediate, and advanced literacy.

Revising the Performance-Level Descriptions

At the conclusion of the September standard setting, 12 of the panelists were asked to stay for an extended session to write performance-level de-

---

[5]Data from the prison sample and the state samples were not ready in time for the September standard setting. Because the 2003 data file was incomplete, the 1992 data were used to generate the population proportions rather than the 2003 data.

scriptions for the NAAL items. At least one member from each of the six tables participated in the extended session, and there was representation from each of the three areas of expertise (adult education, middle and high school English language arts, and industrial and organizational psychology). The 12 participants were split into 3 groups, each focusing on one of the three NAAL content areas. Panelists were instructed to review the test items that would fall into each performance level (based on the Round 3 median cut scores) and prepare more detailed versions of the performance-level descriptions, including specific examples from the stimuli and associated tasks. The revised descriptions are shown in Table 5-4.

RESULTS FROM THE STANDARD-SETTING SESSIONS

Comparison of Results from Differing Response Probability Instructions

The purpose of using the different instructions in the July session was to evaluate the extent to which the different response probability criteria influenced panelists' judgments about bookmark placements. It would be expected that panelists using the higher probability criteria would place their bookmarks earlier in the ordered item booklets, and as the probability criteria decrease, the bookmarks would be placed later in the booklet. For example, panelists working with rp50 instructions were asked to select the items that individuals at a given performance level would be expected to get right 50 percent of the time. This is a relatively low criterion for success on a test question, and, as a result, the panelist should require the test taker to get more items correct than if a higher criterion for success were used (e.g., rp67 or rp80). Therefore, for a given performance level, the bookmark placement should be in reverse order of the values of the response probability criteria: the rp80 bookmark placement should come first in the booklet, the rp67 bookmark should come next, and the rp50 bookmark should be furthest into the booklet.

Tables 5-5a, 5-5b, and 5-5c present the results from the July standard setting, respectively, for the prose, document, and quantitative areas. The first row of each table shows the median bookmark placements for basic, intermediate, and advanced based on the different response probability instructions. For example, Table 5-5a shows that the median bookmark placements for the basic performance level in prose were on item 6 under the rp80 and rp67 instructions and on item 8 under the rp50 instructions.

Ideally, panelists would compensate for the different response criteria by placing their bookmarks earlier or later in the ordered item booklet, depending on the response probability instructions. When panelists respond to the bookmark instructions by conceptualizing a person whose skills match the performance-level descriptions, the effect of using different response probability instructions would shift their bookmark placements in such a way that they compensated exactly for the differences in the translation of bookmark placements into cut scores. When panelists are informing their judgments in this way, the cut score associated with the bookmark placement would be identical under the three different response probability instructions, even though the bookmark locations would differ. As the tables show, however, this does not appear to be the case. For example, the second row of Table 5-5a shows that the median cut scores for basic were different: 226, 211, and 205.5, respectively, for rp80, rp67, and rp50.

It is not surprising that panelists fail to place bookmarks in this ideal way, for the ideal assumes prior knowledge of the likelihood that persons at each level of literacy will answer each item correctly. A more relevant issue is whether judges have a sufficient subjective understanding of probability to change bookmark placements in response to different instructions about response probabilities. Our analysis yields weak evidence in favor of the latter hypothesis.[6]

We conducted tests to evaluate the statistical significance of the differences in bookmark placements and in cut scores. The results indicated that, for a given literacy area and performance level, the bookmark placements were tending in the right direction but were generally not statistically significantly different under the three response probability instructions. In contrast, for a given literacy area and performance level, the differences among the cut scores were generally statistically significant. Additional details about the analyses we conducted appear in Appendix C.

Tables 5-5a, 5-5b, and 5-5c also present the mean and standard deviations of the cut scores under the different response probability instructions. The standard deviations provide an estimate of the extent of variability among the panelists' judgments. Although the bookmark method does not strive for consensus among panelists, the judgments should not be widely disparate. Comparison of the standard deviations across the different response probability instructions reveals no clear pattern; that is, there is no indication that certain response probability instructions were superior to the others in terms of the variability among panelists' judgments.

A more practical way to evaluate these differences is by looking at the

---

[6]In addition, a follow up questionnaire asked panelists what adjustments they would have made to their bookmark placements had they been instructed to use different rp criteria. For each of the three rp criteria, panelists were asked if they would have placed their bookmarks earlier or later in the ordered item booklet if they had been assigned to use a different rp instruction. Of the 37 panelists, 27 (73 percent) indicated adjustments that reflected a correct understanding of the rp instructions.

TABLE 5-4 Performance-Level Descriptions and Subject-Area Descriptions with Exemplar NAAL Items

A. Overall Description

Level	Description	Sample Tasks Associated with Level
Nonliterate in English	May independently recognize some letters, numbers, and/or common sight words in English in frequently encountered contexts.	• Identify a simple letter, word, number, or date on a consumer food item or road sign • Read aloud a number or date • Identify information in a contextually-based format (e.g., locate and/or read aloud the company name provided on a bill statement)
Below Basic	May independently be able to locate and make use of simple words, phrases, numbers, and quantities in short texts or displays (e.g., charts, figures, forms) in English that are based on commonplace contexts and situations; may sometimes be able to perform simple one-step arithmetic operations.	• Underline or otherwise identify a specific sentence in a government form or newspaper article • Calculate change in a situation involving money
Basic	Is independently able to read and understand simple words, phrases, numbers, and quantities in English when the information is easily identifiable with a minimal amount of distracting information; able to locate information in short texts based on commonplace contexts and situations and enter such information into simple forms; is able to solve simple one-step problems in which the operation is stated or easily inferred.	• Read a short story or newspaper article and underline or circle the sentence that answers a question (e.g., why an event occurred or what foods an athlete ate) (prose) • Complete a telephone message slip with information about the caller (document) • Calculate total amount of money to be deposited into a bank account (quantitative)
Intermediate	Is independently able to read, understand, and use written material in English sufficiently well to locate information in denser, less commonplace texts that	• Use an almanac or other reference material to find three food sources that contain Vitamin E (prose) • Identify information on a government form (e.g., when

continued

	may contain a greater number of distractors; able to construct straightforward summaries, and draw simple inferences; able to make use of quantitative information when the arithmetic operation or mathematical relationship is not specified or easily inferred; able to generate written responses that demonstrate these skills.	• an employee is eligible for medical insurance) (document) • Record several transactions on a check ledger and calculate account balance after each transaction (quantitative)
Advanced	Is independently able to read, understand, and use more complex written material in English sufficiently well to locate and integrate multiple pieces of information, perform more sophisticated analytical tasks such as making systematic comparisons, draw more sophisticated inferences from that material, and can make use of quantitative information when multiple operations or more complex relationships are involved; able to generate written responses that demonstrate these skills.	• Read a newspaper article and identify the argument used by the author (prose) • Interpret a timetable (e.g., bus, airplane, or train schedule or a television program listing) and use that information to make a decision (document) • Calculate the tip on a restaurant food order (quantitative)

The NAAL measures competence across a broad range of literacy development. Nonetheless, there exist meaningful distinctions in literacy outside of this range, including degrees of competence well above those described as required for "Advanced Literacy" and below what is required for "Basic Literacy." The "Below Basic Literacy" and "Advanced Literacy" levels, by definition, encompass all degrees of literacy below or above, respectively, those levels described in the above performance-level descriptors.

TABLE 5-4 Continued

B. Prose Literacy Content Area

Level	An individual who scores at this level independently and in English:	Sample of NAAL tasks associated with the level
Below Basic	May sometimes be able to locate information in short texts when the information is easily identifiable.	• Use the text of a short paragraph to answer a question where a literal match occurs (e.g., use the statement, "Terry is from Ireland" to answer the question, "What country is Terry from?") • Underline or otherwise identify a specific sentence in a government form or newspaper article
Basic	Is able to read, understand, follow directions, copy, and locate information in short, commonplace texts (e.g., simple newspaper articles, advertisements, short stories, government forms) when the information is easily identifiable with a minimal number of distractors in the main text. May be able to work with somewhat complex texts to complete a literal match of information in the question and text.*	• Read a short story or newspaper article and underline or circle the sentence that answers a question (e.g., why an event occurred) • Locate specific information on a government form (e.g., definition of "blind" on a Social Security Administration informational handout)
Intermediate	Is able to read and understand moderately dense, less commonplace text that may contain long paragraphs, a greater number of distractors, a higher level vocabulary, longer sentences, more complex sentence structure; able to summarize; make simple inferences, determine cause and effect, and recognize author's purpose; able to generate written responses (e.g., words, phrases, lists, sentences, short paragraphs) that demonstrate these skills.*	• Locate information in a short newspaper article or government form (e.g., a government form regarding Social Security benefits) • Use an almanac or other reference material (e.g., to find three food sources that contain Vitamin E) • Read a short poem and identify or infer the situation described by the poem • Write a letter to a credit department informing them of an error on a bill statement

| Advanced | Is able to read lengthy, complex, abstract texts that are less commonplace and may include figurative language and/or unfamiliar vocabulary; able to synthesize information and make complex inferences; compare and contrast viewpoints; able to generate written responses that demonstrate these skills.* | • Read a newspaper article and identify the argument used by the author
• Orally summarize a short newspaper article
• Identify differences between terms found on a benefits handout (e.g., educational assistance and tuition aid benefits)
• Read a short poem and identify or infer the author's purpose
• Compare and contrast viewpoints in an editorial |

*When presented with a task that measures these skills, the individual would be likely to respond correctly 2 out of 3 times.

C. Document Literacy Content Area

Level	An individual who scores at this level independently and in English:	Sample of NAAL tasks associated with the level
Below Basic	May sometimes be able to follow written instructions on simple displays (e.g., charts, figures, or forms); may sometimes be able to locate easily identified information or to enter basic personal information on simple forms; may be able to sign name in right place on form.	• Put a signature on a government form (e.g., Social Security card) • Read a pay stub and identify the current net pay amount
Basic	Is able to read, understand, and follow one-step instructions on simple displays (e.g., government, banking, and employment application forms, short newspaper articles or advertisements, television or public transportation schedules, bar charts or circle graphs of a single variable); able to locate and/or enter easily identifiable information that primarily involves making a literal match between the question and the display.*	• Identify a single piece of information on a document (e.g., the time when, or room number where, a meeting will take place) • Use a television program listing to identify a television program that airs at a specific time on an specific channel • Record the name of caller and caller's telephone number on a message slip

continued

TABLE 5-4 Continued

C. Document Literacy Content Area

Level	An individual who scores at this level independently and in English:	Sample of NAAL tasks associated with the level
Intermediate	Is able to locate information in dense, complex displays (e.g., almanacs or other reference materials, maps and legends, government forms and instruction sheets, supply catalogues and product charts, more complex graphs and figures that contain trends and multiple variables) when repeated cycling or re-reading is involved; able to make simple inferences about the information displayed; able to generate written responses that demonstrate these skills.*	• Identify a specific location on a map • Complete a bank deposit slip or check • Write the shipping information on a product order form • Make a decision based on information given in a schedule of events (e.g., television program listing)
Advanced	Is able to integrate multiple pieces of information located in complex displays; able to compare and contrast information, and to analyze and synthesize information from multiple sources; able to generate written responses that demonstrate these skills.*	• Locate specific information in an almanac, transportation timetable, utility bill, or television program listing • Determine the appropriateness of a product or statement based upon information given in a display • Interpret a display that utilizes multiple variables (e.g., a chart with blood pressure, age, and physical activity), compare information from two displays of data, or transfer data from one display to another • Use a map and follow directions to identify one or more change(s) in location • Make a decision based on information given in a schedule of events where the time given is not written explicitly on the schedule (e.g., reader must infer that 8:15 a.m. is between 8:00 a.m. and 8:30 a.m.)

*When presented with a task that measures these skills, the individual would be likely to respond correctly 2 out of 3 times.

D. Quantitative Literacy Content Area

Level	An individual who scores at this level independently and in English:	Sample of NAAL tasks associated with the level
Below Basic	May sometimes be able to perform simple arithmetic operations in commonly used formats or in simple problems when the mathematical information is very concrete and mathematical relationships are primarily additive.	• Calculate change in a situation involving money • Add two numbers entered on an order form or bank deposit slip
Basic	Is able to locate and use easily identified numeric information in simple texts or displays; able to solve simple one-step problems when the arithmetic operation is specified or easily inferred, the mathematical information is familiar and relatively easy to manipulate, and mathematical relationships are primarily additive.*	• Complete a bank deposit slip and calculate the total dollar amount of the deposit • Compute or compare information (e.g., ticket prices to two events)
Intermediate	Is able to locate numeric information that is embedded in texts or in complex displays and use that information to solve problems; is able to infer the arithmetic operation or mathematical relationship when it is not specified; is able to use fractions, decimals, or percents and to apply concepts of area and perimeter in real-life contexts.*	• Record several transactions on a check ledger and calculate account balance after each transaction • Use a transportation schedule to make a decision regarding travel plans

continued

TABLE 5-4 Continued

D. Quantitative Literacy Content Area

Level	An individual who scores at this level independently and in English:	Sample of NAAL tasks associated with the level
Advanced	Is able to locate and use numeric information in complex texts and displays; able to solve problems that involve multiple steps and multiple comparisons of displays when the operation(s) is/are not specified or easily inferred, the mathematical relationships are more complex, and the mathematical information is more abstract and requires more complex manipulations.*	• Compute amount of money needed to purchase one or more items and/or the amount of change that will be returned • Compute and compare costs for consumer items (e.g., miles per gallon, energy efficiency rating, cost per ounce for food items) • Use information given in a government form to compute values (e.g., monthly or annual Social Security payments)

*When presented with a task that measures these skills, the individual would be likely to respond correctly 2 out of 3 times.

impact data. The final row of Tables 5-5a, 5-5b, and 5-5c compares the percentage of the population scoring below each of the cut scores when the different response probability instructions were used. Comparison of the impact data reveals that the effects of the different response probability instructions were larger for the cut scores for the document and quantitative areas than for prose.

These findings raise several questions. First, the findings might lead one to question the credibility of the cut scores produced by the bookmark method. However, there is ample evidence that people have difficulty interpreting probabilistic information (Tversky and Kahneman, 1983). The fact that bookmark panelists have difficulties with this aspect of the procedure is not particularly surprising. In fact, the developers of the procedure appear to have anticipated this, saying "it is not reasonable to suggest that lack of understanding of the response probability criterion invalidates a cut score judgment any more than a lack of understanding of [item response theory] methods invalidates the interpretation of a test score" (Mitzel et al., 2001, p. 262).

In our opinion, the bookmark procedure had been implemented very carefully with strict attention to key factors that can affect the results (Cizek, Bunch, and Koons, 2004; Hambleton, 2001; Kane, 2001; Plake, Melican, and Mills, 1992: Raymond and Reid, 2001). The standard-setting panelists had been carefully selected and had appropriate background qualifications. The instructions to panelists were very clear, and there was ample time for clarification. Committee members and staff observing the process were impressed with how it was carried out, and the feedback from the standard-setting panelists was very positive. Kane (2001) speaks of this as "procedural evidence" in support of the appropriateness of performance standards, noting that "procedural evidence is a widely accepted basis for evaluating policy decisions" (p. 63). Thus, while the findings indicated that panelists had difficulty implementing the response probability instructions *exactly* as intended, we judged that this did not seem to be sufficient justification for discrediting the bookmark method entirely.

The second issue presented by the findings was that if the different response probability instructions had produced identical cut scores, it would not have mattered which response probability the committee decided to use for the bookmark procedure. However, the findings indicated that different cut scores were produced by the different instructions; hence, the committee had to select among the options for response probability values.

As discussed in Chapter 3, the choice of a response probability value involves weighing both technical and nontechnical information to make a judgment about the most appropriate value given the specific assessment context. We had hoped that the comparison of different response probability instructions would provide evidence to assist in this choice. However,

TABLE 5-5a Median Bookmark Placements and Cut Scores for the Three Response Probability (RP) Instructions in the July 2004 Standard Setting with NALS Prose Items (n = 39 items)

	Basic			Intermediate			Advanced		
RP Instructions:	(1) 80%	(2) 67%	(3) 50%	(4) 80%	(5) 67%	(6) 50%	(7) 80%	(8) 67%	(9) 50%
Median bookmark placement	6	6	8	20	20	23.5	32	33	36.5
Median cut score	226.0	211.0	205.5	289.0	270.0	277.0	362.0	336.0	351.5
Mean cut score	236.2	205.3	207.2	301.0	273.0	270.9	357.3	341.6	345.8
Standard deviation	15.5	6.9	14.3	13.9	14.3	18.7	33.0	22.7	33.7
Percent below median cut score	20.6	15.5	14.1	56.2	43.6	48.2	93.9	84.5	90.9

NOTE: Number of panelists for the rp80, rp67, and rp50 conditions, respectively, were 9, 10, and 8.

TABLE 5-5b Median Bookmark Placements and Cut Scores for the Three Response Probability (RP) Instructions in the July 2004 Standard Setting with NALS Document Items (n = 71 items)

	Basic			Intermediate			Advanced		
RP Instructions:	(1) 80%	(2) 67%	(3) 50%	(4) 80%	(5) 67%	(6) 50%	(7) 80%	(8) 67%	(9) 50%
Median bookmark placement	13	12.5	23	43.5	51	54	64	70.5	68
Median cut score	213.0	189.0	191.0	263.5	255.0	213.5	330.0	343.5	305.0
Mean cut score	215.3	192.3	189.5	264.1	257.3	230.2	333.1	345.1	306.7
Standard deviation	8.1	8.5	2.6	11.7	10.3	5.1	36.7	29.7	21.3
Percent below median cut score	18.2	12.0	12.4	43.6	38.0	18.6	83.9	89.8	70.2

NOTE: Number of panelists for the rp50, rp67, and rp80 conditions, respectively, were 8, 10, and 8.

TABLE 5-5c Median Bookmark Placements and Cut Scores for the Three Response Probability (RP)Instructions in the July 2004 Standard Setting with NALS Quantitative Items (n = 42 items)

	Basic			Intermediate			Advanced		
RP Instructions:	(1) 80%	(2) 67%	(3) 50%	(4) 80%	(5) 67%	(6) 50%	(7) 80%	(8) 67%	(9) 50%
Median bookmark placement	14	10.5	11	30	25	26	39	38	39
Median cut score	283.0	244.0	235.0	349.0	307.0	284.0	389.0	351.5	323.0
Mean cut score	279.1	243.6	241.1	334.9	295.2	289.4	384.2	367.5	339.9
Standard deviation	11.5	29.5	12.9	23.1	17.6	8.7	26.3	39.3	22.5
Percent below median cut score	51.7	29.2	25.4	88.9	67.6	52.4	97.8	90.0	77.0

NOTE: Number of panelists for the rp50, rp67, and rp80 conditions, respectively, were 9, 10, and 9.

none of the data suggested that one response probability value was "better" than another.

In follow-up debriefing sessions, panelists commented that the rp50 instructions were difficult to apply, in that it was hard to determine bookmark placement when thinking about a 50 percent chance of responding correctly. This concurs with findings from a recent study conducted in connection with standard setting on the NAEP (Williams and Schulz, 2005). As stated earlier, the developers of the bookmark method also believe this value to be conceptually difficult for panelists.

A response probability of 80 percent had been used in 1992, in part to reflect what is often considered to be mastery level in the education field. The committee debated about the appropriateness of this criterion versus the 67 percent criterion, given the purposes and uses of the assessment results. The stakes associated with the assessment are low; that is, no scores are reported for individuals, and no decisions affecting an individual are based on the results. A stringent criterion, like 80 percent, would be called for when it is important to have a high degree of certainty that the individual has truly mastered the specific content or skills, such as in licensing examinations.

A response probability of 67 percent is recommended in the literature by the developers of the bookmark procedure (Mitzel et al., 2001) and is the value generally used in practice. Since there was no evidence from our comparison of response probabilities to suggest that we should use a value other than the developer's recommendation, the committee decided to use a response probability of 67 percent for the bookmark procedure for NALS and NAAL. Therefore, all panelists in the September standard setting used this criterion. In determining the final cut scores from the bookmark procedure, we used all of the judgments from September but only the judgments from July based on the rp67 criterion.

We are aware that many in the adult education, adult literacy, and health literacy fields have grown accustomed to using the rp80 criterion in relation to NALS results, and that some may at first believe that use of a response probability of 67 constitutes "lowering the standards." We want to emphasize that this represents a fundamental, albeit not surprising, misunderstanding. Changing the response probability level does not alter the test in any way; the same content and skills are evaluated. Changing the response probability level does not alter the distributions of scores. Distributions of skills are what they are estimated to be, regardless of response probability levels. The choice of response probability levels should not in principle affect proportions of people in regions of the distribution, although some differences were apparent in our comparisons. Choice of response probability levels does affect a user's attention in terms of condensed, everyday-language conceptions of what it means to be at a level (e.g., what it means to be "proficient").

It does appear that some segments of the literacy community prefer the higher response probability value of 80 percent as a reporting and interpretive device, if for nothing other than continuity with previous literacy assessments. The response probability level of 80 percent is robust to the fact that a response probability level is mapped to a verbal expression, such as "can consistently" or "can usually" do items of a given difficulty (or worse, more simplistic interpretations, such as "can" as opposed to "cannot" do items of a given difficulty level). It is misapplying this ambiguous mapping from precise and invariant quantitative descriptions to imprecise, everyday verbal descriptions that gives the impression of lowering standards. Changing the response probability criterion in the report may be justified by the reasons discussed above, but we acknowledge that disadvantages to this recommendation include the potential for misinterpretations and a less preferable interpretation in the eyes of some segments of the user community.

In addition, use of a response probability of 67 percent for the bookmark standard-setting procedure does not preclude using a value of 80 percent in determining exemplary items for the performance levels. That is, for each of the performance levels, it is still possible to select exemplar items that demonstrate the types of questions individuals have an 80 percent chance of answering correctly. Furthermore, it is possible to select exemplary items that demonstrate other probabilities of success (67 percent, 50 percent, 35 percent, etc.). We discussed this issue in Chapter 3 and return to it in Chapter 6.

Comparison of Results from the July and September Bookmark Procedure

Table 5-6 presents the median cut scores that resulted from the rp67 instructions for the July standard setting (column 1) along with the median cut scores that resulted from the September standard setting (column 2). Column 3 shows the overall median cut scores that resulted when the July and September judgments were combined, and column 5 shows the overall mean cut score. To provide a sense of the spread of panelists' judgments about the placement of the bookmarks, two measures of variability are shown. The "interquartile range" of the cut scores is shown in column 4. Whereas the median cut score represents the cut score at the 50th percentile in the distribution of panelists' judgments, the interquartile range shows the range of cut score values from the 25th percentile to the 75th percentile.

TABLE 5-6 Summary Statistics from the Committee's Standard Settings for Adu

	(1) July Median Cut Score[a]	(2) September Median Cut Score[b]	(3) Overall Median Cut Score[c]
Prose Literacy			
(1) Basic	211	219	211
(2) Intermediate	270	281	270
(3) Advanced	336	345	345
Document Literacy			
(4) Basic	189	210	203
(5) Intermediate	255	254	254
(6) Advanced	344	345	345
Quantitative Literacy			
(7) Basic	244	244	244
(8) Intermediate	307	295	296
(9) Advanced	352	356	356

[a]The July standard setting used the items from the 1992 NALS. The cut scores are based on the bookmark placements set by panelists using the rp67 guidelines.

[b]The September standard setting used items from the 2003 NAAL. All panelists used rp67 guidelines.

Column 6 presents the standard deviation, and column 7 shows the range bounded by the mean plus and minus one standard deviation.

Comparison of the medians from the July and September standard-setting sessions reveals that the September cut scores tended to be slightly higher than the July cut scores, although overall the cut scores were quite similar. The differences in median cut scores ranged from 0 to 21, with the largest difference occurring for the basic cut score for document literacy. Examination of the spread in cut scores based on the standard deviation reveals more variability in the advanced cut score than for the other performance levels. Comparison of the variability in cut scores in each literacy area shows that, for all literacy areas, the standard deviation for the advanced cut score was at least twice as large as the standard deviation for the intermediate or basic cut scores. Comparison of the variability in cut scores across literacy areas shows that, for all of the performance levels, the standard deviations for the quantitative literacy cut scores were slightly higher than for the other two sections. There was considerable discussion (and some disagreement) among the panelists about the difficulty level of the quantitative section, which probably contributed to the larger variability in these cut scores. We address this issue in more detail later in this chapter. Appendixes C and D include additional results from the bookmark standard setting.

(4) Interquartile Range[d]	(5) Overall Mean Cut Score	(6) Standard Deviation	(7) Mean ± One Standard Deviation
206-221	214.2	11.0	199.6-221.6
264-293	275.9	16.2	254.2-86.7
336-366	355.6	33.5	311.9-378.8
192-210	200.1	13.4	189.8-216.6
247-259	254.0	9.1	244.7-262.8
324-371	343.0	30.8	314.2-375.9
230-245	241.3	19.7	223.8-263.3
288-307	293.8	17.1	279.4-313.5
343-398	368.6	41.8	313.9-397.6

[c]The overall median is the median cut score when both the July rp67 and September data were combined.

[d]Range of cut scores from the first quartile (first value in range) to the third quartile (second value in range).

Estimating the Variability of the Cut Scores Across Judges

The *Standards for Educational and Psychological Testing* (American Educational Research Association, American Psychological Association, National Council on Measurement in Education, 1999) recommend reporting information about the amount of variation in cut scores that might be expected if the standard-setting procedure were replicated. The design of our bookmark sessions provided a means for estimating the extent to which the cut scores would be likely to vary if another standard setting was held on a different occasion with a different set of judges.

As described earlier, participants in the July and September standard-setting sessions were divided into groups, each of which focused on two of the three literacy areas. At each session, panelists worked on their first assigned literacy area during the first half of the session (which can be referred to as "Occasion 1") and their second assigned literacy area during the second half of the session (referred to as "Occasion 2"). This design for the standard setting allowed for cut score judgments to be obtained on four occasions that were essentially replications of each other: two occasions from July and two occasions from September. Thus, the four occasions can be viewed as four replications of the standard-setting procedures.

The median cut score for each occasion was determined based on the panelists' Round 3 bookmark placements; these medians are shown in

TABLE 5-7 Confidence Intervals for the Bookmark Cut Scores

| | July | | September | |
	Occasion 1 Median n = 5	Occasion 2 Median n = 5	Occasion 1 Median n = 10	Occasion 2 Median n = 10
Prose Literacy				
Basic	197.0	211.0	208.0	227.0
Intermediate	270.0	263.0	267.5	293.0
Advanced	343.0	336.0	345.0	382.5
Document Literacy				
Basic	202.0	185.0	210.0	201.0
Intermediate	271.0	247.0	258.0	248.5
Advanced	378.0	324.0	364.5	325.0
Quantitative Literacy				
Basic	216.0	271.0	244.0	245.0
Intermediate	276.0	309.0	298.5	292.0
Advanced	347.0	410.0	381.0	349.5

[a]Each median was weighted by the number of panelists submitting judgments.
[b]The standard error reflects the variation in cut scores across the four occasions and was calculated as: $\dfrac{\text{standard deviation.}}{\sqrt{4}}$

Table 5-7. The average of these occasion medians was calculated by weighting each median by the number of panelists. The 95 percent confidence intervals for the weighted averages were computed, which indicate the range in which the cut scores would be expected to fall if the standard-setting session was repeated. For example, a replication of the standard-setting session would be likely to yield a cut score for the prose basic level literacy in the range of 200.5 to 225.5. We revisit these confidence intervals later in the chapter when we make recommendations for the cut scores.

CONTRASTING GROUPS STANDARD-SETTING METHOD

In a typical contrasting groups procedure, the standard-setting panelists are individuals who know the examinees firsthand in teaching, learning, or work environments. Using the performance-level descriptions, the panelists are asked to place examinees into the performance categories in which they judge the examinees belong without reference to their actual performance on the test. Cut scores are then determined from the actual test scores attained by the examinees placed in the distinct categories. The goal is to set the cut score such that the number of misclassifications is roughly the same in both directions (Kane, 1995); that is, the cut score that mini-

Weighted Average of the Medians[a]	Standard Deviation	Standard Error[b]	95% Confidence Interval for the Weighted Average[c]
213.0	12.7	6.4	200.5 to 225.5
275.7	14.6	7.3	261.3 to 290.0
355.7	22.6	11.3	333.5 to 377.8
201.5	9.8	4.9	191.9 to 211.1
255.2	9.9	5.0	245.5 to 264.8
346.8	26.6	13.3	320.7 to 372.9
244.2	18.7	9.4	225.9 to 262.5
294.3	11.7	5.9	282.8 to 305.8
369.7	27.2	13.6	343.0 to 396.4

[c]The confidence interval is the weighted average plus or minus the bound, where the bound was calculated as the standard score at the .05 confidence level multiplied by the standard error.

mizes the number of individuals who correctly belong in an upper group but are placed into a lower group (false negative classification errors) and likewise minimizes the number of individuals who correctly belong in a lower group but are placed into an upper group (false positive classification errors).

Because data collection procedures for NALS and NAAL guarantee the anonymity of test takers, there was no way to implement the contrasting groups method as it is typically conceived. Instead, the committee designed a variation of this procedure that utilized the information collected via the background questionnaire to form groups of test takers. For example, test takers can be separated into two distinct groups based on their responses about the amount of help they need with reading: those who report they need a lot of help with reading and those who report they do not need a lot of help. Comparison of the distribution of literacy scores for these two groups provides information that can be used in determining cut scores.

This approach, while not a true application of the contrasting groups method, seemed promising as a viable technique for generating a second set of cut scores with which to judge the reasonableness of the bookmark cut scores. This QCG method differs from a true contrasting groups approach in two key ways. First, because it was impossible to identify and contact respondents after the fact, no panel of judges was assembled to classify individuals into the performance categories. Second, due to the nature of the background questions, the groups were not distinguished on the basis of characteristics described by the performance-level descriptions. Instead, we used background questions as proxies for the functional consequences of the literacy levels, and, as described in the next section, aligned the information with the performance levels in ways that seemed plausible. We note that implementation of this procedure was limited by the available background information. In particular, there is little information on the background questionnaire that can serve as functional consequences of advanced literacy. As discussed in Chapter 4, additional background information about advanced literacy habits (e.g., number and character of books read in the past year, types of newspapers read, daily or weekly writing habits) would have helped refine the distinction between intermediate and advanced literacy skills.

Implementing the QCG Method Through Analyses with Background Data

From the set of questions available in both the NALS and NAAL background questionnaires, we identified the following variables to include in the QCG analyses: education level, occupation, two income-related variables (receiving federal assistance, receiving interest or dividend income), self-rating of reading skills, level of assistance needed with reading, and participation in reading activities (reading the newspaper, using reading at work). We examined the distribution of literacy scores for specific response options to the background questions.

The below basic and basic levels originated partly from policy distinctions about the provision of supplemental adult education services; thus, we expected the cut score between below basic and basic to be related to a recognized need for adult literacy services. Therefore, for each literacy area, the bookmark cut score between below basic and basic was compared with the QCG cut score that separated individuals with 0-8 years of formal education (i.e., no high school) and those with some high school education. To determine this QCG cut score, we examined the distributions of literacy scores for the two groups to identify the point below which most of those with 0-8 years of education scored and above which most of those with some high school scored. To accomplish this, we determined the median score (50th percentile) in each literacy area for those with no high school education and the median score (50th percentile) for those with some high school education. We then found the midpoint between these two medians (which is simply the average of the two medians).[7] Table 5-8 presents this information. For example, the table shows that in 1992 the median prose score for those with no high school was 182; the corresponding median for those with some high school was 236. The midpoint between these two medians is 209. Likewise, for 2003, the median prose score for those with no high school was 159 and for those with some high school was 229. The midpoint between these two medians is 194.

We also judged that self-rating of reading skills should be related to the distinction between below basic and basic, and the key relevant contrast would be between those who say they do not read well and those who say they do read well. Following the procedures described above, for each literacy area, we determined the median score for those who reported that they do not read well (e.g., in 1992, the value for prose was 140) and those who reported that they read well (e.g., in 1992, the value for prose was 285). The midpoint between these two values is 212.5. The corresponding median prose scores for the 2003 participants were 144 for those who report they do not read well and 282 for those who report that they read well, which results in a midpoint of 213.

We then combined the cut scores suggested by these two contrasts (no high school versus some high school; do not read well versus read well) by averaging the four midpoints for the 1992 and 2003 results (209, 194, 212.5, and 213). We refer to this value as the QCG cut score. Combining the information across multiple background variables enhances the stability of the cut score estimates. Table 5-8 presents the QCG cut scores for the basic performance level for prose (207.1), document (205.1), and quantitative (209.9) literacy.

The contrast between the basic and intermediate levels was developed to reflect a recognized need for GED preparation services. Therefore, the bookmark cut score between these two performance levels was compared with the contrast between individuals without a high school diploma or GED certificate and those with a high school diploma or GED. Furthermore, because of a general policy expectation that most individuals can and should achieve a high school level education but not necessarily more, we expected the contrast between the basic and intermediate levels to be associated with a number of other indicators of unsuccessful versus successful

---

[7]We could have used discriminant function analysis to determine the cut score, but in the usual normal assumption, the maximally discriminating point on the literacy scale would be the point at which equal proportions of the higher group were below and the lower group were above. Assuming common variance and normality for the two groups, this is in fact the midpoint between the two group medians (or the mean of the medians). If the two groups have different variances, the point will be higher or lower than the median, in the direction of the mean of the group with a smaller variance.

TABLE 5-8 Comparison of Weighted Median Scaled Scores for Groups Contrasted to Determine the QCG Cut Scores for Basic Literacy

| | Weighted Median Score[a] | |
Groups Contrasted	1992	2003
Prose Literacy		
Education:		
No high school	182	159
Some high school	236	229
Average of medians	209.0	194.0
Self-perception of reading skills:		
Do not read well	140	144
Read well	285	282
Average of medians	212.5	213.0

Contrasting groups cut score for prose: 207.1[b]

	1992	2003
Document Literacy		
Education:		
No high school	173	160
Some high school	232	231
Average of medians	202.5	195.5
Self-perception of reading skills:		
Do not read well	138	152
Read well	279	276
Average of medians	208.5	214.0

Contrasting groups cut score for document: 205.1

functioning in society available on the background questionnaire, specifically the contrast between:

• Needing a lot of help with reading versus not needing a lot of help with reading.
• Never reading the newspaper versus sometimes reading the newspaper.
• Working in a job in which reading is never used versus working in a job in which reading is used.
• Receiving Aid to Families with Dependent Children or food stamps versus receiving interest or dividend income.

Following the procedures described above for the basic performance

TABLE 5-8 Continued

	Weighted Median Score[a]	
Groups Contrasted	1992	2003
Quantitative Literacy		
Education:		
No high school	173	165
Some high school	233	231
Average of medians	203.0	198.0
Self-perception of reading skills:		
Do not read well	138	166
Read well	285	288
Average of medians	211.5	227.0

Contrasting groups cut score for quantitative: 209.9

[a]For 1992, the median scores are calculated on a sample representing the entire adult population. For 2003, the median scores are calculated on a sample that excludes respondents with no responses to literacy tasks due to various "literacy-related reasons," as determined by the interviewer. These excluded respondents correspond to roughly 2 percent of the adult population. Assuming that these respondents are at the lower end of the literacy scale (since they do not have answers for literacy-related reasons), their exclusion causes an upward bias in the calculated medians as an estimate of the true median of the full adult population. The impact of this bias on the standard setting is likely to be small for two reasons. First, a comparison of the medians for 1992 and 2003 suggest that the medians are relatively close and that the bias is probably not large. Second, the averaging procedure in the QCG calculation dilutes the effect of the biased 2003 results by averaging them with the unbiased 1992 results.

[b]The cut score is the overall average of the weighted medians for the groups contrasted.

level, we determined the cut score for the contrasted groups in the above list, and Table 5-9 presents these medians for the three types of literacy. For example, the median prose score in 1992 for those with some high school was 236; the corresponding median for those with a high school diploma was 274; and the midpoint between these medians was 255. We determined the corresponding medians from the 2003 results (which were 229 for those with some high school and 262 for those with a high school diploma, yielding a midpoint of 245.5). We then averaged the midpoints resulting from the contrasts on these five variables to yield the QCG cut score. These QCG cut scores for prose (243.5), document (241.6), and quantitative (245.4) literacy areas appear in Table 5-9.

The contrast between the intermediate and advanced levels was intended to relate to pursuit of postsecondary education or entry into profes-

TABLE 5-9 Comparison of Weighted Median Scaled Scores for Groups Contrasted to Determine the QCG Cut Scores for Intermediate Literacy

	Weighted Median Score[a]	
Groups Contrasted	1992	2003
Prose Literacy		
Education:		
Some high school	236	229
High school diploma	274	262
Average of medians	255.0	245.5
Extent of help needed with reading:		
A lot	135	153
Not a lot	281	277
Average of medians	208.0	215.0
Read the newspaper:		
Never	161	173
Sometimes, or more	283	280
Average of medians	222.0	226.5
Read at work:		
Never	237	222
Sometimes, or more	294	287
Average of medians	265.5	254.5
Financial status:		
Receive federal assistance	246	241
Receive interest, dividend income	302	296
Average of medians	274.0	268.5

Contrasting groups cut score for prose: 243.5[b]

Document Literacy		
Education:		
Some high school	232	231
High school diploma	267	259
Average of medians	249.5	245.0
Extent of help needed with reading:		
A lot	128	170
Not a lot	275	273
Average of medians	201.5	221.5
Read the newspaper:		
Never	154	188
Sometimes, or more	278	275
Average of medians	216.0	231.5
Read at work:		
Never	237	228
Sometimes, or more	289	282
Average of medians	263.0	255.0

TABLE 5-9 Continued

	Weighted Median Score[a]	
Groups Contrasted	1992	2003
Financial status:		
Receive federal assistance	242	240
Have interest/dividend income	295	288
Average of medians	268.5	264.0

Contrasting groups cut score for document: 241.6

Quantitative Literacy

Education:		
Some high school	233	231
High school diploma	275	270
Average of medians	254.0	250.5
Extent of help needed with reading:		
A lot	114	162
Not a lot	282	285
Average of medians	198.0	223.5
Read the newspaper:		
Never	145	197
Sometimes, or more	284	287
Average of medians	214.5	242.0
Read at work:		
Never	236	233
Sometimes, or more	294	294
Average of medians	265.0	263.5
Financial status:		
Receive federal assistance	240	237
Have interest/dividend income	303	305
Average of medians	271.5	271.0

Contrasting groups cut score for quantitative: 245.4

[a]For 1992, the median scores are calculated on a sample representing the entire adult population. For 2003, the median scores are calculated on a sample that excludes respondents with no responses to literacy tasks due to various "literacy-related reasons," as determined by the interviewer. These excluded respondents correspond to roughly 2 percent of the adult population. Assuming that these respondents are at the lower end of the literacy scale (since they do not have answers for literacy-related reasons), their exclusion causes an upward bias in the calculated medians as an estimate of the true median of the full adult population. The impact of this bias on the standard setting is likely to be small for two reasons. First, a comparison of the medians for 1992 and 2003 suggest that the medians are relatively close and that the bias is probably not large. Second, the averaging procedure in the QCG calculation dilutes the effect of the biased 2003 results by averaging them with the unbiased 1992 results.

[b]The cut score is the overall average of the weighted medians for the groups contrasted.

TABLE 5-10 Comparison of Weighted Median Scaled Scores for Groups
Contrasted to Determine the QCG Cut Scores for Advanced Literacy

Groups Contrasted	Median Score[a]	
	1992	2003
Prose Literacy		
Education:		
High school diploma	274	262
College degree	327	316
Average of medians	300.5	289.0
Occupational status:		
Low formal training requirements	267	261
High formal training requirements	324	306
Average of medians	295.5	283.5

Contrasting groups cut score for prose: 292.1[b]

Document Literacy		
Education:		
High school diploma	267	259
College degree	319	304.5
Average of medians	293.0	281.8
Occupational status:		
Low formal training requirements	264	258
High formal training requirements	315	298
Average of medians	289.5	278.0

Contrasting groups cut score for document: 285.6

sional, managerial, or technical occupations. Therefore, the bookmark cut
score between intermediate and advanced literacy was compared with the
contrast between those who have a high school diploma (or GED) and
those who graduated from college. We expected that completing
postsecondary education would be related to occupation. Thus, for each
type of literacy, we determined the median score for occupations with
minimal formal training requirements (e.g., laborer, assembler, fishing,
farming) and those occupations that require formal training or education
(e.g., manager, professional, technician). These QCG cut scores for prose
(292.1), document (285.6), and quantitative (296.1) literacy appear in Table
5-10.

In examining the relationships described above, it is important to note
that for those who speak little English, the relationship between literacy

TABLE 5-10 Continued

Groups Contrasted	Median Score[a]	
	1992	2003
Quantitative Literacy		
Education:		
High school diploma	275	270
College degree	326	324
Average of medians	300.5	297.0
Occupational status:		
Low formal training requirements	269	267
High formal training requirements	323	315
Average of medians	296.0	291.0

Contrasting groups cut score for quantitative: 296.1

[a]For 1992, the median scores are calculated on a sample representing the entire adult population. For 2003, the median scores are calculated on a sample that excludes respondents with no responses to literacy tasks due to various "literacy-related reasons," as determined by the interviewer. These excluded respondents correspond to roughly 2 percent of the adult population. Assuming that these respondents are at the lower end of the literacy scale (since they do not have answers for literacy-related reasons), their exclusion causes an upward bias in the calculated medians as an estimate of the true median of the full adult population. The impact of this bias on the standard setting is likely to be small for two reasons. First, a comparison of the medians for 1992 and 2003 suggest that the medians are relatively close and that the bias is probably not large. Second, the averaging procedure in the QCG calculation dilutes the effect of the biased 2003 results by averaging them with the unbiased 1992 results.

[b]The cut score is the overall average of the weighted medians for the groups contrasted.

levels in English and educational attainment in the home country may be skewed, since it is possible to have high levels of education from one's home country yet not be literate in English. To see if inclusion of non-English speakers would skew the results in any way, we examined the medians for all test takers and just for English speakers. There were no meaningful differences among the resulting medians; thus we decided to report medians for the full aggregated dataset.

Procedures for Using QCG Cut Scores to Adjust Bookmark Cut Scores

Most authorities on standard setting (e.g., Green, Trimble, and Lewis, 2003; Hambleton, 1980; Jaeger, 1989; Shepard, 1980; Zieky, 2001) suggest that, when setting cut scores, it is prudent to use and compare the results from different standard-setting methods. At the same time, they acknowledge that different methods, or even the same method replicated with different panelists, are likely to produce different cut scores. This presents a dilemma to those who must make decisions about cut scores. Geisinger (1991, p. 17) captured this idea when he noted that "running a standard-setting panel is only the beginning of the standard-setting process." At the conclusion of the standard setting, one has only *proposed* cut scores that must be accepted, rejected, or adjusted.

The standard-setting literature contains discussions about how to proceed with making decisions about proposed cut scores, but there do not appear to be any hard and fast rules. Several quantitative approaches have been explored. For example, in the early 1980s, two quantitative techniques were devised for "merging" results from different standard-setting procedures (Beuck, 1984; Hofstee, 1983). These methods involve obtaining additional sorts of judgments from the panelists, besides the typical standard-setting judgments, to derive the cut scores. In the Beuck technique, panelists are asked to make judgments about the optimal pass rate on the test. In the Hofstee approach, panelists are asked their opinions about the highest and lowest possible cut scores and the highest and lowest possible failing rate.[8]

Another quantitative approach is to set reasonable ranges for the cut scores and to make adjustments within this range. One way to establish a range is by using estimates of the standard errors of the proposed cut scores (Zieky, 2001). Also, Huff (2001) described a method of triangulating results from three standard-setting procedures in which a reasonable range was determined from the results of one of the standard-setting methods. The cut scores from the two other methods fell within this range and were therefore averaged to determine the final set of cut scores.

While these techniques use quantitative information in determining final cut scores, they are not devoid of judgments (e.g., someone must decide whether a quantitative procedure should be used, which one to use and how to implement it, and so on). Like the standard-setting procedure itself, determination of final cut scores is ultimately a judgment-based task that authorities on standard setting maintain should be based on both quantitative and qualitative information.

For example, *The Standards for Educational and Psychological Testing* (American Educational Research Association, American Psychological Association, and the National Council on Measurement in Education, 1999, p. 54) note that determining cut scores cannot be a "purely technical mat-

---

[8]The reader is referred to the original articles or Geisinger (1991) for additional detail on how the procedures are implemented.

ter," indicating that they should "embody value judgments as well as technical and empirical considerations." In his landmark article on certifying students' competence, Jaeger (1989, p. 500) recommended considering all of the results from the standard setting together with "extra-statistical factors" to determine the final cut scores. Geisinger (1991) suggests that a panel composed of informed members of involved groups should be empowered to make decisions about final cut scores. Green et al. (2003) proposed convening a separate judgment-based procedure wherein a set of judges synthesizes the various results to determine a final set of cut scores or submitting the different sets of cut scores to a policy board (e.g., a board of education) for final determination.

As should be obvious from this discussion, there is no consensus in the measurement field about ways to determine final cut scores and no absolute guidance in the literature that the committee could rely on in making final decisions about cut scores. Using the advice that can be gleaned from the literature and guidance from the *Standards* that the process should be clearly documented and defensible, we developed an approach for utilizing the information from the two bookmark standard-setting sessions and the QCG procedure to develop our recommendations for final cut scores.

We judged that the cut scores resulting from the two bookmark sessions were sufficiently similar to warrant combining them, and we formed median cut scores based on the two sets of panelist judgments. Since we decided to use the cut scores from the QCG procedure solely to complement the information from the bookmark procedure, we did not want to combine these two sets of cut scores in such a way that they were accorded equal weight. There were two reasons for this. One reason, as described above, was that the background questions used for the QCG procedure were correlates of the constructs evaluated on the assessment and were not intended as direct measures of these constructs. Furthermore, as explained earlier in this chapter, the available information was not ideal and did not include questions that would be most useful in distinguishing between certain levels of literacy.

The other reason related to our judgment that the bookmark procedure had been implemented appropriately according to the guidelines documented in the literature (Hambleton, 2001; Kane, 2001; Plake, Melican, and Mills, 1992: Raymond and Reid, 2001) and that key factors had received close attention. We therefore chose to use a method for combining the results that accorded more weight to the bookmark cut scores than the QCG cut scores.

The cut scores produced by the bookmark and QCG approaches are summarized in the first two rows of Table 5-11 for each type of literacy. Comparison of these cut scores reveals that the QCG cut scores are always lower than the bookmark cut scores. The differences among the two sets of

TABLE 5-11 Summary of Cut Scores Resulting from Different
Procedures

	Basic	Intermediate	Advanced
Prose			
QCG cut score	207.1	243.5	292.1
Bookmark cut score	211	270	345
Interquartile range of bookmark cut score	206-221	264-293	336-366
Adjusted cut scores	211.0	267.0	340.5
Average of cut scores	209.1	256.8	318.6
Confidence interval for cut scores	200.5-225.5	261.3-290.0	333.5-377.8
Document			
QCG cut score	205.1	241.6	285.6
Bookmark cut score	203	254	345
Interquartile range of bookmark cut score	192-210	247-259	324-371
Adjusted cut scores	203.0	250.5	334.5
Average of cut scores	204.1	247.8	315.3
Confidence interval for cut scores	191.9-211.1	245.5-264.8	320.7-372.9
Quantitative			
QCG cut score	209.9	245.4	296.1
Bookmark cut score	244	296	356
Interquartile range of bookmark cut score	230-245	288-307	343-398
Adjusted cut scores	237.0	292.0	349.5
Average of cut scores	227.0	275.2	326.1
Confidence interval for cut scores	225.9-262.5	282.8-305.8	343.0-396.4

cut scores are smaller for the basic and intermediate performance levels for
prose and document literacy, with differences ranging from 2 to 26 points.
Differences among the cut scores are somewhat larger for all performance
levels in the quantitative literacy area and for the advanced performance
level for all three types of literacy, with differences ranging from 34 to 60
points. Overall, this comparison suggests that the bookmark cut scores
should be lowered slightly.

We designed a procedure for combining the two sets of cut scores that
was intended to make only minor adjustments to the bookmark cut scores,
and we examined its effects on the resulting impact data. The adjustment
procedure is described below and the resulting cut scores are also presented
in Table 5-11. The table also includes the cut scores that would result from
averaging the bookmark and QCG cut scores, which, although we did not
consider this as a viable alternative, we provide as a comparison with the
cut scores that resulted from the adjustment.

ADJUSTING THE BOOKMARK CUT SCORES

We devised a procedure for adjusting the bookmark cut scores that involved specifying a reasonable range for the cut scores and making adjustments within this range. We decided that the adjustment should keep the cut scores within the interquartile range of the bookmark cut scores (that is, the range encompassed by the 25th and 75th percentile scaled scores produced by the bookmark judgments) and used the QCG cut scores to determine the direction of the adjustment within this range. Specifically, we compared each QCG cut score to the respective interquartile range from the bookmark procedure. If the cut score lay within the interquartile range, no adjustment was made. If the cut score lay outside the interquartile range, the bookmark cut score was adjusted using the following rules:

- If the QCG cut score is lower than the lower bound of the interquartile range (i.e., lower than the 25th percentile), determine the difference between the bookmark cut score and the lower bound of the interquartile range. Reduce the bookmark cut score by half of this difference (essentially, the midpoint between the 25th and 50th percentiles of the bookmark cut scores).
- If the QCG cut score is higher than the upper bound of the interquartile range (i.e., higher than the 75th percentile), determine the difference between the bookmark cut score and the upper bound of the interquartile range. Increase the bookmark cut score by half of this difference (essentially the midpoint between the 50th and 75th percentile of the bookmark cut scores).

To demonstrate this procedure, the QCG cut score for the basic performance level in prose is 207.1, and the bookmark cut score is 211 (see Table 5-11). The corresponding interquartile range based on the bookmark procedure is 206 to 221. Since 207.1 falls within the interquartile range, no adjustment is made. The QCG cut score for intermediate is 243.5. Since 243.5 is lower than the 25th percentile score (interquartile range of 264 to 293), the bookmark cut score of 270 needs to be reduced. The amount of the reduction is half the difference between the bookmark cut score of 270 and the lower bound of the interquartile range (264), which is 3 points. Therefore, the bookmark cut score would be reduced from 270 to 267.

Application of these rules to the remaining cut scores indicates that all of the bookmark cut scores should be adjusted except the basic cut scores for prose and document literacy. The adjusted cut scores produced by this adjustment are presented in Table 5-11.

Rounding the Adjusted Cut Scores

In 1992, the test designers noted that the break points determined by the analyses that produced the performance levels did not necessarily occur at exact 50-point intervals on the scales. As we described in Chapter 3, the test designers judged that assigning the exact range of scores to each level would imply a level of precision of measurement that was inappropriate for the methodology adopted, and they therefore rounded the cut scores. In essence, this rounding procedure reflected the notion that there is a level of uncertainty associated with the specification of cut scores.

The procedures we used for the bookmark standard setting allowed determination of confidence intervals for the cut scores, which also reflect the level of uncertainty in the cut scores. Like the test designers in 1992, we judged that the cut scores should be rounded and suggest that they be rounded to multiples of five. Tables 5-12a, 5-12b, and 5-12c show, for prose, document, and quantitative literacy, respectively, the original cut scores from the bookmark procedure and the adjustment procedure after rounding to the nearest multiple of five. For comparison, the table also presents the confidence intervals for the cut scores to indicate the level of uncertainty associated the specific cut scores.

Another consideration when making use of cut scores from different standard-setting methods is the resulting impact data; that is, the percentages of examinees who would be placed into each performance category based on the cut scores. Tables 5-12a, 5-12b, and 5-12c show the percentage of the population who scored below the rounded cut scores. Again for comparison purposes, the table also presents impact data for the confidence intervals.

Impact data were examined for both the original cut scores that resulted from the bookmark procedure and for the adjusted values of the cut scores. Comparison of the impact results based on the original and adjusted cut scores shows that the primary effect of the adjustment was to slightly lower the cut scores, more so for quantitative literacy than the other sections. A visual depiction of the differences in the percentages of adults classified into each performance level based on the two sets of cut scores is presented in Figures 5-1 through 5-6, respectively, for the prose, document, and quantitative sections. The top bar shows the percentages of adults that would be placed into each performance level based on the adjusted cut scores, and the bottom bar shows the distribution based on the original bookmark cut scores.

Overall, the adjustment procedure tended to produce a distribution of participants across the performance levels that resembled the distribution produced by the original bookmark cut scores. The largest changes were in the quantitative section, in which the adjustment slightly lowered the cut scores. The result of the adjustment is a slight increase in the percentages of individuals in the basic, intermediate, and advanced categories.

In our view, the procedures used to determine the adjustment were sensible and served to align the bookmark cut scores more closely with the relevant background measures. The adjustments were relatively small and made only slight differences in the impact data. The adjusted values remained within the confidence intervals. We therefore recommend the cut scores produced by the adjustment.

RECOMMENDATION 5-1: The scale score intervals associated with each of the levels should be as shown below for prose, document, and quantitative literacy.

	Nonliterate in English	Below Basic	Basic	Intermediate	Advanced
Prose:	Took ALSA	0-209	210-264	265-339	340-500
Document:	Took ALSA	0-204	205-249	250-334	335-500
Quantitative:	Took ALSA	0-234	235-289	290-349	350-500

We remind the reader that the nonliterate in English category was intended to comprise the individuals who were not able to answer the core questions in 2003 and were given the ALSA instead of NAAL. Below basic is the lowest performance level for 1992, since the ALSA did not exist at that time.[9]

DIFFICULTIES WITH THE UPPER AND LOWER ENDS OF THE SCORE SCALE

With respect to setting achievement levels on the NAAL, we found that there were significant problems at both the lower and upper ends of the literacy scale. The problems with the lower end relate to decisions about the

---

[9]For the 2003 assessment, the nonliterate in English category is intended to include those who were correctly routed to ALSA based on the core questions, those who should have been routed to ALSA but were misrouted to NAAL, and those who could not participate in the literacy assessment because their literacy levels were too low. The below basic category is intended to encompass those who were correctly routed to NAAL, and they should be classified into below basic using their performance on NAAL.

TABLE 5-12a Comparison of Impact Data for Prose Literacy Based on Rounded Bookmark Cut Scores, Rounded Adjusted Cut Scores, and Rounded Confidence Interval for Cut Scores

	Basic	Intermediate	Advanced
Rounded[a] bookmark cut score	210	270	345
Percent below cut score:			
1992	16.5[b,c]	46.8	87.4
2003	15.4[c,d]	46.8	88.8
Rounded[a] adjusted cut score	210	265	340
Percent below cut score:			
1992	16.5[b,c]	43.7	85.7
2003	15.4[c,d]	43.6	87.1
Rounded[e] confidence interval	201-226	261-290	334-378
Percent below cut scores:			
1992	13.8-22.7[b,c]	41.2-59.4	83.2-95.6
2003	12.6-21.5[c,d]	40.9-60.1	84.6-96.5

[a]Rounded to nearest multiple of five.

[b]Includes those who took NALS and scored below the cut score as well as those who were not able to participate in the assessment for literacy-related reasons (having difficulty with reading or writing or unable to communicate in English or Spanish); nonparticipants for literacy-related reasons comprised 3 percent of the sample in 1992.

[c]This is an underestimate because it does not include the 1 percent of individual who could not participate due to a mental disability such as retardation, a learning disability, or other mental/emotional conditions. An upper bound on the percent below basic could be obtained by including this percentage.

[d]Includes those who took NAAL and scored below the basic cut score, those who took ALSA, and those who were not able to participate in the assessment for literacy-related reasons (having difficulty with reading or writing or unable to communicate in English or Spanish); nonparticipants for literacy-related reasons comprised 2 percent of the sample in 2003.

[e]Rounded to nearest whole number.

nature of the ALSA component. ALSA was implemented as a separate low-level assessment. ALSA and NAAL items were not analyzed or calibrated together and hence were not placed on the same scale. We were therefore not able to use the ALSA items in our procedures for setting the cut scores. These decisions about the ways to process ALSA data created a de facto cut score between the nonliterate in English and below basic categories. Consequently, all test takers in 2003 who performed poorly on the initial screening questions (the core questions) and were administered ALSA are classified into the nonliterate in English category (see footnote 9).

TABLE 5-12b Comparison of Impact Data for Document Literacy Based on Rounded Bookmark Cut Scores, Rounded Adjusted Cut Scores, and Rounded Confidence Interval for Cut Scores

	Basic	Intermediate	Advanced
Rounded[a] bookmark cut score	205	255	345
Percent below cut score:			
1992	16.8[b,c]	40.8	89.2
2003	14.2[c,d]	39.4	91.1
Rounded[a] adjusted cut score	205	250	335
Percent below cut score			
1992	16.8	37.8	85.8
2003	14.2	36.1	87.7
Rounded[e] confidence interval	192-211	246-265	321-373
Percent below cut scores:			
1992	12.9-18.9	35.5-47.0	79.9-95.6
2003	10.5-16.3	33.7-46.0	81.6-96.9

See footnotes to Table 15-12a.

TABLE 5-12c Comparison of Impact Data for Quantitative Literacy Based on Rounded Bookmark Cut Scores, Rounded Adjusted Cut Scores, and Rounded Confidence Interval for Cut Scores

	Basic	Intermediate	Advanced
Rounded[a] bookmark cut score	245	300	355
Percent below cut score:			
1992	33.3[b,c]	65.1	89.3
2003	27.9[c,d]	61.3	88.6
Rounded[a] adjusted cut score	235	290	350
Percent below cut score			
1992	28.5	59.1	87.9
2003	23.1	55.1	87.0
Rounded[e] confidence interval	226-263	283-306	343-396
Percent below cut scores:			
1992	24.7-42.9	55.0-68.5	85.6-97.1
2003	19.2-37.9	50.5-64.9	84.1-97.2

See footnotes to Table 15-12a.

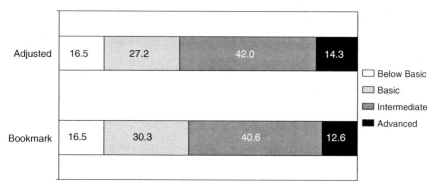

FIGURE 5-1 Comparison of the percentages of adults in each performance level based on the bookmark cut scores and adjusted cut scores for 1992 prose literacy.

FIGURE 5-2 Comparison of the percentages of adults in each performance level based on the bookmark cut scores and adjusted cut scores for 2003 prose literacy. *The nonliterate in English category comprises 4.7% of the 2003 population. This percentage plus those in the below basic category would be equivalent to the 1992 below basic category.

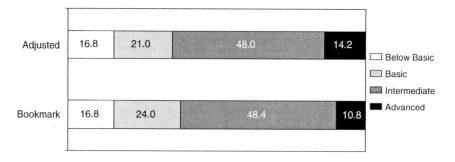

FIGURE 5-3 Comparison of the percentages of adults in each performance level based on the bookmark cut scores and adjusted cut scores for 1992 document literacy.

FIGURE 5-4 Comparison of the percentages of adults in each performance level based on the bookmark cut scores and adjusted cut scores for 2003 document literacy.

*The nonliterate in English category comprises 4.7% of the 2003 population. This percentage plus those in the below basic category would be equivalent to the 1992 below basic category.

FIGURE 5-5 Comparison of the percentages of adults in each performance level based on the bookmark cut scores and adjusted cut scores for 1992 quantitative literacy.

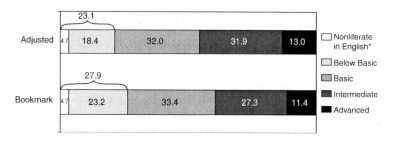

FIGURE 5-6 Comparison of the percentages of adults in each performance level based on the bookmark cut scores and adjusted cut scores for 2003 quantitative literacy.

*The nonliterate in English category comprises 4.7% of the 2003 population. This percentage plus those in the below basic category would be equivalent to the 1992 below basic category.

This creates problems in making comparisons between the 1992 and 2003 data. Since ALSA was not a part of NALS in 1992, there is no way to identify the group of test takers who would have been classified into the nonliterate in English category. As a result, the below basic and nonliterate in English categories will need to be combined to examine trends between 1992 and 2003.

With regard to the upper end of the scale, we found that feedback from the bookmark panelists, combined with our review of the items, suggests that the assessment does not adequately cover the upper end of the distribution of literacy proficiency. We developed the description of this level based on what we thought was the natural progression of skills beyond the intermediate level. In devising the wording of the description, we reviewed samples of NALS items and considered the 1992 descriptions of NALS Levels 4 and 5. A number of panelists in the bookmark procedure commented about the lack of difficulty represented by the items, however, particularly the quantitative items. A few judged that an individual at the advanced level should be able to answer all of the items correctly, which essentially means that these panelists did not set a cut score for the advanced category. We therefore conclude that the assessment is very weak at the upper end of the scale. Although there are growing concerns about readiness for college-level work and preparedness for entry into professional and technical professions, we think that NAAL, as currently designed, will not allow for detection of problems at these levels of proficiency. It is therefore with some reservations that we include the advanced category in our recommendation for performance levels, and we leave it to NCES to ultimately decide on the utility and meaning of this category.

With regard to the lower and upper ends of the score scale, we make the following recommendation:

RECOMMENDATION 5-2: Future development of NAAL should include more comprehensive coverage at the lower end of the continuum of literacy skills, including assessment of the extent to which individuals are able to recognize letters and numbers and read words and simple sentences, to allow determination of which individuals have the basic foundation skills in literacy and which individuals do not. This assessment should be part of NAAL and should yield information used in calculating scores for each of the three types of literacy. At the upper end of the continuum of literacy skills, future development of NAAL should also include assessment items necessary to identify the extent to which policy interventions are needed at the postsecondary level and above.

6

Communicating and Using the Results of Literacy Assessments

Experience with the initial release and subsequent media coverage of the results of the 1992 National Adult Literacy Survey (NALS) highlighted the critical importance of clearly communicating the assessment results so they are interpreted correctly, inform the public, and are useful to the various audiences concerned about adult literacy in the United States. In particular, because media coverage is such a central factor in how the performance levels and associated findings are understood and used, the committee included this important issue as one of the topics discussed at its public forum in February 2004. We draw on the advice provided by the stakeholders and journalists in attendance at the forum to make recommendations about reporting and communicating about results of the National Assessment of Adult Literacy (NAAL).

In this chapter, we first discuss strategies for ensuring that appropriate information and accurate messages reach the various audiences for the NAAL results. We then discuss strategies for devising and formulating methods for communicating the results. The chapter concludes with examples of how the NAAL results can be used by different fields.

COMMUNICATING RESULTS

Types of Information That Need to Be Communicated

In reporting NAAL results, the Department of Education should strive to communicate succinct and accurate messages that address two basic questions:

- To what extent have adults' literacy skills changed between 1992 and 2003?
- What is the status of adults' literacy skills now?

In communicating these messages, however, the department needs to be keenly aware of the audiences for the information and what they seek to learn from the reports. One of the recurring points that participants made during the public forum was that the results of the adult literacy assessments are not reported in a vacuum. Journalists, the public, and even specialized audiences have preexisting views about literacy that affect how they interpret the assessment results. For example, many journalists and members of the public think of literacy as a dichotomy (literate versus illiterate), rather than as a continuum of skills. Those with more sophisticated notions of the concept may wonder how literacy applies in different real-world contexts: What does a particular performance level mean in terms of how those falling within the category function as citizens, workers, family members, or consumers? If these preexisting frames are not adequately considered in communicating the assessment results, the kinds of distortions that occurred in 1993 could happen again. Mindful of that possibility, two public forum participants, one representing journalists and another representing policy makers, suggested ways to prevent this, saying:

> Journalists only need two levels—literate and not literate. If you don't tell us where the break point is, we'll make one ourselves. [But] if literacy is truly more complex, if you truly need more than two levels and a more nuanced discussion, then one way to do it is to talk about contexts. For example, here's what people need in the work environment, in the home environment, in the school environment, in order to obtain additional training. (Richard Colvin, Hechinger Institute, Columbia University)

> The same is true for state legislators and state policy makers—if you don't tell them what the message is, they'll [create] the message. (Milton Goldberg, Education Commission of the States)

This advice suggests how the department might think about the substance of its message and its dissemination strategies. The substantive challenge will be to convey the message that literacy is not a unidimensional concept or an all-or-nothing state, and that NAAL provides a nuanced portrait of adult literacy in the United States at the beginning of the 21st century. That message will be most understandable to the public and useful to policy makers if it is anchored in the competencies and life circumstances associated with each performance level and each of the three types of literacy. So, for example, in describing the distribution of survey respondents across performance levels, the department should identify concrete tasks (drawn from the survey) that adults in each category are likely to be able to do and ones that they have a low probability of accomplishing. Illustrative examples should be directly tied to their roles as citizens, workers, family members, and consumers.

Equally important is for the department to provide a picture of the life circumstances associated with those scoring at each performance level, for example, the proportion earning a middle-class wage, the likelihood of voting, and the likelihood of pursuing postsecondary education. Because policy interest and needs are greatest for those with the lowest literacy skills, it is especially critical that policy makers and the press be given a full and useful representation of this group—one that will aid in crafting policy strategies of benefit to them.

While it is clear that the public wants information about the percentage of adults in the country who truly have substantial difficulties with reading and that policy interventions are needed for this group, other audiences are more concerned about policy interventions at higher points on the continuum of literacy skills. For example, Beth Beuhlmann, with the Center for Workforce Preparation at the U.S. Chamber of Commerce, pointed out that about 80 percent of jobs currently require some form of postsecondary education. Christopher Mazzeo, with the National Governors' Association, noted that preparedness for work and for higher education is "of paramount concern for every state and for adults at all ages, not just for the 18-24 age group." Audiences concerned about workforce issues will look to NAAL for information about the extent to which the adult population is ready to meet the demands of the workplace in the 21st century. As forum participants pointed out, employers using the 1992 NALS results were concerned about increasing the numbers of adults with skills described by Levels 4 and 5; that is, moving more of the adult population from Level 3 to the higher levels. Thus, it is likely that employers and those involved with postsecondary education will be most interested in the percentage of adults in the committee's recommended category of intermediate literacy and will focus on interventions that increase the numbers of adults in the committee's category of advanced literacy.

Meeting the needs of these varied audiences will require careful thought about the formats and types of information included on NAAL reports, and we encourage the department to adapt versions of the reports to meet the needs of the various audiences. The alternate versions of the performance-level descriptions included in this report could provide a basis for these efforts. Appendix A includes the sample performance-level descriptions that were used to elicit comments during the public forum. Chapter 5 presents the performance-level descriptions used in the committee's standard-setting sessions as well as revisions developed after the standard settings (see Tables 5-2, 5-3, and 5-4); these versions provided overall descriptions as well as subject-specific descriptions. We suggest that the department consider these alternate versions and formulate performance-level descriptions tailored to the needs of specific audiences.

Our suggestions concerning the development of reports of NAAL results that are appropriate and useful to interested stakeholders are encapsulated in the following two recommendations:

RECOMMENDATION 6-1: NAAL results should be presented with implications of their relevance for different contexts in which adults function, such as employment and the workplace, health and safety, home and family, community and citizenship, consumer economics, and leisure and recreation, as well as the different aspects of life affected by literacy.

RECOMMENDATION 6-2: The Department of Education should prepare different versions of the performance-level descriptions that are tailored to meet the needs of various audiences. Simple descriptions of the performance levels should be prepared for general audiences to enhance public understanding. More technical and more detailed descriptions should be developed to be responsive to the needs of other users.

Policy Interventions for Low-Literate Adults

With the development of NAAL and the Adult Literacy Supplemental Assessment, the department focused specific attention on gathering information about low-literate adults. It is hoped that there will be renewed interest among policy makers and educators in meeting the needs of this group. It is therefore critical that the department report results in ways that allow for the identification and design of appropriate services for low-literate adults and for recruiting new populations of adults who could benefit from these services. The nonliterate in English and below basic categories are likely to be heterogeneous, encompassing English speakers who have weak literacy skills, non-English speakers who are highly literate in their native languages but not literate in English, and non-English speakers who are not literate in any language. Distinctly different services and strategies will be needed for these groups. To allow these distinctions to be made and valid conclusions to be drawn, we make the following recommendation about reporting results for those with low levels of literacy:

RECOMMENDATION 6-3: Reports of the percentages of adults in the nonliterate in English and below basic categories should distinguish among native English speakers and non-English speakers. This will allow for more appropriate conclusions to be drawn about (1) the extent of literacy problems among native English-speaking adults in the United States and (2) the share of adults in the United States who are still learning English and therefore cannot handle literacy tasks in English.

In addition, we note that attention should be focused on determining the skill levels and needs of non-English speakers in the United States. Over the past decade, there has been a significant increase in the number of non-English speakers residing in this country. In 1990, 13.8 percent of the U.S. population over age 5 spoke a language other than English at home; in 2000, this figure increased to 17.9 percent. The percentage of U.S. residents who speak Spanish at home is now reported to be 10.7 percent of the population, compared to 7.5 percent in 1990, and 2.7 percent of the U.S. population speak languages associated with Asia and the Pacific Islands, compared to 1.9 percent in 1990 (http://www.censusscope.org/us/chart_language.html).

English for speakers of other languages (ESOL) is the fastest growing segment of the adult literacy education system (http://www.ed.gov/about/offices/list/ovae/pi/AdultEd/aefacts.html). ESOL currently constitutes 43 percent of the overall system, with the proportion of English language learners in the system being as high as 73 percent in California (http://www.ed.gov/about/offices/list/ovae/pi/AdultEd/datatables/2002-2003enroll.xls). Being able to read, write, and speak in English accrues significant benefits in this society. NAAL results can do much to clarify the needs of this group and inform policy interventions aimed at providing services appropriate for different groups of immigrants and refugees. We therefore encourage the department to conduct analyses that will answer such questions as:

- What are the literacy levels of the immigrant population in this country, both in the native languages and in English?
- What languages are spoken by the immigrant population, and how did individuals with different language backgrounds perform on NAAL?
- What is the relationship between earnings and various levels of literacy, including English literacy, native language literacy, and biliteracy?
- What is the relationship between education level and English literacy for immigrants, and does it matter if their education was obtained in the United States or in their native country?

The Department of Education commissioned a special study on the literacy levels of non-English speakers who participated in the 1992 NALS (see Greenberg et al., 2001), and we encourage the department to conduct a similar study again. At a time when legalization of undocumented immigrants as well as a revised citizenship examination are part of the U.S.

policy agenda, information on the language and literacy abilities of immigrants and refugees can provide valuable insights.

If data on those who speak a language other than English at home are not disaggregated and analyzed separately, the true nature of the literacy problem is likely to be obscured. For example, early reports of the 1992 NALS merely noted that 25 percent of those scoring in the lowest level were foreign-born and that the majority of immigrants fell into Levels 1 and 2. Early reports did not provide information on whether the difficulties encountered by individuals in Levels 1 and 2 required remedial services (i.e., services for adults who went to U.S. schools but never attained functional literacy skills) or developmental services (services for those who are not yet proficient in English). Not providing a separate description of the skills and backgrounds of those who speak a language other than English at home is likely to confuse both the nature and the extent of the literacy problem in the United States and fails to provide policy makers with the data they need to make informed decisions about various groups of adult learners.

RECOMMENDATION 6-4: The Department of Education should commission a special study on the literacy levels of non-English speakers who participated in NAAL. The study report should be given the same prominence as other reports and should be published and disseminated in a timely manner after the main release of NAAL results and in similar ways as the main report. In addition, federal and state agencies that provide substantial services for immigrants (the departments of Labor, Education, and Health and Human Services, along with the Department of Homeland Security and its citizenship services) should be given briefings that outline the profiles of the non-English-speaking population. Information should also be marketed through channels that are commonly used by those serving immigrants and refugees.

Exemplifying the Performance Levels

Presentations of the 1992 results included samples of released NALS items that illustrated the skills represented by each of the performance levels. According to participants in the committee's public forum, this was a particularly useful feature of the reports. For instance, Tony Sarmiento, with Senior Service America, said that whenever he has made presentations of NALS results, he has relied more on the sample items than on the performance-level descriptions. In addition, participants in the two bookmark standard-setting sessions conducted by the committee reported using sample items as instructional guides in their adult education classrooms. We encourage the department to again use released items to exemplify the levels. However, we suggest a change in procedures, as described below.

In 1992, released NALS items were "mapped" to performance levels using the same item response theory methods that provided estimates of response probabilities (see Chapter 3 for details). Items were mapped to the performance level at which there was an 80 percent probability of an examinee's responding correctly. Item mapping is a useful tool for communicating about test performance, but we think that more than one response probability should be considered for each item. That is, an item may map to one level based on a response probability of 80 percent; however, it will map to another, lower level based on a lower response probability (e.g., 67 percent).

Many of the NALS results that were publicly reported in 1993 displayed items mapped only to a single performance level, the level associated with a response probability of 80 percent. This type of mapping procedure tends to lead to a misperception that individuals who score at the specific level will respond correctly to the item and those at lower levels will respond incorrectly. This all-or-nothing focus on the mapped items ignores the continuous nature of response probabilities. That is, for any given item, individuals at every score point have some probability of responding correctly.

We encourage the use of exemplar items to illustrate what adults who score at each of the performance levels are likely to be able to do. For some audiences, it may be sufficient to simply report the percentage of adults at the given performance level who responded correctly to the item. For other audiences, item mapping procedures will be more appropriate.

When item mapping procedures are used, we encourage use of displays that emphasize the continuous nature of response probabilities. Items should be mapped using different response probability values so as to communicate about the types of things that adults at each performance level would be likely to do at different levels of accuracy (e.g., 50, 67, and 80 percent of the time). Displays showing what adults would be likely to do 80 percent of the time will be important to maintain consistency with item mapping procedures used in 1992, and we note that those in the health literacy field specifically requested this during our public forum. Displays showing other levels of accuracy (e.g., other response probability values) will provide additional information about adults' literacy skills. Mapping items to more than one level will stimulate understanding of the strengths and weaknesses of those scoring at each level. We therefore make the following recommendation:

RECOMMENDATION 6-5: The Department of Education should carefully consider the ways in which released items are used to illustrate the skills represented by the performance levels. For the simplest displays, the department should avoid the use of response probabilities and just indicate the proportion of people in a given level (e.g., basic) who can do the item. If the department decides to use an item mapping procedure to illustrate performance on NAAL, items should be mapped to more than one performance level. The displays should demonstrate that individuals at each performance level have some likelihood of responding correctly to each item. Such displays will allow interpretations about what individuals at each level are and are not likely to be able to do.

Simplifying Presentations of NAAL Results with Composite Scores

Many reports of the NALS results displayed graphs and tables separately for each of the literacy scales. However, due to the high intercorrelations among the types of literacy, the relationships portrayed and the conclusions drawn about the information in the displays tended to be similar regardless of the literacy scale (e.g., the relationships between self-perception of reading skills and NALS literacy scores were nearly identical for prose, document, and quantitative literacy). We think that this redundancy deserves some attention as the department and others plan their reports of NAAL results.

Some of the participants in the focus group discussions sponsored by the department (see U.S. Department of Education, 1998) commented that having results reported as five performance levels for each of three types of literacy was too much information to present during discussions with policy makers and other audiences. They commented that they would often select results for a single literacy area (i.e., prose) to use in their discussions. We therefore suggest that the department find ways to simplify and reduce the amount of information in NAAL results. One way to do this is to form a composite of the three literacy scores that can be used for presentations to certain audiences, and we explored several ways to accomplish this as described below.

As detailed in Chapter 5, we initially planned to conduct our standard settings by combining all of the items into a single ordered item booklet, which would have yielded a single set of cut scores. This was not possible, however, since the items were not scaled together. This made it impossible to compare the difficulty levels of the items across literacy areas; for example, it was not possible to determine whether a prose item was more or less difficult than a document or quantitative item.

Another way to accomplish this would be to have identical cut scores for the three types of literacy. In this case, a simple average of the three scores could be formed and the cut scores applied to this composite score. This would have been a feasible alternative if our standard-setting procedures had yielded identical (or at least similar) cut scores for each of the three types of literacy. This was not the case, however; the cut scores were quite different for the three types.

We were not able to devise a means for combining prose, document, and quantitative scores in order to report NAAL results according to a single set of performance levels. To compensate for this, we developed a set of overall performance-level descriptions (see Table 5-3). These overall descriptions combine the features included in the subject-specific levels, but they differ in that they do not include cut scores. We suggest that these overall performance-level descriptions be used as one way to reduce the amount of information to present to more general audiences.

Not all audiences will be interested in NAAL results grouped into the performance level categories. For some purposes, reporting at the scale score level using descriptive statistics (e.g., means and standard deviations) will be more appropriate. In these circumstances, when the focus of an analysis or display is scale scores, we urge the department and others to develop a composite score that is the simple average of prose, document, and quantitative scores. This will serve to reduce the number of displays required and will simplify the information for the user. We therefore recommend the following:

RECOMMENDATION 6-6: The Department of Education and others reporting and using NAAL results should consider the purposes of and audiences for their reports as well as the messages they seek to convey. Whereas performance levels will be most appropriate for some purposes, scale scores will be most appropriate for others. When scale scores are used, a composite score that is a simple average of the prose, document, and quantitative scores should be used.

COMMUNICATION STRATEGIES

Ensuring that an accurate, nuanced message is effectively conveyed is a difficult task, particularly given the broad range of media likely to report on the NAAL results and the varying interests of policy makers and other stakeholders. Consequently, the Department of Education will need to consider a variety of dissemination strategies, beyond publication of the results, press releases, and news conferences.

Participants in the committee's public forum proposed a number of dissemination and communication strategies that the department could consider. For instance, in Canada, informational packets about literacy results are tailored specifically for different constituencies. Other proposed strategies include prerelease briefings for Washington-based media, web-based presentations with the Department of Education staff available to answer questions and provide information in response to online inquiries, collaboration with organizations providing professional development to journalists specializing in education and business, and opinion pieces prepared for agency officials that highlight key findings and that can be distributed to a variety of media outlets. Similarly, in-person, hard-copy, and virtual presentations can be made to organizations, such as the National Governors' Association and the National Conference of State Legislatures, whose members decide the priority and level of resources allocated to adult literacy efforts. Attempts should also be made to communicate with community-based organizations and other nongovernmental agencies (e.g., National Council of La Raza, the Center for Law and Social Policy) who both seek and provide information on populations in need.

Whatever communication strategies the Department of Education decides to employ, there should be a well-crafted plan designed to convey a clear, accurate, and consistent message or "story" about the NAAL results and their meaning. An effective way to proceed would be to consult with communication professionals to develop materials tailored to specific audiences and then to identify vehicles for disseminating them. The ways in which different audiences are likely to interpret and understand these materials can be tested using focus groups representing stakeholders, media, policy makers, and members of the public. The materials and dissemination strategies can then be revised before their release.

Key actors in any communication strategy are the secretary of education and other agency officials. They need to be thoroughly briefed about the results, their meaning, and implications. Agency officials should be aware that they will be asked simplistic questions, such as "How many Americans are illiterate?" Consequently, it is especially important that they have sufficient information to allow them to give nuanced responses that are both faithful to the survey results and understandable to the public. The Department of Education should involve leaders in the literacy field as much as possible, so they can reinforce the major messages and provide a consistent picture of the results.

In addition, there needs to be a strategy for communicating with members of Congress. Education committee members and staff in both the House of Representatives and the Senate should be included in prebriefing sessions and perhaps could be involved in developing dissemination strategies. Larger House and Senate briefings should be arranged soon after the main release of NAAL results and scheduled at times when staff members can attend. There should be bipartisan involvement in making these invitations. Our recommendations with regard to communication and dissemination strategies are summarized in the following recommendation.

RECOMMENDATION 6-7: Before releasing results from the 2003 NAAL, the Department of Education should enlist the services of communication professionals to develop materials that present a clear, accurate, and consistent message. It should then pilot test the interpretation of those materials with focus groups including stakeholders, media, and members of the public, and revise them as appropriate before release. A briefing strategy should be developed that includes prebriefing sessions for department policy makers and congressional staff members. These groups should be briefed in detail on the supportable inferences from the findings before the official release of NAAL results.

The Department of Education can also do much to enhance understanding of adult literacy in this country by making NAAL data public and encouraging research on the results. After the initial release of NALS in 1992, the department funded a number of special studies on specific population groups (e.g., language minorities, prisoners, older adults, workers, low-literate adults). These studies offered significant insight into the literacy levels of these populations and have been widely cited and used over the past decade. We encourage the department to again commission extensive follow-up studies on NAAL results. The department can also provide support for smaller scale research studies on NAAL data in the same way that it does through the secondary analysis grant program of the National Assessment of Educational Progress (NAEP) (http://www.nces.ed.gov/nationsreportcard/researchcenter/funding.asp).

In order to encourage researchers to use NAAL data, the data have to be publicly available in a format that is accessible by the most commonly used statistical software. We note specifically that the NAAL data files are currently designed so that they can be analyzed only with software, called "AM," developed by the contractor. Having the data files accessible only by proprietary software will severely limit the extent to which researchers can make use of NAAL results.

In addition, the software is designed to produce plausible values that are conditioned on the set of background variables specified for a given analysis. As a consequence, the plausible values that are generated for one analysis (using one set of background variables) differ from those generated for another that uses another set of background variables. This feature of the AM software has the potential to cause confusion among researchers accessing NAAL data. We suggest that the department determine a means for developing a set of plausible values in the publicly available data file so that all researchers will work with a common data file.

EXAMPLES OF WAYS NAAL RESULTS MAY BE USED

NAAL results will be used by a variety of audiences and in a variety of ways. For some of these audiences, the report of NAAL findings will be a one-day story. The findings are likely to create a public stir on the day they are released, but public attention will probably be brief. For other audiences, however, NAAL results will receive long-term attention. For instance, NALS results, reported over a decade ago, are still frequently cited by the adult literacy and adult education fields (e.g., Sticht, 2004). Similarly, the health literacy field has relied on NALS results for a wealth of information and as the basis for numerous studies, some conducted only recently (e.g., Rudd, Kirsch, and Yamamoto, 2004). Below we present two examples of long-term uses of adult literacy results, one drawn from the health literacy field and one from the civic literacy field. We include these examples not only to consider the types of information that should be reported to enable such uses but also to prompt the various literacy fields to consider ways in which they can use NAAL results.

Health Literacy

Findings from the 1992 NALS sparked interest in literacy and possible links to health outcomes among researchers in health education, public health, medicine, and dentistry (American Medical Association, 1999; Berkman et al., 2004; Institute of Medicine, 2004; Rudd, Moeykens, and Colton, 2000). As was true in the education sector, some initial misinterpretations of the findings fueled headlines and misuse of the term "illiteracy." The body of literature developed since the publication of NALS, however, has established the field called health literacy, which is now on the national agenda. The report, *Communicating Health*, recommends actions to support the education sector and improve the communication skills of health professionals (U.S. Department of Health and Human Services, Office of Disease Prevention and Health Promotion, 2003). The National Institutes of Health have called for research examining the pathways between education and health (RFA OB-03-001, Pathways Linking Education to Health; see http://www.grants.nih.gov/grants/guide/rfa-files/RFA-OB-03-001.html) and through calls for proposals examining health literacy supported by several institutes (PAR-04-117, Understanding and Promoting Health Literacy, see http://www. grants1.nih.gov/grants/guide/pa-files/PAR-04-117.html).

Findings from well over 400 published studies of health materials indicate a mismatch between average high school reading skills in the United States and the reading-level demands of materials across a broad spectrum of health topic areas. Many of these studies measured the ability of patients to read and comprehend materials developed and designed to offer them key information and directions. The documented mismatch between the demands of the materials and the reading skills of the intended audience speaks to poor communication on the part of health professionals as well as to limited abilities of patients to use health materials (Rudd, Moeykens, and Colton, 2000).

Over 50 studies have linked untoward health outcomes among patients with limited reading skills (as measured by instruments that correlate well with reading assessments such as the Wide Range Achievement Test) compared with outcomes among those with stronger reading skills (Berkman et al., 2004). Measures of health outcomes included general public health information, such as knowledge about the effects of smoking, knowledge of HIV transmission risk, and the use of screening services. Medical outcomes included such measures as knowledge of their disease, the risk of hospitalization, and glycemic control in diabetes care (Berkman et al., 2004; Institute of Medicine, 2004).

A recent Institute of Medicine report, *Health Literacy: A Prescription to End Confusion*, cites the finding that 90 million adults have difficulty understanding and acting on health information based on findings from health studies and an understanding of the implications of the NALS results (Institute of Medicine, 2004; Rudd, Kirsch, and Yamamoto, 2004). Among the recommendations of the Institute of Medicine report are the following:

• The U.S. Department of Health and Human Services and other government and private funders should support research leading to the development of causal models explaining the relationships among health literacy, the education system, the health system, and relevant social and cultural systems.

• Federal agencies responsible for addressing disparities should support the development of conceptual frameworks on the intersection of culture and health literacy to direct in-depth theoretical explorations and formulate the conceptual underpinnings that can guide interventions.

• Professional schools and professional continuing education programs in health and related fields should incorporate health literacy into their curricula and areas of competence.

Measures of functional literacy skills fueled this development. Many health-related items and associated tasks were included in the 1992 NALS and covered a wide spectrum of health activities, including health promotion, health protection, disease prevention, health care and maintenance, and access and systems navigation. For example, items included a food label, an article on air quality, an advertisement for sunscreen, a medicine box dosage chart, and information from a benefits package. Because the tasks associated with these items were developed and rated in the same way that nonhealth-related tasks were, the findings for literacy skills in health contexts remain the same as that for prose, document, and quantitative scores for application of literacy skills in other everyday contexts (Rudd, Kirsch, and Yamamoto, 2004).

Diffusion of information across fields is slow, and the findings from the 1992 NALS are still new to many in the health fields. With NAAL, which augments existing materials with additional items and tasks, health literacy findings will be reported. Having NAAL results focused on health contexts will garner significant attention among health researchers, practitioners, and policy makers.

The approximately 300 studies published between 1970 and 1999 and the additional 300 studies between 2000 and 2004 attest to a rapidly increasing interest in the relationship between literacy and health outcomes. The field of inquiry is expanding to new health topics and new health disciplines, including pediatrics, oral health, mental health, environmental health, and public health.

Although some health researchers continue to develop literacy-related assessments suitable for use in health settings, the health sector continues to rely on the education field to measure literacy skills, monitor change, and inform researchers and practitioners in other related fields. Furthermore, the health field has an interest in making comparisons over time and in examining trend data. Consequently, careful attention will need to be given to the measurement and reporting changes enacted with NAAL in order to not confuse users and hamper progress in this nascent field of inquiry.

Civic Literacy

Participation in civic and political engagement, a crucial aspect of public life in a democratic society, is contingent on many of the fundamental literacy skills presumed to be measured by NALS and NAAL. These skills include such tasks as reading the news sections or opinion pieces in a newspaper, deciphering documents like an election ballot, and understanding numbers associated with public issues like the allocation of local government resources. Studies of the 1992 NALS results (Smith, 2002; Venezky and Kaplan, 1998; Venezky, Kaplan, and Yu, 1998) reported that the likelihood of voting increased as literacy increased, even when controlling for other factors, such as age, educational attainment, and income. Newspaper readership also increased as literacy increased and was positively associated with voting behavior. More generally, research on civic and political engagement suggests that characteristics known or believed to be related to literacy (e.g., education, following the news, knowledge of politics, being in a white-collar occupation) are direct and indirect precursors of a variety of types of civic and political participation (Brady, 1996; Delli Carpini and Keeter, 1996; Verba, Lehman Schlozman, and Brady, 1995).

It is possible that NAAL results can enhance understanding of the extent to which adults have the fundamental literacy skills needed for participating in civic affairs and carrying out their civic responsibilities. According to the frameworks the National Assessment Governing Board developed for the civic assessment of NAEP (National Assessment Governing Board, 1998), fundamental skills required for civic functioning include both content knowledge about civics as well as intellectual skills that can be applied to the content, such as knowing how to identify, describe, explain, and analyze information and arguments and evaluating positions on public issues. While NAAL does not contain any questions that specifically address civic content knowledge, the assessment does evaluate some of the intellectual skills described by NAEP's frameworks.

For instance, the committee's advanced category for prose literacy encompasses the skills of making complex inferences, comparing and contrasting viewpoints, and identifying an author's argument (e.g., in a newspaper). Likewise, the prose intermediate category includes being able to recognize an author's purpose and to locate information in a government form. Using the performance-level descriptions and samples of released NAAL items, it may be possible to glean information relevant for evaluating adults' skills in areas fundamental to civic engagement and civic participation.

Knowledge about adults' proficiency in this important area can be used both to formulate methods to improve their skills as well as to evaluate the extent to which civic and political materials are accessible to adults. The changes implemented by those working in the health literacy area provide a model. For example, after the release of NALS results in 1992, the health literacy field sought to evaluate the level of reading needed to understand health and safety information and to enact changes to make the information more accessible. Similar strategies could be used in the civic literacy field to evaluate the match (or mismatch) between individuals' literacy skills and the level of reading and vocabulary required on such documents as election ballots, pamphlets explaining rights and responsibilities, and flyers stating candidates' stands on political issues. Such strategies can lead to increased awareness of adults' understanding of civic and political issues and development of more accessible materials.

A negative example may serve to reinforce the importance of discussing the implications of literacy data. The report on NALS results for non-English speakers was not published until 2001 (eight years after the main Department of Education report, *Adult Literacy in America*). Neither analyses, findings, nor implications for this group of adults were widely discussed or disseminated. As a result, the realization that a significant portion of the population of greatest need was comprised of immigrants who had not yet learned English was slow to enter the policy debate and the public consciousness. If future reports are published in a timely manner, interested audiences will be able to gain a more nuanced picture of the literacy abilities and needs of the U.S. population, and policy makers will find it easier to make informed decisions.

7

Recommendations for
Future Literacy Assessments

In today's society, literacy is a critical skill, one that has the power to enhance the number and variety of opportunities available to individuals and that can enable them to lead productive lives and become informed community members and citizens. The 1992 assessment of adults' literacy skills yielded a tremendous wealth of information on the literacy needs of adults living in the United States, information that served to strengthen and refocus efforts on new and existing programs. We expect that the results from the 2003 assessment will be equally useful.

Conducting regular and periodic large-scale assessments of adult literacy provides a means for determining what literacy hurdles this country has overcome and which hurdles still lie ahead. The committee understands that there are currently no plans to conduct a follow-up to the National Assessment of Adult Literacy (NAAL). We think, however, that ongoing assessment of the literacy skills of the nation's adults is important, and that planning for a follow-up to NAAL should begin now. In this chapter, in an effort to be forward looking, we offer suggestions for ways to improve the assessment instrument and expand the literacy skills assessed.

Through our own research and analyses of the National Adult Literacy Survey (NALS) and NAAL and in listening to stakeholders and standard-setting participants—members of policy-making, curriculum-building, and practitioner communities—the committee came to realize that there may be ways the assessment could be altered and expanded to enable better understanding of literacy issues in the United States. Throughout this report, we have alluded to certain weaknesses in NALS and NAAL and have pointed

182

out areas of concern for users of NAAL results. In this chapter we restate some of the weaknesses and concerns with the intent that our recommendations will stimulate reflective and proactive thinking for future literacy assessment developments. Some of our suggestions are speculative and far-reaching, but we raise these issues as a means of opening the dialogue with the Department of Education about what an assessment like NAAL could, and perhaps should, encompass.

The committee addresses four areas of concern. First, we revisit the issue of the type of inferences that policy makers, media, and the public wanted to make about NALS results when they were released in 1993. There are alternative approaches to test development, such as those used for licensing and certification tests, which produce assessment results that support standards-based inferences. We encourage exploration of the feasibility of these methods for future literacy assessments. We describe an approach that could be considered, which we refer to as a "demand-side analysis of critical skills," and explain how it can be used to enhance and expand NAAL.

Second, there are ways to improve on the information currently collected about adults' quantitative skills, and we make suggestions for strengthening and expanding this portion of the assessment. Third, we provide a rationale for expanding the test development and administration processes to better evaluate the literacy needs of growing populations of nonnative English speakers.

Finally, we propose ways to broaden the conception of literacy on which NALS and NAAL were based. The definitions of literacy that guided test development for NALS and NAAL placed constraints on the inferences made about the results and the generalizability of the findings. Defining literacy in a meaningful way is perhaps the most fundamental aspect of constructing a literacy assessment. If the definition of literacy that underpins item development is narrow and limited, then the inferences based on the assessment results will likewise be narrow and limited. We suggest ways to broaden the conception of literacy that underlies NAAL.

DEMAND-SIDE ANALYSIS OF CRITICAL SKILLS

Formal large-scale assessment programs are designed to fulfill a variety of needs, ranging from a simple information-gathering survey used to evaluate program needs, to assessments used for more high-stakes purposes, such as grade promotion, high school graduation, and professional licensure.

NALS and NAAL are examples of assessments used primarily to evaluate program needs. For instance, the findings from NALS generated intense interest and funding for literacy education programs for adults who spoke

English or who were trying to learn English. Similarly, the results of NAAL are likely to be used to shape and refocus existing programs as well as target additional needy populations. The approach to test development for NALS and NAAL reflected these intended purposes.

Many audiences for the assessment results sought to make standards-based inferences about NALS: they wanted to know how many adults were "illiterate" and how many had the skills needed to function adequately in society. As we have discussed, however, the test development process used for NALS and repeated for NAAL was not intended to support such claims. An alternative approach to test development, similar to that used for certification and licensing tests, would allow such inferences to be made about the results.

Test development for credentialing examinations typically begins with identification of the critical skills that an individual should master in order to obtain the specific credential. Often this is handled by gathering feedback (e.g., via surveys or focus groups) from the community of experts and practitioners who work in the specific domain. Experts and practitioners help to define the set of knowledge, skills, and competencies that individuals should be able to demonstrate; they also assist with the development and review of test items and actively participate in the determination of the cut score required to pass the exam.

NALS and NAAL currently draw test questions from six contexts in which adults utilize their literacy skills: work, health and safety, community and citizenship, home and family, consumer economics, and leisure and recreation. Our suggested approach to test development would involve a systematic review of each of these contexts to determine the critical literacy demands required to function adequately, which would then serve as the foundation for the test development process. Included in this approach would be a review of print materials in each context that adults are expected to read, understand, and use. This task could also include focus groups or other types of discussion with low-literate adults who could talk about what they see as the literacy skills they need in their home and work lives.

Standard setting, that is, determinations of the level of proficiency that adults need or should have, would be a natural outgrowth of such an approach, including, if desired, the setting of multiple standards. For instance, performance levels could be established that reflect judgments about the levels of proficiency adults need in order to excel, to function adequately, or simply to get by in this country. This approach to test development could produce assessment results intended to support claims about the levels of literacy judged to be adequate. The psychometric literature provides documentation of these procedures for professional licensing and certification that could serve as a resource for this approach in the context of literacy assessment.[1]

We recognize that, in the case of literacy assessment, this is no easy task and that previous attempts to characterize adequate literacy skills for adults have not been entirely successful (e.g., the work conducted as part of the Adult Performance Level Study described in Adult Performance Level Project, 1975). Furthermore, the construct of literacy is much broader than the set of skills and competencies evaluated by credentialing tests. Nevertheless, we encourage further exploration of the feasibility of this strategy toward test design. The work of Sticht (1975) would be relevant in this endeavor.

Providing Scores for the Context Areas

Systematic sampling of the literacy demands in the six contexts, via a demand-side analysis, could be used to support the existing prose, document, and quantitative scores, but it could also result in separate scores for the different contexts. For example, NAAL could be better designed to measure literacy skills that are directly relevant to citizenship. Prose, document, and quantitative literacy items, drawn from civic and politically relevant real-world examples, could be added to the assessment to inform the development of instructional materials for adult education and citizenship preparation classes. Prose items could measure understanding of a proposal on a ballot and in a voter information pamphlet, or they could measure skill in identifying political candidates' perspectives about certain issues; quantitative items could measure understanding of the allocation of public funds. The addition of civic-related materials would enhance NAAL by lending much-needed guidance to those who are working to ensure access to the democratic process for all. Including a number of test items regarding literacy and citizenship in future generations of NAAL would offer the opportunity to evaluate the extent to which adults' literacy skills are sufficient to make informed decisions regarding civic matters.

Development of the health literacy score could be used as a model for exploring the feasibility of reporting literacy scores in other NAAL content domains. The health literacy community was active in the design of new items for NAAL that would support a health literacy score. NAAL items drawn from the health and safety context were developed and included on the assessment in such a way that they contribute to prose, document, and quantitative literacy scores but also yield a separate health literacy score.

---

[1]Procedures used to develop the National Board for Professional Teaching Standards' advanced certification program for teachers provides one example (see http://www.nbpts.org).

Similar procedures could be used to provide literacy information for each of the specified contexts. We believe it is worthwhile considering the feasibility of this approach.

Expanding Information Collected on the Background Questionnaire

Feedback from experts in each of the contexts could also be used to expand and focus the information collected on the background questionnaire. As it currently exists, the background questionnaire is a tremendous resource, but there are ways in which it could be improved. As described in Chapters 4 and 5, we were not able to conduct some of the desired analyses, either because the data were not available from the background questionnaire or because the information collected did not allow for fine enough distinctions to use in setting standards. Changes were made to the 2003 background questionnaire as a result of the efforts to create a health literacy score, and questions were added to gather background information with regard to health and safety issues. Similar procedures could be used to link demand-side analyses with the construction of the background questionnaire items for the various contexts, with input and guidance provided by panels of domain-specific experts, stakeholders, and practitioners.

For example, with respect to the context of community and citizenship, NAAL currently includes measures of voting and volunteering in its background survey. Future surveys should draw more effectively on the existing literature to include a larger and more carefully designed battery of items measuring both attitudinal and behavioral dimensions of civic and political engagement. Doing so would allow for much richer and more definitive analyses of the relationship between literacy and effective democratic citizenship.

The following two recommendations convey the committee's ideas with regard to the test development approach and revisions to the background questionnaire.

RECOMMENDATION 7-1: The Department of Education should work with relevant domain-specific experts, stakeholders, and practitioners to identify the critical literacy demands in at least six contexts: work, health and safety, community and citizenship, home and family, consumer economics, and leisure and recreation. Future generations of NAAL should be designed to measure these critical skills and should be developed from the outset to support standards-based inferences about the extent to which adults are able to perform these critical skills.

RECOMMENDATION 7-2: The background questionnaire included in NAAL should be updated and revised. The Department of Education should work with relevant domain-specific experts, stakeholders, and practitioners to identify the key background information to collect with regard to at least six contexts: work, health and safety, community and citizenship, home and family, consumer economics, and leisure and recreation. Relevant stakeholders should be involved in reviewing and revising questions to be included on the background questionnaire.

Maintaining the Integrity of Trends

The validity of any assessment rests on the strengths of the item pool for that assessment. Although much time and many resources have been invested in development and testing the current NAAL item pool, these items will eventually become obsolete. As with any large-scale assessment, review and revision of the item pool requires continuous efforts. Items need to incorporate current and future uses of texts, behaviors, and practices, as well as adoption of components that reflect current bodies of research in domain-specific areas. We recognize that altering the test development approach or making changes in the item pool has the potential to interfere with efforts to monitor trends. We therefore suggest that while each new generation of NAAL should update the assessment items to reflect current literacy requirements and expectations in each context, some time-invariant items should also be retained to enable trend analysis. We therefore recommend the following:

RECOMMENDATION 7-3: The Department of Education should work with relevant domain-specific experts, stakeholders, and practitioners to monitor literacy requirements in at least six contexts: work, health and safety, community and citizenship, home and family, consumer economics, and leisure and recreation. For every administration of the adult literacy assessment, the Department of Education should document changes in the literacy demands in these contexts. Each new instrument should update the assessment items to reflect current literacy requirements and expectations in each context but should also retain some time-invariant items to enable trend analysis.

Consideration of Written Expression and Computer Skills

During both standard settings, panelists raised questions about the role of written expression in NALS and NAAL. Many of the assessment questions require written responses, but the quality of the writing is not considered in the scoring process. For instance, some assessment questions require the test taker to write a brief letter, but it is the content of the response that is scored, not the writing: a one- or two-sentence response is accorded the same weight as a one- or two-paragraph response. Although adding a full measure of written expression is not a simple endeavor, we think that writing is a critical aspect of literacy and of functioning in modern society. We suggest that writing be explored as part of a demand-side analysis by evaluating the extent to which written expressive skills are critical for functioning in the six contexts specified.

A demand-side analysis could also cover the need for computer and technological literacy skills in each of the contexts, such as using a computer to handle daily activities, accessing and navigating the Internet to research and locate information, and deciphering multimedia. These skills include the motor skills needed to manage a keyboard, a mouse, and menus, but they also go far beyond them to include the kinds of reading that are required to navigate in hypermedia. As government and private industry shift critical literacy tasks, such as interaction with forms and applications, to online media, assessing functional literacy without considering the role of computer usage will understate the complexity of such daily tasks and may tend to overestimate the functional literacy of the population. Furthermore, it will be impossible to assess computer-mediated communication skills without computer-mediated testing. Therefore, we suggest that computer skills be considered in a demand-side analysis.

We acknowledge that developing assessments of these skills introduces a host of complexities, not the least of which is defining the specific domain to be assessed and determining a means for reliably scoring responses to the tasks. We further recognize that such assessments are labor-intensive and may prove to be too expensive to be conducted on a large-scale basis. It may be possible, however, to implement assessments of these skills on a smaller scale, such as through a subsample of participants or focused special studies. Therefore, we encourage further exploration of the feasibility of assessing these skills on future generations of the assessment.

IMPROVING THE ASSESSMENT OF QUANTITATIVE SKILLS

The second area in which changes are warranted is the quantitative literacy scale. As described in Chapter 4, analyses of the dimensionality of NALS, conducted by the committee and others (e.g., Reder, 1998a, 1998b), revealed very high correlations among the three literacy scales. These factor analytic studies suggest that a single dimension, not three, underlies performance on the assessment. In part, this may be due to the fact that every item that measures quantitative literacy is embedded in a text-based or document-based stimulus. To perform the required mathematics, test takers must first be able to handle the reading tasks presented by the stimulus materials as well as the reading required in the instructions for the question. Thus, every item in the quantitative literacy scale confounds skill in mathematics with factors associated with understanding text-based or document-based materials.

Mathematical demands in society are not easily separated from the task of reading; hence, the overlapping nature of the stimuli used for NALS and NAAL mirrors tasks that occur in real-life situations. Nevertheless, the overlap presents problems when interpreting the results. A difficult quantitative literacy item may be so because it requires a good deal of text-based or document-based interpretation, while the mathematical skill required to complete the item may be as simple as adding two amounts of money. This characteristic of the quantitative tasks was noted by participants in both of the committee's standard-setting sessions. Some panelists commented that they were surprised by the extent of reading required for the questions that were intended to measure quantitative skills, cautioning that the NALS and NAAL quantitative scale should not be construed as a mathematics test. Panelists were also surprised at the level of mathematical skill evaluated on NALS and NAAL, observing that most questions required only very basic mathematics (e.g., addition, subtraction, simple multiplication, division).

Research has shown that skill in mathematics may correlate even more strongly with economic success than reading (Murnane, Willet, and Levy, 1995). We therefore think it is important to understand the mathematical skill level of the adult population.

When NALS was first developed, scant attention was paid to mathematics in the adult basic education and literacy education system. Since then, the emphasis on numeracy—the mathematics needed to meet the demands of society, which differs somewhat from school or highly formal mathematics—has been increasing. This emphasis on numeracy skills is reflected in decisions made about the Adult Literacy and Lifeskills Survey, the successor to the International Adult Literacy Survey. In 2002, Statistics Canada and other organizations who work on international literacy assessments reexamined the components of the International Adult Literacy Survey and recommended that the quantitative literacy scale of the Adult Literacy and Lifeskills Survey be replaced by a broader numeracy construct (Murray, 2003). The Organisation for Economic Co-Operation and Development Programme for International Student Assessment (http://www.pisa.oecd.org) and the Center for Literacy Studies' Equipped for the Future program (http://www.eff.cls.utk.edu) are two other large-scale endeavors that include mathematics or numeracy as separate from skill in reading and writing.

Neither NALS nor NAAL was meant to be a formal test of mathematical proficiency in higher level domains, such as algebra, geometry, or calculus, and we are not suggesting that this should be the case. That said, it is the committee's view that the mathematical demands in a technological society require more than a basic grasp of whole numbers and money, as currently reflected in the NAAL. A fuller development of a quantitative literacy scale could include such skills as algebraic reasoning (with an emphasis on modeling rather than symbol manipulation), data analysis, geometric and measurement tasks, and the various forms and uses of rational numbers, in addition to the basic operations with time and money that are assessed in the NAAL. These arguments suggest that mathematical skill and literacy could be assessed more accurately as separate and more fully developed constructs, less tied to prose or document literacy, yet still reflective of the types of tasks encountered by adults in everyday situations.

In line with the demand-side analysis of critical skills discussed in the preceding section, the committee suggests that a reconceptualization of the quantitative literacy scale include an examination of the research into the mathematical and commingled mathematical and reading demands of society as well the aspects that contribute to the complexity of a variety of mathematical tasks. NALS put mathematics on the map by including quantitative literacy, but it would be useful if future assessments of adult literacy were to go further. Expansion of the quantitative literacy construct would enable a more accurate assessment of those at higher levels of mathematical skill. NAAL results could be used to generate discussion about college remediation programs with the same vigor that energizes discussion of literacy skills at the lower end of the scale.

There is a significant body of international research on numeracy and cognitive assessments of adult problem-solving skills that could be used as a starting point for rethinking the quantitative literacy scale. Other entities available as resources for rethinking measurement of quantitative literacy include Adults Learning Mathematics—A Research Forum (http://www.alm-online.org/) and the Adult Numeracy Network (http://www.shell04.theworld.com/std/anpn/), an affiliate of the National Council of Teachers of Mathematics.

We therefore recommend the following:

RECOMMENDATION 7-4: The Department of Education should consider revising the quantitative literacy component on future assessments of adult literacy to include a numeracy component assessed as a separate construct, less tied to prose or document literacy but still reflective of the types of tasks encountered by adults in everyday situations. The numeracy skills to include on the assessment should be identified as part of an analysis of critical literacy demands in six content areas. The types of numeracy skills assessed on the Adult Literacy and Lifeskills Survey could serve as a starting place for identifying critical skills.

IMPROVING THE INFORMATION COLLECTED ABOUT ADULT NON-ENGLISH SPEAKERS

The third area in which the committee thinks significant modifications of future NAAL instruments should be made is with regard to collecting information about the literacy skills of non-English speaking adults. As described in Chapter 6, language-minority adults are an ever-increasing segment of the U.S. population. Since immigration to the United States is likely to continue and demand for services to non-English speakers is likely to remain high, much more needs to be known about the backgrounds and skills of this population. Data on the language skills and literacy profiles of non-English speakers are needed so that policy makers, program administrators, practitioners, and employers can make informed decisions about their education and training needs.

Immigrant adults make up a significant proportion of the working poor in the United States, and a high number of immigrants among this group are not fully literate in English. Limited English language and literacy skills of immigrants are seen as a significant threat to U.S. economic advancement (United Way, Literacy@Work: The L.A. Workforce Literacy Project, September 2004), yet analyses of the NALS data on Spanish speakers (Greenberg et al., 2001) show that bilingual adults have higher earnings as a group than those who are monolingual in either English or Spanish. Thus, social, political, and economic concerns warrant a more focused effort at gathering information about adults who speak English as a second language than NAAL administrative procedures allowed.

We addressed this issue in our letter report to the National Center for Education Statistics issued in June 2003,[2] and we repeat our concerns here with the hope that future assessments of adult literacy will allow for expanded and more structured information to be collected about non-English speakers. We recognize that NAAL is intended to be an assessment of English literacy skills only, and we are not suggesting that it should be expanded to assess competence in other languages. We nevertheless maintain that it is important to enable the survey results to portray a nuanced picture of the backgrounds and skills of the entire population.

Procedures for Collecting Background Data on NAAL

Currently NAAL collects background information only from those who speak sufficient English or Spanish to understand and respond to the initial screening and background questions. As described in Chapter 2, when an interviewer arrived at a sampled household, a screening device

---

[2]Available at http://www.nap.edu/catalog/10762.html.

was used to determine if there was an eligible person in the household to participate in the assessment. If the respondent could not understand the English or Spanish spoken by the interviewer (or vice versa), the interviewer could solicit translation assistance from another household member, family friend, or a neighbor available at the time. If an interpreter was not available, the assessment would cease, and the case would be coded as a language problem. Therefore, unless an interpreter happened to be available, no information was collected from those who do not speak English or Spanish. Furthermore, if translation assistance was available, it was only for the initial screening questions that requested information about age, race/ethnicity, and gender. The background questionnaire was available only in English and Spanish, and translation assistance was not allowed. The consequence of these administrative decisions is that an opportunity was missed to gather additional information about individuals in this country who speak languages other than English or Spanish. The information that was obtained about this group of individuals who spoke a language other than English or Spanish relied primarily on happenstance (e.g., if an interpreter happened to be available). A more structured, more in-depth approach might have been used to better capitalize on these important data collection opportunities.

Proposed Changes to Procedures

Much useful information can be gathered through NAAL by allowing speakers of other languages to demonstrate the English literacy skills they do possess while providing information about their capabilities in other languages, capabilities that are likely to influence the acquisition of literacy skills in English. While translating NAAL's background questionnaire into multiple languages may be infeasible, there are alternative ways to collect information about non-English speakers. Language-minority groups often cluster in particular geographic areas. Often, translators are available to assist adults with understanding community information, such as school enrollment procedures, health and safety information, voter information, and the like. We think this resource could be tapped for future administrations of NAAL, and a more structured approach taken to ensure that either bilingual assessors or trained translators are available during interviews with individuals who speak languages other than English or Spanish.

With translators available, more in-depth information could be obtained from individuals who do not speak English or have only minimal English skills than is allowed through the current version of the initial screening device, information that could be used for programmatic purposes. For instance, it would be useful to gather information from this group about their formal education, participation in English language courses, training and work experience in other countries as well as in the United States, and self-perceptions about their oral and written proficiency in English and in other languages (e.g., using questions like the self-report questions currently included on the background questionnaire). We are not proposing that the entire background questionnaire be translated into multiple languages, simply that additional information collected about non-English speakers.

It may also be useful to explore oversampling or special focused studies of language-minority regions so that they will yield sufficient numbers to allow for detailed analyses and provide information for policy makers and practitioners serving those language communities.

Finally, we suggest that non-English speakers be considered in each population group (e.g., the incarcerated) and as part of each focus area (e.g., health and safety) and that background data on non-English speakers be included as part of all major reports and as a separate report on the language and literacy skills of all adults who speak a language other than English at home.

RECOMMENDATION 7-5: The Department of Education should seek to expand the information obtained about non-English speakers in future assessments of adult literacy, including, for example, background information about formal education, participation in English language courses, training and work experience in other countries as well as in the United States, and self-reports about use of print materials in languages other than English. Efforts should also be made to be more structured in the collection of background information about individuals who speak languages other than English or Spanish.

RETHINKING AND BROADENING
THE DEFINITION OF LITERACY

We conclude this chapter by proposing ways to broaden the conception of literacy on which NALS and NAAL were based. For these two assessments, literacy has been construed as an ability, as skills, and as a possession. As a concept, literacy provides a canvas that encompasses practices, behaviors, beliefs, and activities that range from basic reading and writing to the less well-defined notion of higher order problem solving. Literacy has multiple conceptions, which range from a focus on the most fundamental survival skills to more complex definitions that encompass the skills needed to thrive in a variety of contexts, such as the home, the workplace, and the community. The ways in which literacy specialists talk about literacy typically attempt to take into consideration a broad spectrum of knowledge and skills.

Literacy changes over time as expectations for knowledge and skill levels increase, and it changes with the advent of new mediating technologies. While a signature served as demonstration of literacy at one point, no one would argue that signing one's name would signify being literate today. A pen and pencil, typewriter, or keyboard were key mediating tools in the past, but to separate literacy from its most powerful purveyor, digital technology and the Internet, is to lose much of what counts as literacy in this age.

Once again, we encourage discussion and reconsideration of the literacy demands in the tasks of daily living. Inclusion of stakeholders, practitioners, and members of the media in these discussions will not only contribute to an improved test design for assessing critical literacy skills for existing and new domains beyond the six specified previously, but will also contribute to a higher level of reflection on rethinking and broadening the existing definition of literacy. With these comments in mind, we make two additional suggestions for rethinking and retooling how literacy is defined for the NAAL.

A significant departure from the existing NAAL paradigm is to consider future assessments as measuring functional literacy in a wider set of contexts. Although the types of literacy that are prevalent in the world of work would be important to sample, individuals use literacy for many personal purposes as well, including literacy practices connected to religion or their children's schooling. Use of focus groups and a panel of experts for guidance in demand-side analyses would be extremely beneficial in probing the measurement boundaries of future NAAL assessments.

Currently, examinees are allowed assistance only for completion of the background questionnaire. However, literacy is a social practice, and, in the real world, literacy tasks are often done collaboratively. For example, when faced with a literacy task, people often speak with each other, consult resources, and rely on background experiences to solve problems. Low-literate adults in particular have developed ways to compensate for their weak reading skills; many manage to get by in life by using compensatory strategies. We suggest that the Department of Education explore the feasibility of providing assistance as needed for the completion of some proportion of the items in the main assessment as well as in the background questionnaire. This could include, for example, asking for assistance in reading a word or two in a question or asking for clarification about the meaning of a phrase in a document or a quantitative task. When a test taker is not able to answer a question, the interviewer could gather additional information about ways he or she would approach solving the particular problem if it arose in real life. This type of information may provide especially valuable insight into the actual skills of low-literate adults and into effective compensatory strategies.

CONCLUSION

Ultimately, as the literacy assessment instrument evolves, so will the processes by which standards are set and performance levels described. The committee has suggested some far-reaching recommendations for future developments of a literacy assessment, some of which will require significant contemplation regarding test development processes. Most notably, there is a lingering question regarding the adequacy and completeness of the existing prose, document, and quantitative literacy scales, both in relation to the content coverage and the adequacy of measurement at the upper and lower ends of the score distribution. We recommend an alternative approach to test development, one that considers the tasks of daily living to identify the critical literacy demands that will guide development of the item pool. These procedures could change the nature of the assessment, the test administration processes, and the meaning of the scores that are reported. We recognize that such extensive modifications of the assessment make it difficult to measure trends in adult literacy, which is also an important goal. These competing goals must be carefully weighed in the design of future assessments. In all cases, however, regardless of whether any of the proposed changes are implemented, the committee recommends that the process of determining performance levels be carried out concurrently with the process of designing the assessment and constructing the items.

References

Adult Performance Level Project. (1975). *Adult functional competency: A summary.* (ED No. 114 609.) Austin: University of Texas, Division of Extension.

American Educational Research Association, American Psychological Association, and National Council on Measurement in Education. (1999). *Standards for educational and psychological testing.* Washington, DC: American Educational Research Association.

American Medical Association. (1999). Health literacy: Report of the Ad Hoc Committee on Health Literacy for the Council of Scientific Affairs. *Journal of the American Medical Association, 281(6),* 552-557.

Baldwin, J., Kirsch, I.S., Rock, D., and Yamamoto, K. (1995). *The literacy proficiencies of GED examinees: Results from the GED-NALS Comparison Study.* Washington, DC: American Council on Education and Educational Testing Service.

Baron, D. (2002). Will anyone accept the good news on literacy? *The Chronicle of Higher Education,* February 1.

Barton, P.E. (1999). *What jobs require: Literacy, education, and training, 1940-2006.* Princeton, NJ: Educational Testing Service.

Berk, R.A. (1986). A consumer's guide to setting performance standards on criterion-referenced tests. *Review of Educational Research, 56,* 137-172.

Berkman, N.D., De Walt, D.A., Pignone, M.P., Sheridan, S.L., Lohr, K.N., Lux, L., Sutton, S.F., Swinson, T., and Bonito, A.J. (2004). *Literacy and health outcomes.* (Evidence Report/Technology Assessment No. 87 prepared by RTI International-University of North Carolina Evidence-Based Practice Center under Contract No. 290-02-0016. AHRQ Publication No. 04-E007-1.) Rockville, MD: Agency for Healthcare Research and Quality.

Berliner, D.C. (1996). Nowadays, even the illiterates read and write. *Research in the Teaching of English, 30(3),* 334-351.

Beuck, C.H. (1984). A method for researching a compromise between absolute and relative standards in examinations. *Journal of Educational Measurement, 21,* 147-152.

Brady, H.E. (1996). Political participation. In M.X. Delli Carpini and S. Keeter (Eds.), *What Americans know about politics and why it matters.* New Haven, CT: Yale University Press.

Brennan, R.L. (1998). Misconceptions at the intersection of measurement theory and practice. *Educational Measurement: Issues and Practice, 17*(1), 5-9.

Campbell, A., Kirsch, I.S., and Kolstad, A. (1992). *Assessing literacy.* Washington, DC: U.S. Department of Education, National Center for Education Statistics.

Cizek, G.J. (1993). *Reactions to the National Academy of Education report setting performance standards for student achievement.* Washington, DC: National Assessment Governing Board.

Cizek, G.J. (2001a). Conjectures on the rise and call of standard setting: An introduction to context and practice. In G.J. Cizek (Ed.), *Setting performance standards: Concepts, methods, and perspectives.* Mahwah, NJ: Lawrence Erlbaum.

Cizek, G.J. (Ed.), (2001b). *Setting performance standards: Concepts, methods, and perspectives.* Mahwah, NJ: Lawrence Erlbaum.

Cizek, G.J., Bunch, M.B., and Koons, H. (2004). An NCME instructional module on setting performance standards: Contemporary methods. *Educational Measurement: Issues and Practice, 2*(4), 31-50.

Delli Carpini, M.X. and Keeter, S. (1996). *What Americans know about politics and why it matters.* New Haven, CT: Yale University Press.

Egan, K.L. (2001). *Validity and defensibility of cut scores established by the bookmark standard setting methods.* Paper presented at the Council of Chief State School Officers Conferences on Large-Scale Assessment, June, Houston, TX.

Equipped for the Future Assessment Consortium, Center for Literacy Studies at University of Tennessee, and SRI International. (2002). *EFF/NRS data collection project, 2000-2001: An interim report on the development of the EFF assessment framework.* Washington, DC: National Institute for Literacy.

Fry, E. (1977). Fry's readability graph: Clarifications, validity and extension to Level 17. *Journal of Reading, 21,* 242-252.

GED Testing Service. (2004). *Who passed the GED tests? 2002 statistical report.* Washington, DC: American Council on Education.

Geisinger, K.F. (1991). Using standard-setting data to establish cutoff scores. *Educational Measurement: Issues and Practice, 10*(2), 17-22.

Gray, P. (1993). Adding up the under-skilled: A survey finds nearly half of U.S. adults lack the literacy to cope with modern life. *Time,* September 20, *142,* 175.

Green, D.R., Trimble, C.S., and Lewis, D.M. (2003). Interpreting the results of three different standard-setting procedures. *Educational Measurement: Issues and Practice, 22*(1), 22-32.

Greenberg, E., Macia, R., Rhodes, D., and Chan T. (2001). *English literacy and language minorities in the United States.* (No. 2001-464). Washington, DC: U.S. Department of Education, National Center for Education Statistics.

Haigler, K.O., Harlow, C., O'Connor, P., and Campbell, A. (1994). *Literacy behind prison walls: Profiles of the prison population from the National Adult Literacy Survey.* Washington, DC: U.S. Department of Education, National Center for Education Statistics.

Hambleton, R.K. (1980). Test score validity and standard setting methods. In D.C. Berliner, (Ed.), *Criterion-referenced measurement: The state of the art* (pp. 80-123). Baltimore, MD: Johns Hopkins University Press.

Hambleton, R.K. (2001). Setting performance standards on educational assessments and criteria for evaluating the process. In C.J. Cizek (Ed.), *Setting performance standards: Concepts, methods, and perspectives.* Mahwah, NJ: Lawrence Erlbaum.

Hambleton, R.K., and Bourque, M.L. (1991). *The levels of mathematics achievement* (technical report, vol. III). Washington, DC: National Assessment Governing Board.

Hambleton, R.K., Brennan, R.L., Brown, W., Dodd., B., Forsyth, R.A., Mehrens, W.A., Nellhaus, J., Rackase, M., Rindone, D., van der Linden, W.J., and Zqick, R. (2000). A response to "setting reasonable and useful performance standards" in the National Academy of Sciences "Grading the nation's report card." *Educational Measurement: Issues and Practice, 19*(2), 5-14.

Hauck, W.W. (1983). A note on confidence bands for the logistic regression curve. *American Statistician, 37,* 158-160.

Hauser, R.M. and Goldberger, A.S. (1971). The treatment of unobservable variables in path analysis. In H.L. Costner (Ed.), *Sociological methodology* (pp. 81-117). San Francisco: Jossey-Bass.

Hofstee, W.K.B. (1983). The case for compromise in educational selection and grading. In S.B. Anderson and J.S. Helmick (Eds.), *On educational testing* (pp. 109-127). San Francisco: Jossey-Bass.

Huff, K. L. (2001). *Overcoming unique challenges to a complex performance assessment: A novel approach to standard setting.* Paper presented at the annual meeting of the National Council on Measurement in Education, April, Seattle, WA.

Hunyh, H. (2000). *On item mappings and statistical rules for selecting binary items for criterion-referenced interpretation and bookmark standard settings.* Paper presented at the annual meeting of the National Council for Measurement in Education, April, New Orleans.

Institute of Medicine. (2004). *Health literacy: A prescription to end confusion.* Committee on Health Literacy, Board on Neuroscience and Behavioral Health. Washington, DC: The National Academies Press.

Jaeger, R.M. (1989). Certification of student competence. In R.L. Linn (Ed.), *Educational measurement* (3rd ed., pp. 485-514). Washington DC: American Council on Education.

Jaeger, R.M. (1991). Selection of judges for standard-setting. *Educational Measurement: Issues and Practice, 10*(2), 3-6.

Jaeger, R.M., and Mills, C.N. (2001). An integrated judgement procedure for setting standards on complex, large-scale assessments. In G.J. Cizek (Ed.), *Setting performance standards: Concepts, methods, and perspectives.* Mahwah, NJ: Lawrence Erlbaum.

Jordan, H. (1993). Literacy of 90 million is deficient. *Washington Post,* September 8, A1, A15.

Joreskog, K.G., and Goldberger, A.S. (1975). Estimation of a model with multiple indicators and multiple causes of a single latent variable. *Journal of the American Statistical Association, 70,* 631-639.

Kane, M. (1993). *Comments on the NAE evaluation of NAGB achievement levels.* Washington, DC: National Assessment Governing Board.

Kane, M.T. (1995). Examinee-centered vs. task-centered standard setting. In *Proceedings of joint conference on standard setting in large-scale assessments* (pp. 119-139). Washington, DC: National Assessment Governing Board and U.S. Department of Education, National Center for Education Statistics.

Kane, M.T. (2001). So much remains the same: Conception and status of validation in setting standards. In G.J. Cizek (Ed.), *Setting performance standards: Concepts, methods, and perspectives.* Mahwah, NJ: Lawrence Erlbaum.

Kaplan, D.A. (1993). Dumber than we thought: Literacy: A new study shows why we can't cope with everyday life. *Newsweek, 122,* 44-45.

Kingston, N.M., Kahl, S.R., Sweeney, K.P., and Bay, L. (2001). Setting performance standards using the body of work method. In G.J. Cizek (Ed.), *Setting performance standards: Concepts, methods and perspectives* (Chapter 8). Mahwah, NJ: Lawrence Erlbaum.

Kirsch, I.S. (2002). *Literacy standards must not be lowered.* Available: http://www.ets.org/search97cgi/s97_cgi [accessed 2003.]

Kirsch, I.S., Jungeblut, A., Jenkins, L., and Kolstad, A. (1993). *Adult literacy in America: A first look at the results of the national adult literacy survey.* Princeton, NJ: Educational Testing Service.

Kirsch, I.S., Jungeblut, A., and Mosenthal, P.B. (2001). Interpreting the adult literacy scales and literacy levels. Chapter 13 in *Technical report and data file user's manual for the 1992 national adult literacy survey.* (NCES No. 2001-457). Washington, DC: U.S. Department of Education, National Center for Education Statistics.

Kirsch, I., Yamamoto, K., Norris, N., Rock, D., Jungeblut, A., O'Reilly, P., Berlin, M., Mohandjer, L., Waksberg, J., Goksel, H., Burke, J., Rieger, S., Green, J., Klein, M., Campbell, A., Jenkins, L., Kolstad, A., Mosenthal, P., and Baldi, S. (2001). *Technical report and data file user's manual for the 1992 national adult literacy survey.* (NCES No. 2001-457.) Washington, DC: U.S. Department of Education, National Center for Education Statistics.

Langley, P.S. (1999). *Corrections education: A learning profiles special report.* Salt Lake City: Utah State Office of Education. Available: http://64.233.161.104/search?q=cache:K8oNS l03sgEJ:literacynet.org/ll/issue8/columnist2.html+Corrections+education, +Langley&hl=en&start=1 [accessed June 2005].

Lawrence, S., Mears, D., Dubin, G., and Travis, J. (2002). *The practice and promise of prison programming.* Washington, DC: Urban Institute, Justice Policy Center.

Lewis, D.M., Green, D.R., Mitzel, H.C., Baum, K., and Patz, R.J. (1998). *The bookmark standard setting procedure: Methodology and recent implementations.* Paper presented at the National Council for Measurement in Education annual meeting, San Diego, CA.

Mathews, J. (2001). Adult illiteracy, rewritten: Director revises widely quoted 1993 study that said 1 in 5 couldn't read; analysis called overly pessimistic. *Washington Post,* July 17.

Mehrens, W.A. (1995). Methodological issues in standard setting for educational exams. In *Proceedings of the joint conference on standard setting for large-scale assessments* (p. 221-263). Washington, DC: National Assessment Governing Board and National Center for Education Statistics.

Mitzel, H.C., Lewis, D.M., Patz, R.J., and Green, D.R. (2001). The bookmark procedure: Psychological perspectives. Chapter 9 in G.J. Cizek (Ed.), *Setting performance standards: Concepts, methods and perspectives.* Mahwah, NJ: Lawrence Erlbaum.

Mullins, M., and Green, D. (1994). In search of truth and the perfect standard-setting method: Is the Angoff procedure the best available for credentialing. *Clear Exam Review,* winter, 21-24.

Murnane, R.J., Willett, J.B., and Levy, F. 91995). The growing importance of cognitive skills in wage determination. *The Review of Economics and Statistics,* 77(2), 251-266.

Murray, T.S. (2003). *The assessment of literacy, numeracy, and language at the international level: A review.* Paper prepared for the Committee on Performance Levels for Adult Literacy, National Research Council.

National Assessment Governing Board, U.S. Department of Education. (1998). *Civics framework for the 1998 national assessment of educational progress.* Washington, DC: Author. Available: http://www.nagb.org/pubs/civics.pdf [accessed December 2004].

National Center for Education Statistics. (2003). *Digest of education statistics, 2003.* Available: http://nces.ed.gov/programs/digest/d03/index.asp [accessed February 25, 2005].

National Institute for Literacy. (2002). *Correctional education facts.* Washington, DC: Author.

National Reporting System. (2002). *6 levels of ABE or ESL.* Available: http://www.oei-tech.com/nrs/. [accessed September 2005].

National Research Council. (1999). *Grading the nation's report card: Evaluating NAEP and transforming the assessment of educational progress*. J.W. Pellegrino, L.R. Jones, and K.J. Mitchell (Eds.), Committee on the Evaluation of National Assessments of Educational Progress. Commission on Behavioral and Social Sciences and Education. Washington, DC: National Academy Press.

Plake, B.S., Melican, G.S., and Mills, C.N. (1991). Factors influencing intrajudge consistency during standard-setting. *Educational Measurement: Issues and Practice*, 10(2), 15-16.

Ratzan, S.C., and Parker, R.M. (2000). Introduction. In C.R. Selden, M. Zorn, S.C. Ratzan, and R.M. Parker (Eds.), *National library of medicine, current bibliographies in medicine: Health literacy*. (NLM No. CBM 2000-1.) Bethesda, MD: National Institutes of Health, U.S. Department of Health and Human Services.

Raymond, M.R., and Reid, J.B. (2001). Who made thee a judge? Selecting and training participants for standard setting. In G.J. Cizek (Ed.), *Setting performance standards: Concepts, methods, and perspectives*. Mahwah, NJ: Lawrence Erlbaum.

Reder, S. (1998a). Dimensionality and construct validity of the NALS assessment. In M.C. Smith, (Ed.), *Literacy for the twenty-first century: Research, policy, practices and the national adult literacy survey* (pp. 37-57). Westport, CT: Praeger.

Reder, S. (1998b). Literacy selection and literacy development: Structural equation models of the reciprocal effects of education and literacy. In M.C. Smith (Ed.), *Literacy for the twenty-first century: Research, policy, practices and the national adult literacy survey* (pp. 37-57). Westport, CT: Praeger.

Reid, J.B. (1991). Training judges to generate standard-setting data. *Educational Measurement: Issues and Practice*, 10(2), 11-14.

Rock, D.A., Latham, A., and Jeanneret, P.R. (1996). *Estimating prose, document, and quantitative literacy scores from position analysis questionnaire dimensions: An empirical linkage between adult literary skills and job analysis information*. Princeton, NJ: Educational Testing Service.

Rock, D.A., and Yamamoto, K. (1994). *Construct validity of the adult literacy subscales*. Princeton, NJ: Educational Testing Service.

Rudd, R.E., Kirsch, I., and Yamamoto, K. (2004). *Literacy and health in America*. (Global Assessment Policy Report.) Princeton, NJ: Educational Testing Service.

Rudd, R.E., Moeykens, B.A., and Colton, T.C. (2000). Health and literacy: A review of medical and public health literature. In J. Comings, B. Garner, and C. Smith (Eds.), *Annual review of adult learning and literacy* (vol. 1, pp. 158-199). San Francisco: Jossey-Bass.

Shepard, L.A. (1980). Standard setting issues and methods. *Applied Psychological Measurement, 4*, 447-467.

Shepard, L.A. (1983). Setting performance standards. In R.A. Berk (Ed.), *Criterion-referenced measurement: The state of the art* (pp. 169-198). Berkeley, CA: McCutchan.

Shepard, L.A. (1984). Setting performance standards. In R.A. Berk (Ed.), *A guide to criterion-referenced test construction* (pp. 169-198). Baltimore: Johns Hopkins University Press.

Shepard, L.A., Glaser, R., Linn, R.L., and Bohrnstedt, G. (1993). *Setting performances standards for student achievement. A report of the National Academy of Education panel on the evaluation of the NAEP trial state assessment: An evaluation of the 1992 achievement levels*. Stanford, CA: Stanford University, National Academy of Education.

Smith, M.C. (2003). *The national adult literacy survey: A review of primary and secondary analyses of the NALS*. Paper prepared for the Committee on Performance Levels for Adult Literacy, December, National Research Council, Washington, DC.

Sticht, T., (Ed.) (1975). *Reading for working: A functional literacy anthology*. Alexandria, VA: Human Resources Research Organization.

Sticht, T. (2004). Is illiteracy rampant in Los Angeles county? *Los Angeles Times*, September 11. Available: http://www.latimes.com/search/dispatcher.front?Query=adult=literacy andtarget=article. [accessed September 12, 2004].

Stites, R. (2000). *How much literacy is enough? Issues in defining and reporting performance standards for the national assessment of adult literacy.* (No. 2000-07.) Washington, DC: U.S. Department of Education, National Center for Education Statistics.

Sum, A. (1999) *Literacy in the labor force: Results from the national adult literacy survey.* Washington, DC: U.S. Department of Education, National Center for Education Statistics.

Thissen, D., and Wainer, H. (1982). Some standard errors in item response theory. *Psychometrika, 47,* 397-412.

Thissen, D., and Wainer, H. (1990). Confidence envelopes for item response theory. *Journal of Educational Statistics, 15,* 113-128.

Tversky, A., and Kahneman, D. (1983). Extensional versus intuitive reasoning: The conjunction fallacy in probability judgment. *Psychological Review, 90*(4), 293-315.

U.S. Department of Education, National Center for Education Statistics. (1998). *Developing the national assessment of adult literacy: Recommendations from stakeholders.* (Working Paper No. 98-17.) Washington, DC: Author.

U.S. Department of Health and Human Services, Office of Disease Prevention and Health Promotion. (2003). *Communicating health: Priorities and strategies for progress, Action plan to achieve the health communication objectives in healthy people 2010.* Washington, DC: Author.

U.S. Department of Justice, Office of Justice Programs. (2003). *Education and correctional populations.* (Special Report, NCJ No. 195670.) Washington, DC: Bureau of Justice Statistics.

Venezky, R., and Kaplan, D. (1998). Literacy habits and political participation. In M.C. Smith (Ed.), *Literacy for the twenty-first century: Research, policy, practices and the national adult literacy survey* (pp. 109-124). Westport, CT: Praeger.

Venezky, R., Kaplan, D., and Yu, F. (1998). *Literacy practices and voting behavior: An analysis of the 1992 national adult literacy survey.* Washington, DC: U.S. Department of Education, National Center for Education Statistics.

Verba, S., Lehman Schlozman, K., and Brady, H.E. (1995). *Voice and equality: Civic voluntarism in American politics.* Cambridge, MA: Harvard University Press.

Wagner, D.A. (2004). Literacy(ies), culture(s), and development(s): The ethnographic challenge. (A five-volume review.) *Reading Research Quarterly, 39*(2), 234-241.

Wedgeworth, R. (2003). *The number of functionally illiterate adults in the United States is growing: 2003 national assessment of adult literacy likely to show more adults lacking basic reading and writing skills.* Available: http://www.proliteracy.org/downloads/ProLiteracyStateOfLiteracy%2010-25-04.pdf. [accessed February 25, 2005].

Western, B., and Pettit, B. (2000). Incarceration and racial inequality in men's employment. *Industrial and Labor Relations Review, 54,* 3-16.

Williams, N.J., and Schulz, E.M. (2005). *An investigation of response probability (rp) values used in standard setting.* Paper presented at the annual meeting of the National Council on Measurement in Education, April, Montreal.

Zieky, M.J. (2001). So much has changed: How the setting of cutscores has evolved since the 1980s. In G.J. Cizek (Ed.), *Setting performance standards: Concepts, methods, and perspectives.* Mahwah, NJ: Lawrence Erlbaum.

Appendix A

The Committee's Public Forums on Performance Levels for NAAL

Public Forum—February 27, 2004

Panelists

Cynthia Baur, U.S. Department of Health and Human Services
Beth Beuhlmann, U.S. Chamber of Commerce, Workforce Preparation
Richard Colvin, Hechinger Institute
Leslie Farr, Ohio State University
Milton Goldberg, Education Commission of the States (ECS)
Richard Long, International Reading Association
Christopher Mazzeo, National Governors Association
Gemma Santos, Miami Dade Public Schools
Tony Sarmiento, Senior Service America, Inc.
Linda Taylor, Comprehensive Adult Student Assessment System
Robert Wedgeworth, Proliteracy Worldwide

Participants

Joan Auchter, GED Testing Service/American Council on Education
Justin Baer, American Institutes for Research (AIR)
Amy Baide, Department of Homeland Security
Sandra Baxter, The National Institute for Literacy (NIFL)
Jaleh Behroozi, The National Institute for Literacy (NIFL)
Martha Berlin, Westat

Peggy Carr, Department of Education, National Center for Education Statistics (NCES)
June Crawford, The National Institute for Literacy (NIFL)
Elizabeth Greenberg, American Institutes for Research (AIR)
Ricardo Hernandez, Office of Vocational and Adult Education (OVAE)
Shannon Holmes, U.S. Conference of Mayors
Eugene Johnson, American Institutes for Research (AIR)
Linda Johnston Lloyd, Health Resources & Services Administration (HRSA)
Michael Jones, Office of Vocational and Adult Education (OVAE)
Cheryl Keenan, Office of Vocational and Adult Education (OVAE)
Irwin Kirsch, Educational Testing Service (ETS)
Andy Kolstad, National Center for Education Statistics (NCES)
Mark Kutner, American Institutes for Research (AIR)
Mariann Lemke, National Center for Education Statistics (NCES)
Anne Lewis, freelance journalist
Lennox McLendon, National Adult Education Professional Development Consortium
Wendy Mettger, Mettger Communications
Leyla Mohadjer, Westat
Gerri Ratliff, Department of Homeland Security
Lyn Schaefer, GED Testing Service
Peggy Seufert, American Institutes for Research (AIR)
Sondra Stein, The National Institute for Literacy (NIFL)
Lynn Thai, Department of Homeland Security
Peter Waite, Proliteracy America
Dan Wagner, National Center on Adult Literacy
Maria White, Department of Health and Human Services
Sheida White, National Center for Education Statistics (NCES)
Kentaro Yamamoto, Educational Testing Service (ETS)

Representatives from State Departments of Adult Education— April 22-23, 2004

Bob Bickerton, Massachusetts
Steve Coffman, Missouri
Donna Cornelius, Massachusetts
Cheryl King, Kentucky
Tom Orvino, New York
Ann Serino, Massachusetts
Reecie Stagnolia, Kentucky
Linda Young, Oklahoma

Stakeholder Questions and Alternative Versions of Performance-Level Descriptions for the National Assessment of Adult Literacy

1.   In what ways did you use the results from the 1992 NALS? What were the strengths and weaknesses of these performance levels? To what extent did these performance levels provide you with the information that you needed?

2.   NAAL measures skills in the areas of prose, document, and quantitative literacy. To what extent is it useful and informative to have different performance level descriptions for each area? Are results from the three areas of literacy used differently? If so, how?

3.   The attachment presents three alternative versions of performance-level descriptions for the prose literacy scale. Sample 1 is simply a reformatted version of the existing performance-level descriptions with 5 levels. Sample 2 is a 4-level model, and Sample 3 is a 3-level model. Please comment on how many levels are needed. What types of decisions are made at the various levels? What are the critical distinctions that need to be made?

4.   *Level Labels:* The three samples present different labels for the levels. Sample 1 uses numbers (Col. 2). Samples 2 and 3 use phrases as labels (Col. 2). In addition, Sample 3 presents a narrative description of the label (Col. 3). Please comment on these alternative labels. What types of labels are useful and informative? Feel free to make suggestions for alternative labels.

5.   *Level Descriptions:* The three samples present different ways of describing the skills represented by the performance level. Sample 1 describes the tasks associated with the level (Col. 3). Sample 2 describes what an average respondent who scores at this level should be able to do (Col. 3). Sample 3 (Col. 4) describes what the average respondent who scores at this level is able to do and not able to do in probabilistic terms (i.e., likely, not likely). Please comment on these alternative ways of describing the skills associated with the levels. What types of descriptions are useful and informative? Feel free to make suggestions for alternative descriptions.

6.   *Sample Tasks:* The three samples present different ways of exemplifying the tasks respondents who score at the level should be able to do. Samples 1 and 2 (Col. 4) are similar and provide examples drawn from actual assessment. Sample 3 (Col. 5) attempts to generalize from assessment tasks to real world tasks. Please comment on the extent to which these exemplifications are useful and informative.

7.   *Relationships Between Prose Scores and Background Data:* Samples 2 and 3 present the relationships between NAAL scores and key real-world factors as measured on the background questionnaire. Sample 2 (Col. 5) uses societal factors (income, education, voting) and Sample 3 (Col. 6) uses reading related factors. (Please be aware that the percentages in-

cluded in these examples are purely hypothetical. If we were to recommend this format, the percentages would be based on analyses with NAAL data.) Please comment on the utility of this type of information.

SAMPLES ARE ON THE FOLLOWING PAGES

Sample 1: Five-Level Model, Based on Current PLDs for Prose Literacy

(Col. 1) Level	(Col. 2) Label	(Col. 3) Description of tasks	(Col. 4) Sample NAAL tasks associated with the level
I	Level 1	Most of the tasks in this level require the reader to read relatively short text to locate a single piece of information which is identical to or synonymous with the information given in the question or directive. If plausible but incorrect information is present in the text, it tends not to be located near the correct information.	• Locate one piece of information in a sports article. • Identify the country in a reading passage. • Underline sentence explaining action stated in short article.
II	Level 2	Some tasks in this level require readers to locate a single piece of information in the text; however, several distractors or plausible but incorrect pieces of information may be present, or low-level inference may be required. Other tasks require the reader to integrate two or more pieces of information or to compare and contrast easily identifiable information based on a criterion provided in the question or directive.	• Underline the meaning of a term given in government brochure on supplemental security income. • Locate two features of information in sports article. • Interpret instructions from an appliance warranty.
III	Level 3	Tasks in this level tend to require readers to make literal or synonymous matches between the text and information given in the task, or to make matches that require low-level inferences. Other tasks ask readers to integrate information from dense or lengthy text that contains no organizational aids	• Write a brief letter to complain about an error on a bill. • Read a news article and identify a sentence that provides interpretation of a situation. • Read lengthy article to identify two behaviors that meet a stated condition.

		such as headings. Readers may also be asked to generate a response based on information that can be easily identified in the text. Distracting information is present, but is not located near the correct information.	
IV	Level 4	These tasks require readers to perform multiple-feature matches and to integrate or synthesize information from complex or lengthy passages. More complex inferences are needed to perform successfully. Conditional information is frequently present in tasks in this level and must be taken into consideration by the reader.	• State in writing an argument made in a newspaper article. • Explain differences between two types of employee benefits. • Contrast views expressed in two editorials on technologies available to make fuel-efficient cars.
V	Level 5	Some tasks in this level require the reader to search for information in dense text which contains a number of plausible distractors. Others ask readers to make high-level inferences or use specialized background knowledge. Some tasks ask readers to contrast complex information.	• Compare approaches stated in a narrative on growing up. • Summarize two ways lawyers may challenge prospective jurors. • Interpret a phrase from a lengthy news article.

Sample 2: Four-Level Model for Prose Literacy

(Col. 1) Level	(Col. 2) Label	(Col. 3) The average respondent who scores at this level should be able to:	(Col. 4) Sample of NAAL tasks the average respondent should be able to:	(Col. 5) Relationships with societal factors
I	Below Basic	• Identify letters and numbers. • Point to orally presented words. • Read aloud words, phrases, or short sentences.	• Locate specific information on a food label. • Identify a specific word in an advertisement. • Locate an address in an advertisement.	• >50% of being poor or near poor • >50% chance of not having a U.S. high school diploma • <50% chance of voting in most recent election
II	Basic	• Locate a single piece of information in a brief written text that uses organizational aids such as headings. • Make simple inferences. • Provide appropriate answers to questions that require integrating two or more pieces of information.	• Locate one piece of information in a sports article. • Identify the country in a reading passage. • Interpret brief instructions from warranty information.	• 25-50% of being poor or near poor • 50% chance of having at least a high school diploma • 50-60% chance of voting in most recent election

III	Intermediate	• Generate a response based on information that is easily identifiable in dense or lengthy text. • Integrate information from dense or lengthy text.	• Write a brief letter to complain about an error on a bill. • Read a magazine article and identify the facts that support a specific inference.	• 10-25% of being poor or near poor • 50% chance of having at least some college • 60-70% chance of voting in recent election
IV	Advanced	• Search for information that is in dense texts. • Integrate or synthesize information from complex texts. • Perform complex inferences.	• State in writing an argument made in a newspaper article. • Explain the differences between two types of employee benefits. • Contrast views expressed in two editorials.	• <10% of being poor or near poor • 50% chance of having at least an associates college degree • 70-80% chance of voting in recent election

NOTES: NAAL background data will be analyzed to provide information about the likely relationships between literacy levels and the three societal factors included in Column 5; the current figures are for demonstration purposes only. Many of these descriptions may not generalize to English language learners (ELL). ELLs may be literate in languages other than English, and the relationships with societal factors (Col. 5) may be different for ELLs than for native English speakers. The response mode may also affect ELLs' performance, since writing skills in English may develop at a slower pace than reading or speaking skills.

Sample 3: Three-Level Model for Prose Literacy

(Col. 1) Level	(Col. 2) Label	(Col. 3) Description of label for individuals who score at this level:	(Col. 4) The average respondent who scores at this level:	(Col. 5) Sample real-world tasks the average respondent at this level should be able to do:	(Col. 6) Relationship to reading-oriented factors
I	Minimally Literate in English	Are not able to independently handle most of the tasks of daily living that require literacy skills in English.	• Is *likely* to be able to identify letters and numbers; point to words when they are presented orally; orally read individual words, phrases, or short sentences. • Is *not likely* to able to read connected text.	• Place signature in proper place on a form. • Follow a simple recipe. • Identify an address in an advertisement.	• >80% chance of never reading the newspaper • >80% chance of needing a lot of help with printed information
II	Somewhat Literate in English	Should be able to independently handle some of the tasks of daily living that require literacy skills in English.	• Is *likely* to be able to locate a single piece of information in a brief written text with organizational aids, such as headings; to integrate two or more pieces of information; and to compare and contrast easily identifiable information.	• Follow directions on a medicine bottle. • Read aloud to a child in preschool or elementary grade.	• 40-80% chance of never reading the newspaper • 40-80% chance of needing a lot of help with printed information

		• Is *not likely* to be able to integrate or synthesize information from dense text with no organizational aids.	
III	Fully Literate in English	Should be able to independently handle most of the tasks of daily living that require literacy skills in English.	• Is *likely* to be able to integrate or synthesize information from dense or lengthy text that contains no organizational aids; and to generate a response based on information that can be identified in the text.	• Read and understand *New York Times*. • Understand a proposition on a ballot.	• <10% chance of never reading the newspaper • <10% chance of needing a lot of help with printed information

NOTES: NAAL background data will be analyzed to provide information about the likely relationships between literacy levels and the reading oriented factors in Column 6; the current figures are for demonstration purposes only. These descriptions may not generalize to English language learners (ELL). ELLs may be literate in languages other than English, and their performance on real world tasks (Col. 5 and 6) may be different than for native English speakers. The response mode may also affect ELLs' performance, since writing skills in English may develop at a slower pace than reading or speaking skills.

Appendix B

Examination of the Dimensionality of NALS

CONFIRMATORY FACTOR ANALYSIS OF NALS

The National Adult Literacy Survey (NALS) used a balanced incomplete block (BIB) spiraling design for assigning items to test booklets and booklets to test takers, much like what is done for NAEP. There are 26 NALS test booklets. Each booklet contains 3 blocks of items, and test takers are given about 15 minutes per block. Each block of items appears in three different test booklets; each block appears with every other block at least once.

In 1992, all test takers were given a set of six "core" questions to familiarize them with the examination and testing procedures. The core questions were relatively easy and consisted of two questions per literacy area (prose, document, and quantitative).

NALS included some questions/tasks that had been developed for the 1985 Young Adult Literacy Survey (n = 85) and some newly developed questions/tasks (n = 81). Table B-1 shows the distribution of the tasks across the three literacy areas.

For this analysis, six booklets were selected, and the responses of the household survey participants (n = 24,944) were studied. This analysis replicated some of the procedures that had been used for prior dimensionality analyses (e.g., Rock and Yamamoto, 2001) but selected different blocks of items. Table B-2 shows the booklets and blocks of items included in the analysis along with the distribution of the tasks across the three literacy areas and the number of test takers who received each of the tasks.

Using LISREL, six confirmatory factor analyses were run in which a

TABLE B-1 Distribution of NALS Tasks Across the Three Literacy Areas

Scale	Prose	Doc.	Quant.	Total	Task Blocks
1992 New Tasks	27	26	28	81	7
1985 Old Tasks	14	56	15	85	6
Total 1992 Tasks	41	82	43	166	13

TABLE B-2 Booklets and Blocks of Items Included in the Exploratory Factor Analysis

Booklet (Blocks)	N	Prose Tasks	Doc. Tasks	Quant. Tasks	# of Tasks
1 (1, 2, 13)	957	11	22	10	43
6 (9, 7, 10)	895	12	16	12	40
8 (8, 6, 12)	920	11	25	10	46
12 (12, 5, 3)	855	11	23	8	42
15 (2, 4, 6)	925	8	32	11	51
17 (4, 9, 11)	929	11	11	17	39

three-factor model was specified. Analyses were run separately for each test booklet. Because the six core items evidenced limited variability, the analyses were repeated with these six items removed. Tables B-3 and B-4 present the results with the core items included and excluded, respectively.

Correlations between the literacy scales were quite high. When the core items were included in the analyses, correlations between the prose and document scales ranged from .89 to .94 for the six booklets, from .77 to .97 for the document and quantitative scales, and from .80 to .97 for the prose and quantitative scales. When the core items were removed from the analyses, correlations between the prose and document scales ranged from .86 to .94 for the five booklets (data matrix for Booklet 1 was not positive definite), from .75 to .95 for the document and quantitative scales, and from .79 to .97 for the prose and quantitative scales.

Model fit was evaluated using the root mean square error of approximation (RMSEA). Fit tended to decrease slightly when the core items were

TABLE B-3 LISREL Results for a Three-Factor Model When the Six Core Tasks Were Included in the Analyses

		Intercorrelations		
Booklet	RMSEA*	Prose/Doc.	Doc./Quant.	Prose/Quant.
1	.06	.92	.85	.88
6	.07	.92	.98	.91
8	.08	.89	.85	.97
12	.05	.91	.97	.95
15	.08	.94	.77	.80
17	.08	.94	.89	.88

*The RMSEA provides an estimate of the fit of the model to the data.

TABLE B-4 LISREL Results for a Three-Factor Model When the Six Core Tasks Were Excluded from the Analyses

		Intercorrelations		
Booklet	RMSEA*	Prose/Doc.	Doc./Quant.	Prose/Quant.
1	Did not converge			
6	.08	.91	.95	.90
8	.10	.87	.81	.97
12	.05	.86	.94	.97
15	.10	.94	.75	.79
17	.08	.92	.89	.87

*The RMSEA provides an estimate of the fit of the model to the data.

removed. These results suggest that a three-factor model provided acceptable fit to the data.

EXAMINATION OF THE RELATIONSHIPS BETWEEN LITERACY SCORES AND SOCIAL AND ECONOMIC CHARACTERISTICS

Another set of statistical analyses addressed questions about the relationships between the prose, document, and quantitative scores and an array of literacy outcomes. First, were the dimensions of literacy associated differentially with social and economic characteristics? For example, was prose more highly associated with outcome x than with outcome y, while quantitative was more highly associated with outcome *y* than with outcome *x*? If so, there would be empirical support for use of each separate dimension to guide adult education policy and the activities of adult educators. If not, either the assessments do not measure the dimensions independently, or there is little practical significance to the distinctions among them.

Second, were some dimensions of literacy more highly related to the social and economic characteristics than others? For example, is prose the most important type of literacy, or are document and quantitative equally important? The answer to the second question is both simpler and more important if the answer to the first is that the dimensions of literacy are not associated differentially with their correlates. That is, if one weighted combination of the prose, document, and quantitative scores adequately describes the relationship of measured literacy to the several possible correlates, the weights of prose, document, and quantitative become more instructive.

These analyses were based upon the national and state household samples from the 1992 NALS.[1] The total sample size was 25,987. The possible literacy correlates used in the analysis were similar to those used in the panel's search for break points in the distributions of literacy scores (as described in Chapter 4):

- years of school completed,
- immigration within the last five years,
- reporting at least one health impairment,
- reporting a health problem that limits work,
- reporting not reading well,
- voting within the last five years,
- being in the labor force,
- weekly earnings (log),
- reporting never reading newspaper,
- reporting reading no books,
- working in an occupation with high formal training requirements (professional, technical, managerial, nonretail sales),
- working in an occupation with low formal training requirements (skilled worker, semi-skilled worker, labor, service work, farm work),
- using Food Stamps within the past year,
- having interest income in the past year,
- reporting use of reading on the job,
- reporting help needed with written material, and
- reporting use of math on the job.

---

[1]Thus, the sample of incarcerated persons was not included.

The prose, document, and quantitative scores used were the first set of plausible values in the public release of the data (http://www.nces.ed.gov/naal/analysis/resources.asp).

The analyses were based on a multiple-indicator, multiple-cause (MIMIC) model (Hauser and Goldberger 1971; Joreskog and Goldberger 1975), estimated by maximum likelihood. Rather than estimating separate regressions, one for each of the correlates of prose, document, and quantitative, the model posits that there is one linear composite of prose, document, and quantitative—much like the predicted values in a single regression equation—and that the statistical effects of prose, document, and quantitative on the correlates are completely described by the relationships of the correlates with the composite variable. An equivalent way of describing the model is that the statistical effects of prose, document, and quantitative on each of the correlates are in the same proportion.

This model was estimated in the total household sample of NALS and in groups defined by race-ethnicity (black, Hispanic), gender, and age (16-29, 20-44, 45-59, and 60 and older). The constrained model of the effects of prose, document, and quantitative on literacy correlates never fits statistically. This is to be expected because the sample is so large that any deviation from the model, no matter how trivial in substance, is statistically reliable. However, the actual deviations of the data from the constraints of the model are neither large nor numerous.[2] Typical deviations from the model are that (a) using mathematics on the job is *more* highly correlated with quantitative literacy, (b) voting within the past five years is *less* highly correlated with document literacy, and (c) earnings are *more* highly correlated with quantitative literacy. Nevertheless the model provides a useful framework for assessing the relative importance of prose, document, and quantitative.

As shown in summary in Table B-5, estimates from the constrained model are roughly similar across all of the groups. For fully constrained models, the left hand panel shows the effects of each of the dimensions of literacy. Prose, document, and quantitative are in the score metric, and the coefficients show effects on grouped levels of educational attainment.[3] The right hand panel shows corresponding standardized coefficients. That is,

---

[2]For example, in the total sample, the model yields a likelihood ratio fit statistic of 2093.5 with 32 degrees of freedom, but the adjusted goodness of fit index (AGFI) is 0.949, a value that is commonly regarded as acceptable.

[3]The choice of educational attainment as the outcome variable is completely arbitrary. Any of the correlates could have been used because the effects of P, D, and Q on each outcome are in the same proportion in the constrained model.

TABLE B-5 Constrained Associations of Literacy Dimensions with Life Outcomes

Population	Test Score Coefficients			Standardized Coefficients		
	Prose	Doc.	Quant.	Prose	Doc.	Quant.
Total	6.907 (0.170)	1.378 (0.179)	4.766 (0.151)	0.532 (0.013)	0.107 (0.014)	0.394 (0.012)
Black	6.932 (0.167)	0.751 (0.175)	4.943 (0.139)	0.548 (0.013)	0.060 (0.014)	0.432 (0.012)
Hispanic	4.601 (0.117)	2.185 (0.135)	4.349 (0.116)	0.417 (0.011)	0.200 (0.012)	0.414 (0.011)
Female	7.404 (0.173)	1.386 (0.176)	4.131 (0.151)	0.574 (0.013)	0.110 (0.014)	0.347 (0.013)
Male	6.595 (0.171)	1.129 (0.183)	5.436 (0.153)	0.506 (0.013)	0.085 (0.014)	0.441 (0.012)
Ages 16-29	6.038 (0.148)	1.089 (0.155)	2.748 (0.132)	0.625 (0.015)	0.113 (0.016)	0.295 (0.014)
Ages 30-44	7.999 (0.172)	1.095 (0.185)	4.227 (0.156)	0.610 (0.013)	0.083 (0.014)	0.335 (0.012)
Ages 45-59	8.611 (0.187)	0.880 (0.211)	5.329 (0.173)	0.587 (0.013)	0.059 (0.014)	0.381 (0.012)
Ages 60-99	5.899 (0.151)	3.310 (0.167)	4.353 (0.128)	0.436 (0.011)	0.236 (0.012)	0.382 (0.011)

NOTE: Standard errors are in parentheses.

the variables are all expressed in standard-deviation units. All three types of literacy have statistically significant associations with the correlates. The effect of document literacy is much less than that of prose or quantitative literacy and the effect of prose literacy is slightly larger than that of quantitative literacy. Model fit deteriorates markedly, however, if the effect of either document or quantitative literacy is ignored.

Thus, while the panel notes the apparently prime importance of prose literacy, the other dimensions should not be ignored, and for some purposes it may be useful to construct a composite of the three literacy scores. It is not clear how to interpret the separate effects of the three literacy dimensions because they are so highly confounded by design in NALS and NAAL. That is, as long as the same task yields items scored on multiple dimensions, prose, document, and quantitative scores are intrinsically confounded.

REFERENCES

Hauser, R.M., and Goldberger, A.S, (1971). The treatment of unobservable variables in path analysis. In H.L. Costner (Ed.), *Sociological methodology 1971* (pp. 81-117). San Francisco: Jossey-Bass.

Joreskog, KG., and Goldberger, A.S. (1975). Estimation of a model with multiple indicators and multiple causes of a single latent variable. *Journal of the American Statistical Association, 70*, 631-639.

Appendix C

July 2004 Bookmark Standard-Setting Session with the 1992 NALS Data

As described in the body of the report, the Committee on Performance Levels for Adult Literacy convened two bookmark standard-setting sessions in 2004, one in July to gather panelists' judgments about cut scores for the 1992 National Adult Literacy Survey (NALS) and another in September to collect judgments about cut scores for the 2003 National Assessment of Adult Literacy (NAAL). This appendix details how the bookmark procedure was implemented and reports results for the July session, and Appendix D presents similar information for the September session. Following the text are the background materials, which include the agenda, participant questionnaires, tables, and figures for the July session. The appendix concludes with technical details about the data files that the committee used for the standard settings; this information is provided to assist the U.S. Department of Education and its contractors with any follow-up analyses that need to be conducted with respect to the cut scores for the performance levels.

BOOKMARK STANDARD SETTING WITH THE 1992 NALS DATA

The July 2004 session was held to obtain panelists' judgments about cut scores for the 1992 NALS and to collect their feedback about the performance-level descriptions. Several consultants assisted the committee with the standard setting, including Richard Patz, one of the original developers of the bookmark procedure.

A total of 42 panelists participated in the standard setting. Background information on the panelists was collected by means of a questionnaire (a blank questionnaire is included in Background Materials at the end of this appendix). A majority (85 percent, n = 28) had managerial responsibilities for adult education in their states or regional areas, although many panelists were instructors as well as program coordinators or directors. Most panelists worked in adult basic education (66 percent, n = 22), general educational development or GED (54 percent, n = 18), or English language instruction (51 percent, n = 17) settings. Almost half (45 percent, n = 15) reported they were very familiar with NALS prior to participating in the standard-setting activities; 42 percent (n = 14) reported that they were somewhat familiar with NALS. Only four participants (12 percent) who completed the questionnaire said they were unfamiliar with NALS prior to the standard setting.

Panelists were assigned to tables using a quasi-stratified-random procedure intended to produce groups with comparable mixtures of perspectives and experience. To accomplish this, panelists were assigned to one of nine tables after being sorted on the following criteria: (1) their primary professional responsibilities (instructor, coordinator or director, researcher), (2) the primary population of adults they worked with as indicated on their resumes, and (3) the areas in which they worked as indicated on their resumes. The sorting revealed that panelists brought the following perspectives to the standard-setting exercise: adult basic education (ABE) instructor, English for speakers of other languages (ESOL) instructor, GED instructor, program coordinator or director, or researcher. Panelists in each classification were then randomly assigned to one of the nine tables so that each group included at least one person from each of the classifications. Each table consisted of four or five panelists and had a mixture of perspectives: instructor, director, researcher, ESOL, GED, and ABE.

Once panelists were assigned to tables, each table was then randomly assigned to two of the three literacy areas (prose, document, or quantitative). The sequence in which they worked on the different literacy scales was alternated in an attempt to balance any potential order effects (see Table C-1). Three tables worked with the prose items first (referred to as Occasion 1 bookmark placements) and the document items second (referred to as Occasion 2 bookmark placements); three tables worked with the document items first (Occasion 1) and the quantitative items second (Occasion 2); and three tables worked with the quantitative items first (Occasion 1) and the prose items second (Occasion 2).

Ordered Item Booklets

For each literacy area, an ordered item booklet was prepared that rank-ordered the test questions from least to most difficult according to the responses of NALS examinees. The ordered item booklets consisted of all the available NALS tasks for a given literacy area, even though with the balanced incomplete block spiraling design used for the assessment, no individual actually responded to all test questions. The tasks were arranged in the ordered item booklets so that the question appeared first (one question per page) followed by the stimulus materials (e.g., a newspaper article, a bus schedule, a graph) and the scoring rubric. Accompanying each ordered item booklet was an item map that listed each item number and a brief description of the item. The number of items in each NALS ordered item booklet was 39 for prose literacy, 71 for document literacy, and 42 for quantitative literacy.

Training Procedures

Two training sessions were held, one just for the table leaders, the individuals assigned to be discussion facilitators for the tables of panelists, and one for all panelists. The role of the table leader was to serve as a discussion facilitator but not to dominate the discussion or to try to bring the tablemates to consensus about cut scores. Table leaders also distributed standard-setting materials to each table member, guided the discussions of the content and context characteristics that differentiated NALS test items from each other, led the discussion of the impact data for the final round of bookmark placements, and ensured that security procedures were followed. Table leader training was held the day before the standard setting to familiarize the table leaders with their roles, the NALS materials, and the agenda of activities for the standard-setting weekend. (The agenda for the July session is included in Background Materials at the end of this appendix.) Panelist training was held the morning of the standard setting. Richard Patz facilitated both training sessions and used the same training materials for both sessions. This helped ensure that the table leaders were well acquainted with the bookmark process.

The training began with an overview of NALS (skills assessed by the tasks in the three literacy areas, administrative procedures, etc.), followed by background about the committee's charge and the timing of its work. Panelists were told that the cut scores that resulted from the bookmark procedure would be the group's recommendations to the committee but that it would ultimately be up to the committee to determine the final cut scores to recommend to the Department of Education. Panelists then received instruction in the elements and procedures of the bookmark method.

Conducting the Standard Setting

Once the training session was completed, the bookmark process began by having each panelist respond to all the questions in the NALS test booklet for their assigned literacy scale. For this task, the test booklets contained the full complement of NALS items for each literacy scale, arranged in the order that test takers would see them but not ranked-ordered as in the ordered item booklets. Afterward, the table leader facilitated discussion of differences among items with respect to knowledge, skills, and competencies required and familiarized panelists with the scoring rubrics. Panelists were expected to take notes during the discussion, which would be used in making their judgments.

Panelists then received the ordered item booklets. They discussed each item and noted characteristics they thought made one item more difficult than another. The table leader distributed the performance-level descriptions.[1] Each table member then individually reviewed the performance-level descriptions, the items in the ordered item booklet, the scoring rubrics, and their notes about each item and proceeded to independently place bookmarks to represent cut points for basic, intermediate, and advanced literacy; this first bookmark placement constituted Round 1.

On the second day of standard setting, each table received a summary of the Round 1 bookmark placements made by each table member and were provided the medians of the bookmark placements (calculated for each table). Table leaders facilitated discussion among table members about their respective bookmark placements, moving from basic to intermediate to advanced literacy, without asking for consensus. Panelists were given just under two hours to deliberate about differences in their bookmark placements before independently making judgments for Round 2. Throughout the standard setting, staff members, consultants, assistants, and four committee members observed the interactions among the panelists as they discussed the characteristics of the items and their reasons for selecting their bookmark placements.

For Round 3, each table again received a summary of the Round 2 bookmark placements made by each table member as well as the medians for the table. In addition, each table received impact data, that is, the proportion of the 1992 population who would have been categorized at the below basic, basic, intermediate, or advanced literacy level based on the table's median cut points. After discussion of the variability of Round 2 judgments and the impact of their proposed cut points on the percentages of adults who would be placed into each of the four literacy groups, each panelist made his or her final judgments about bookmark placements for the basic, intermediate, and advanced literacy levels. This final set of judgments concluded Round 3.

After Round 3, panelists were asked to provide feedback about the

---

[1]The performance-level descriptions used in July are presented in Table 5-2 of the report.

performance-level descriptions by reviewing the items that fell between each of their bookmarks and editing the descriptions accordingly. That is, the items in the booklet up to, but not including, the first bookmark described the basic literacy level. Panelists reviewed these items and revised the descriptions to better fit the items that fell within this level. They were asked to do the same for the intermediate and advanced performance-level descriptions.

On the afternoon of the second day, the processes described above were repeated for the second literacy area. Round 1 was completed on the second day; Rounds 2 and 3 were completed on the third day. The standard setting concluded with a group session to obtain feedback from the panelists.

Using Different Response Probability Instructions

In conjunction with the July standard setting, the committee collected information about the impact of varying the instructions given to panelists with regard to the criteria used to judge the probability that an examinee would answer a question correctly (the response probability). The NALS results were reported in 1992 using a response probability of 80 percent, a level commonly associated with mastery tests. Some researchers have questioned the need for such a strict criterion for an assessment like NALS, for which there are no individual results, and recommend instead using a more moderate response probability level of 67 percent (e.g., Kolstad, 2001). The authors of the bookmark method also recommend a 67 percent response probability level (Mitzel et al., 2001). Because the issue of response probability had received so much attention in relation to NALS results, the committee arranged to collect data from panelists about the impact of using different (50, 67, or 80 percent) response probability values. Specifically, we were interested in evaluating (1) the extent to which panelists understand and can make sense of the concept of response probability level when making judgments about cut scores and (2) the extent to which panelists make different choices when faced with different response probability levels. Panelists were told that they would be given different instructions to use in making their judgments and that they should not discuss the instructions with each other.

As described earlier, the panelists were grouped into nine tables of four or five panelists each. Each group was given different instructions and worked with different ordered item booklets. Three tables (approximately 15 panelists) worked with booklets in which the items were ordered with a response probability of 80 percent and received instructions to use 80 percent as the likelihood that the examinee would answer an item correctly. Similarly, three tables used ordered item booklets and instructions consistent with a response probability of 67 percent, and three tables used ordered item booklets and instructions consistent with a response probability of 50 percent.

Panelists received training in small groups about their assigned response probability instructions. The additional training session gave detailed instructions to panelists on one of three difficulty levels (50, 67, or 80 percent). These specialized instructions are summarized in Background Materials at the end of this appendix. Each table of panelists used the same response probability level for the second content area as they did for the first.

Refining the Performance-Level Descriptions

The performance-level descriptions used at the July standard setting consisted of overall and subject-specific descriptors for the top four performance levels. In accord with typical bookmark procedures, concrete examples of stimulus materials (e.g., newspaper articles, almanac) or types of tasks (e.g., read a bus schedule, fill out an employment application form) had been intentionally omitted from the performance-level descriptions because including specific examples tends to overly influence panelists' judgments about the bookmark placements. Omission of specific examples allows the panelists to rely on their own expertise in making judgments.

Panelists' written comments about and edits of the performance levels were reviewed. Many panelists commented about the lack of concrete examples, saying that a few examples would have helped them. Some were concerned that NALS did not have enough items at the upper end of the spectrum for them to confidently make a distinction between intermediate and advanced categories. They also suggested edits, such as adding the modifier "consistently" to the levels higher than below basic, asked for clarification of adjectives such as "dense" versus "commonplace" text and "routine" versus "complex" arithmetic operations. In addition, the panelists raised questions about the scope of the NALS quantitative assessment and the extent to which it was intended to evaluate arithmetic skills versus functional quantitative reasoning. They also pointed out inconsistencies in the wording of the descriptions, moving from one level to the next. The committee used this feedback to rethink and reword the level descriptions in ways that better addressed the prose, document, and quantitative literacy demands suggested by the assessment items.

Revised descriptions were used for the September standard-setting session. The following types of changes were made. The introduction to the descriptions was rewritten to include the phrase, "An individual who scores at this level, independently, and in English . . . ," reflecting the nature of the NALS and NAAL as tests of literacy in English in which examinees complete the test items with minimal or no help from the interviewer or other family members or individuals. In addition, the subject-area descriptions were revised to better reflect the range of literacy skills needed for the NALS items without specifying the types of NALS items or stimuli used. Four panelists who had participated in the July standard-setting session were invited to review the revised performance-level descriptions prior to the September standard setting, and their feedback was used to further refine the descriptions.[2]

Panelists' Evaluation of the Standard Setting

At the end of the July standard-setting session, panelists were asked to complete a satisfaction questionnaire (a blank questionnaire is included in Background Materials at the end of this appendix). Almost all of the participants reported that they were either very satisfied (59 percent, n = 20) or satisfied (35 percent, n = 12) with the standard-setting training, while only two participants reported that they were not satisfied with the training they received. Almost three-quarters of the participants (74 percent, n = 25) reported being very satisfied with their table interactions and discussions; roughly a quarter (26 percent, n = 9) reported that they were satisfied with the logistical arrangements. The contributions and guidance of the table leaders were perceived as mainly very satisfactory (53 percent, n = 18) or satisfactory (32 percent, n = 11). Only two participants (6 percent) indicated that their table leaders were not satisfactory. Both of these individuals wrote on their evaluations that their table leaders were overly talkative and did not facilitate discussions among the table members. The majority of comments indicated that participants thought their table leaders were well organized, adept at facilitating discussion, and kept the table members focused on the standard setting tasks.

The organization of the standard-setting session was well received: over half of the participants (68 percent, n = 23) were very satisfied and 32 percent (n = 11) reported satisfaction with the session. Participants also reported being satisfied with their work during the standard setting—94 percent of the participants reported that they were either very satisfied (44 percent, n = 15) or satisfied (50 percent, n = 17) with the cut scores decided by their table, indicating a high level of participant confidence in both the process and the product of the standard-setting session. In addition, 85 percent (n = 29) and 12 percent (n = 4) reported that participation in the standard-setting session was very valuable or valuable to them, respectively.

---

[2]The performance-level descriptions used in September are presented in Table 5-3 of the report.

Besides giving feedback on the standard-setting session, panelists were also very helpful in suggesting ways in which the September standard-setting session would benefit from the perspective of those who had just completed the process. For example, the participants reflected a range of adult education areas, such as ABE, GED, and ESL. While the experiences and perspectives of these individuals were useful and appropriate for the standard-setting task, the July participants asked that the committee consider broadening the array of perspectives for the September gathering by including middle school or high school language arts teachers and professionals familiar with human relations, employment testing, or skills profiling. The July participants commented that the table discussions needed these additional perspectives to better conceptualize the range of literacy skills within the performance levels. In addition, the panelists commented that they would have liked to have seen a broader representation of community types (e.g., rural, suburban, urban) reflected in the table discussions because the needs of adult learners and their environments play a factor in program availability and access to various literacy materials represented in NALS. The committee agreed and solicited participation from members of these professional and geographic areas for the September standard setting.

RESULTS OF
STANDARD SETTING WITH 1992 DATA

In an effort to provide results that can be fully understood and replicated, this section provides complete results from the July standard setting reported separately by literacy area.

Prose Literacy

A complete listing of all judgments made by each panelist who reviewed the prose literacy scale at the July standard-setting session is presented in Tables C-2A, C-2B, and C-2C respectively, for Basic, Intermediate, and Advanced. The information included in the table consists of each participant's bookmark placement for each round, as well as the corresponding scale score.[3] The table number and response probability (rp) level used by each panelist are provided, as well as an indication of whether a

---

[3]The item parameters used for the July standard setting were those available in the public data file. The transformation constants used to convert theta estimates to scaled scores follow—prose: 54.973831 and 284.808948; document: 55.018198 and 279.632461; quantitative: 58.82459 and 284.991949.

given literacy scale was reviewed by the panelist first (i.e., Occasion 1) or second (i.e., Occasion 2).

Figure C-1 illustrates the bookmark placement results on the scale score metric by round and table. The top three graphs present the results for Occasion 1 (Tables 1, 4, and 7), and the bottom three graphs show the results for Occasion 2 (Tables 2, 5, and 8). The lines are differentiated by performance level to indicate panelists' cut score recommendations: the upward-facing triangles (Δ) indicate the cut score each panelist recommended for the basic literacy performance standard, the asterisks (*) represent the intermediate literacy performance standard, and the downward-facing triangles (∇) indicate the advanced literacy performance standard. The median Round 3 placement for the table for each cut score is indicated by a standalone symbol (Δ, *, or ∇) on the right-hand side of each graph. The numbers below each graph represent the scale scores corresponding to the median basic, intermediate, and advanced literacy values for the given table.

The graphs in Figure C-1 reflect panelist behavior similar to other, published, bookmark standard-setting sessions (Lewis et al., 1998). That is, as the rounds progress, the variability in bookmark placements tends to decrease, resulting in a relative convergence of bookmark location by the end of the third round. As Figure C-1 illustrates, however, convergence did not always happen, given that bookmark placement reflects individual decisions and biases.

Panelists at Tables 1 and 2 used an 80 percent response probability level (rp80); Tables 4 and 5 were assigned an rp level of 67 percent (rp67); and Tables 7 and 8 were instructed to use a 50 percent response probability level (rp50). Across Tables 1, 4, and 7, there was generally more agreement among panelists in the basic and intermediate cut scores at the conclusion of the Round 3, but the final placements of the advanced cut score varied considerably. A somewhat different pattern is seen across Tables 2, 5, and 8. Panelists at Tables 5 and 8 appeared to reach consensus regarding the cut scores for the basic performance level, Table 2 participants achieved consensus on the cut scores for the intermediate level; and Table 5 achieved consensus on the cut score for the advanced level.

Round 3 data from the two occasions were combined and descriptive statistics calculated. This information is reported by rp level for the prose literacy scale in Table C-3. Across performance levels and rp levels, the standard errors were lowest with the 67 percent response probability level.

Document Literacy

Panelists at six of the nine tables reviewed NALS items from the document literacy scale. A complete listing of all judgments made by each panelist who reviewed the document literacy scale at the July standard-setting session is presented in Tables C-4A, C-4B, and C-4C.

Figure C-2 shows the bookmark placement results on the scale score metric for each of the three Occasion 1 (top three graphs) and Occasion 2 (bottom three graphs) cut scores by round and table. Panelists at Tables 3 and 1 used rp80, panelists at Tables 6 and 4 used rp67, and panelists at Tables 9 and 7 used rp50. Final bookmark placements for Table 9 are taken from Round 2, due to a data processing in the Round 3 results for that table.

As with prose literacy, the variability of bookmark placements decreased as the rounds progressed. At all of the tables, there appeared to be more agreement with regard to the cut scores for the basic and intermediate performance levels than for the advanced level. Although some convergence in the advanced cut scores was observed as the rounds progressed, the Round 3 bookmark placements are quite disparate.

Summary statistics for the Occasion 1 and Occasion 2 combined data are presented in Table C-5. Unlike the data for prose literacy, the standard error of the mean for document literacy across rp levels and performance levels was lowest for rp50 and highest for rp80.

Quantitative Literacy

Panelists at six of the nine tables reviewed NALS items from the quantitative literacy scale. A complete listing of all judgments made by each panelist who reviewed the quantitative literacy scale at the July standard-setting session is presented in Tables C-6A, C-6B, and C-6C. The Occasion 1 (top three graphs) and Occasion 2 (bottom three graphs) bookmark locations and corresponding scale scores reported by each panelist by round and rp level are given in Figure C-3. Panelists at Table 2 and 3 used rp80, panelists at Table 5 and 6 used rp67, and panelists at Tables 8 and 9 used rp50.

Overall, panelists tended to approach consensus on the cut scores for the basic and intermediate performance levels, although this was not true for Tables 3 or 5. Considerable disparity was evident in the cut scores for the advanced level, and this variability was maintained across all three rounds.

Summary statistics on the combined Occasion 1 and Occasion 2 data are given in Table C-7. The standard error was highest in the basic and advanced performance levels for rp67 and in the intermediate performance level for rp80.

Results from Comparison of Different Response Probability Levels

The purpose of using the different response probability instructions was to evaluate the extent to which the different response probability criteria influenced panelists' judgments about bookmark placements. It would be expected that panelists using the lower probability criteria would place their bookmarks later in the ordered item booklets, and, as the probability criteria increase, the bookmarks would be placed earlier in the booklet.

Bookmark placements are converted to scaled scores in two steps. First the item response theory (IRT) model (here, the two-parameter logistic model, or 2PL) is used to calculate the theta value at which an individual would be expected to answer the item correctly at the specified probability level (see equation 3-1 in the technical note to Chapter 3). Then the theta value is transformed to a scale score value using a linear transformation equation.

Typically, the IRT model equation estimates the value of theta associated with a 50 percent probability of correctly answering an item. As described in the technical note to Chapter 3, the equation can be solved for different probabilities of a correct response. Thus, when the response probability value is 67, the theta estimate is the value at which one would have 67 percent chance of answering the item correctly. Likewise, when the response probability is 80, the theta estimates the value at which one would have an 80 percent chance of answering the item correctly. For a given item, the theta values will increase as the response probability moves from 50 to 67 to 80; the scaled scores will similarly increase.

If panelists apply the different response probabilities correctly, they should shift their bookmark placements in such a way that they compensate exactly for the differences in the way the bookmark placements are translated into thetas and to cut scores. That is, ideally, panelists should compensate for the different response criteria by placing their bookmarks earlier or later in the ordered item booklet. If they are compensating exactly for the different instructions, the theta (and scale score) associated with the bookmark placement should be identical under the three different response probability instructions, even though the bookmark locations would differ. Given these expectations for panelists' implementation of the response probability criteria, we further examined both the bookmark placements and the resulting scaled cut scores.

In the body of the report, we presented the median results for the Round 3 judgments, as it is these judgments that are typically used in determining the final cut scores. Here we examine the Round 1 judgments, as these would be expected to be more independent than those made after group discussions.

In addition, we look at the results separately by occasion. That is, as shown in the design for the standard setting (see Table C-1), the order in which the literacy areas were assigned to tables of panelists was alternated so that each literacy area was worked on during Occasion 1 by one table and Occasion 2 by another. The panelists worked with the different areas on different days of the standard setting, with time for interaction with other panelists during the evening. We decided that there might be differences in the way the panelists interpreted and implemented the rp instructions on the first occasion, before there was time for conversation with others (despite the instructions that they should not compare their instructions with each other). We therefore examined results for the first occasion and for the two occasions combined.

Examination of Bookmark Placements

To examine the extent to which panelists adjusted their judgments based on the different response probability instructions, we first examined the bookmark placements. Tables C-8, C-9, and C-10 present the Round 1 median bookmark placements for the different rp values, separated by Occasion 1 and for the two occasions combined. The median bookmark placements for intermediate and advanced on Table C-8 (prose) demonstrate the expected pattern; that is, the median bookmark placements increased as the rp criteria decreased.

Regression analyses were run to evaluate whether the response probability criteria had a statistically significant effect on bookmark placement. To increase statistical power for detecting differences, the analyses were conducted by combining all of the judgments into a single data set, which resulted in a total of 252 judgments. Because panelists each made multiple judgments, robust standard errors were calculated with clusters at the panelist level for evaluating statistical significance. A series of dummy codes were created to represent each combination of literacy area and performance level. The rp values were maintained in their original numeric form (50, 67, and 80).

This regression resulted in an R^2 of .91 (p < .001) and a negative coefficient (–.07) for the rp variable, which approached statistical significance (p = .075). This result suggests a tendency for a negative relationship between rp criteria and bookmark placement. That is, as rp criteria increased, bookmark placement tended to decrease (i.e., bookmarks were placed earlier in the ordered item book). On average, over the different literacy areas and performance levels, a coefficient of –.07 for the rp variable means that panelists using the rp80 instructions placed their bookmarks roughly two items earlier than did the panelists using the rp50 instructions. This is the general pattern that one would expect if panelists were implementing the rp instructions as intended, although the next section shows that the size of the difference is smaller than the ideal adjustment.

Follow-up analyses were run to examine the effect of the rp criteria separately for each combination of literacy area and performance level, which resulted in nine individual regressions (3 literacy areas × 3 performance levels). For these analyses, dummy codes were created to represent the rp50 and rp80 conditions. The coefficients associated with the dummy codes provide an indication of the extent to which the panelists adjusted their judgments according to the response probability instructions. If panelists were appropriately adjusting their judgments, the coefficient associated with rp50 should be positive (bookmark placed later in the ordered item booklet than when rp67 instructions were used), and the coefficient associated with rp80 should be negative (bookmark placed earlier in the ordered item booklet than when rp67 instructions were used).

Tables C-11, C-12, and C-13 present the results for Occasion 1 judgments (first column) and for Occasion 1 and 2 judgments (second column), respectively, for prose, document, and quantitative literacy. For Occasion 1, seven of the nine rp50 coefficients are positive, and five of the nine coefficients for rp80 are negative, although very few of the coefficients are statistically significant, even at the significance level of $p < .10$. Similar results are evident for Occasion 1 and 2 combined: seven of the nine rp50 coefficients are positive, and four of the nine rp80 coefficients are negative. Overall, these results show a statistically weak trend in the direction of the correct adjustment to the different rp conditions.[4]

Examination of Scaled Cut Scores

Regressions were run in a similar fashion when the dependent variable was the scaled cut score. The resulting coefficient for the rp criteria was 1.33, which was statistically significant ($p < .001$). The value of this coefficient suggests a positive relationship between the rp criteria and scaled cut scores; that is, as rp value increases, so do the cut scores. If it were the case that the panelists were insensitive to the rp instructions—making the same bookmark placements on average in all three rp conditions—a positive relationship between the rp condition and the scaled cut scores would result

---

[4]In addition, a follow-up questionnaire asked panelists what adjustments they would have made to their bookmark placements had they been instructed to use different rp criteria. For each of the three rp criteria, panelists were asked if they would have placed their bookmarks earlier or later in the ordered item booklet if they had been assigned to use a different rp instruction. Of the 37 panelists, 27 (73 percent) indicated adjustments that reflected a correct understanding of the rp instructions.

simply from the effect of the rp condition on the equations used to transform the bookmark placements into the corresponding scale scores. The preceding section shows that the panelists were not insensitive to the rp conditions, however, making adjustments that tended in the correct direction with borderline statistical significance. Given the strong relationship between the rp condition and the scaled cut scores, however, it is clear that the size of the adjustment made by the panelists falls short of the ideal.

As before, a series of follow-up regressions were run, one for each combination of literacy area and performance levels. Dummy codes were again created to represent rp50 and rp80 conditions. If panelists were appropriately adjusting their judgments to compensate for the different response probability instructions, the scale score associated with the bookmark placements should, ideally, be identical under the three conditions. For these analyses, the focus is on the statistical significance of the coefficients; that is, ideally, the coefficients associated with the two rp conditions should not be statistically significant.

Tables C-14, C-15, and C-16 present the results for Occasion 1 judgments (first column) and for Occasion 1 and 2 judgments (second column), respectively, for prose, document, and quantitative literacy. For Occasion 1, four of the nine rp50 coefficients are statistically significant, and five of the nine rp80 coefficients are statistically significant. For Occasions 1 and 2 combined, four of the nine rp50 coefficients are statistically significant, and six of the nine rp80 coefficients are statistically significant. These results suggest a strong relationship between the rp condition and the scaled cut scores.

ACKNOWLEDGMENTS

The committee wishes to acknowledge the assistance and contributions of individuals who served as panelists for the bookmark standard setting and provided valuable input on the performance-level descriptions. The complete list of participants appears at the end of Appendix D.

BACKGROUND MATERIALS

July Standard-Setting Session

Tables

Figures

Agenda
Bookmark Standard-Setting Session
for the National Adult Literacy Survey (NALS)
National Research Council, Washington, DC
July 16-19, 2004

Friday, July 16, 2004—The Day Before the Standard-Setting

1:00–2:30 PM	**Welcome, Introductions** Stuart Elliott, Judy Koenig, *NRC* Rich Patz, *Consultant to NRC* **Training for Table Leaders**
2:30–2:45 PM	**Break**
2:45–5:00 PM	**Training for Table Leaders continued**

Saturday, July 17, 2004—Day 1 of Standard-Setting

8:00–8:30 AM	**Participant registration** **Continental breakfast**
8:30–9:00 AM	**Welcome, Introductions** Stuart Elliott, Judy Koenig, *NRC* Rich Patz, *Consultant to NRC*
9:00–10:20 AM	**Training**
10:20–10:30 AM	**Break**
10:30 AM–Noon	**Training continued**
Noon–1:00 PM	**Lunch**
1:00–2:00 PM	**Round 1 (1st subject area)** Participants review all items of NALS (1st subject area) *individually*
2:00–4:00 PM	Participants at each table, *as a group,* study and discuss items in the ordered item booklets

3:30–4:15 PM	Additional training for bookmark procedure
	3:30 – 3:40 PM – Tables 7, 8, 9
	3:45 – 3:55 PM – Tables 4, 5, 6
	4:05 – 4:15 PM – Tables 1, 2, 3

4:00–5:00 PM   Bookmark placement directions given and Round 1 judgments made (judgments are made *individually*)

5:00 PM   First day adjourned

Sunday, July 18, 2004— Day 2 of Standard-Setting

7:30–8:00 AM   Continental breakfast

8:00–9:45 AM   Round 2 (1st subject area)
Tables receive data from their Round 1 judgments
Bookmark directions given for Round 2
As a group, discussion about Round 1 data
Round 2 judgments made *individually*

9:45–10:30 AM   Break

10:30 AM–Noon   Round 3 (2nd subject area)
Tables receive impact data from their Round 2 judgments
Bookmark directions given for Round 3
As a group, discussion about Round 2 data
Round 3 judgments made *individually*
Individually, each panelist suggests edits to performance-level descriptions

1:30–2:30 PM   Round 1 (2nd subject area)
Participants review all items of NALS (2nd subject area) *individually*

2:30–4:30 PM   Participants at each table, *as a group,* study and discuss items in the ordered item booklets

4:30–5:30 PM	Bookmark placement directions given and Round 1 judgments made (judgments are made *individually*)
5:30 PM	Second day adjourned

Monday, July 19, 2004—Day 3 of Standard-Setting

7:30–8:00 AM	Breakfast on one's own; please save receipts
8:00–9:45 AM	Round 2 (2nd subject area) Tables receive data from their Round 1 judgments Bookmark directions given for Round 2 bookmark placement *As a group*, discussion about Round 1 data Round 2 judgments made *individually*
9:45–10:30 AM	Break
10:30 AM–Noon	Round 3 (2nd subject area) Tables receive impact data from their Round 2 judgments placement *As a group*, discussion about Round 2 data Round 3 judgments made *individually* *Individually*, each panelist suggests edits to performance-level descriptions
Noon–1:00 PM	Group discussion
1:00 PM	Standard setting meeting adjourned
1:00–1:30 PM	Box lunch
1:30–2:30 PM	Large-group discussion on NALS performance-level descriptions

Professional and Personal Information Questionnaire
Bookmark Standard-Setting Session for NALS
July 17-19, 2004
National Research Council, Washington, DC

Please answer the following questions in order for us to better understand the characteristics of our group of standard-setting participants.

1. Do your professional responsibilities include direct or managerial responsibilities for the education of adults?

_____ No. Please characterize your professional responsibilities:

_____ Yes. For how many years have you had such responsibilities?

If you answered 'yes' to question 1, please answer the following questions:

2. I am involved in adult education in the following roles (please check all that apply):

_____ I am directly involved as an instructor
_____ I am involved in a managerial capacity

3. How would you characterize the educational setting for these adults (check all that apply):

_____ Traditional high school   _____ English language instruction
_____ Vocational high school   _____ Community college
_____ Alternative high school   _____ 4-year college or university
_____ Adult basic education   _____ Graduate or professional
         program   school
_____ GED program
_____ Other. Please describe: _____

4. How familiar were you with the National Adult Literacy Survey (a.k.a. NALS) before your participation in the standard-setting activities?

_____ Unfamiliar _____ Somewhat familiar _____ Very familiar

Please tell us about yourself (optional):

Gender: _____ Male _____ Female

Age: _____ 20-29 _____ 30-39 _____ 40-49

_____ 50-59 _____ 60-69 _____ 70+

Race/Ethnicity: _____

Specialized Response Probability Instructions Used for the July Standard-Setting Session Instructions for RP50

Items in your booklet are ordered from easiest to most difficult. The easiest items can be answered correctly with a probability of .50 (i.e., 50 percent of the time) by the most people. The most difficult items can be answered correctly with a probability of .50 by the least number of people. In careful consideration of each performance-level description and each item's difficulty, your task is to identify those skills (represented by items) that you expect persons in each literacy performance level to answer correctly with a probability of at least .50.

First, to establish your **Basic Literacy** performance level:

Place your bookmark to identify those items which you believe adults with Basic Literacy skills should be able to answer correctly at least 50 percent of the time. Items coming before your bookmark will be answered correctly at least 50 percent of the time by adults in your Basic Literacy performance level. Items coming after your bookmark may be answered correctly, but they will be answered correctly less than 50 percent of the time by some adults in your Basic Literacy performance level. The least literate adult who meets your Basic Literacy standard will be able to answer the items just before your bookmark with probability just at or above .50 (50 percent). This same adult will be able to answer the items just after your bookmark with probability just below .50.

Next, to establish your **Intermediate Literacy** performance level:

Place your bookmark to identify those items which you believe adults with Intermediate Literacy skills should be able to answer correctly at least 50 percent of the time. Items coming before your bookmark will be answered correctly at least 50 percent of the time by adults in your Intermediate Literacy performance level. Items coming after your bookmark may be answered correctly, but they will be answered correctly less than 50 percent of the time by some adults in your Intermediate Literacy performance level. The least literate adult who meets your Intermediate Literacy standard will be able to answer the items just before your bookmark with probability just at or above .50 (50 percent). This same adult will be able to answer the items just after your bookmark with probability just below .50.

Finally, to establish your **Advanced Literacy** performance level:

Place your bookmark to identify those items which you believe adults with Advanced Literacy skills should be able to answer correctly at least 50 percent of the time. Items coming before your bookmark will be answered correctly at least 50 percent of the time by adults in your Advanced Literacy performance level. Items coming after your bookmark may be answered correctly, but they will be answered correctly less than 50 percent of the time by some adults in your Advanced Literacy performance level. The least literate adult who meets your Advanced Literacy standard will be able to answer the items just before your bookmark with probability just at or above .50 (50 percent). This same adult will be able to answer the items just after your bookmark with probability just below .50.

Instructions for RP67

Items in your booklet are ordered from easiest to most difficult. The easiest items can be answered correctly with a probability of .67 (i.e., 67 percent of the time) by the most people. The most difficult items can be answered correctly with a probability of .67 by the least number of people. In careful consideration of each performance-level description and each item's difficulty, your task is to identify those skills (represented by items) that you expect persons in each literacy performance level to answer correctly with probability of at least .67.

First, to establish your **Basic Literacy** performance level:

Place your bookmark to identify those items which you believe adults with Basic Literacy skills should be able to answer correctly at least 67 percent of the time. Items coming before your bookmark will be answered correctly at least 67 percent of the time by adults in your Basic Literacy performance level. Items coming after your bookmark may be answered correctly, but they will be answered correctly less than 67 percent of the time by some adults in your Basic Literacy performance level. The least literate adult who meets your Basic Literacy standard will be able to answer the items just before your bookmark with probability just at or above .67 (67 percent). This same adult will be able to answer the items just after your bookmark with probability just below .67.

Next, to establish your **Intermediate Literacy** performance level:

Place your bookmark to identify those items which you believe adults with Intermediate Literacy skills should be able to answer correctly at least 67 percent of the time. Items coming before your bookmark will be answered correctly at least 67 percent of the time by adults in your Intermediate Literacy performance level. Items coming after your bookmark may be answered correctly, but they will be answered correctly less than 67 percent of the time by some adults in your Intermediate Literacy performance level. The least literate adult who meets your Intermediate Literacy standard will be able to answer the items just before your bookmark with probability just at or above .67 (67 percent). This same adult will be able to answer the items just after your bookmark with probability just below .67.

Finally, to establish your **Advanced Literacy** performance level:

Place your bookmark to identify those items which you believe adults with Advanced Literacy skills should be able to answer correctly at least 67 percent of the time. Items coming before your bookmark will be answered correctly at least 67 percent of the time by adults in your Advanced Literacy performance level. Items coming after your bookmark may be answered correctly, but they will be answered correctly less than 67 percent of the time by some adults in your Advanced Literacy performance level. The least literate adult who meets your Advanced Literacy standard will be able to answer the items just before your bookmark with probability just at or above .67 (67 percent). This same adult will be able to answer the items just after your bookmark with probability just below .67.

Instructions for RP80

Items in your booklet are ordered from easiest to most difficult. The easiest items can be answered correctly with a probability of .80 (i.e., 80 percent of the time) by the most people. The most difficult items can be answered correctly with a probability of .80 by the least number of people. In careful consideration of each performance-level description and each item's difficulty, your task is to identify those skills (represented by items) that you expect persons in each literacy performance level to answer correctly with probability at least .80.

First, to establish your **Basic Literacy** performance level:

Place your bookmark to identify those items which you believe adults with Basic Literacy skills should be able to answer correctly at least 80 percent of the time. Items coming before your bookmark will be answered correctly at least 80 percent of the time by adults in your Basic Literacy performance level. Items coming after your bookmark may be answered correctly, but they will be answered correctly less than 80 percent of the time by some adults in your Basic Literacy performance level. The least literate adult who meets your Basic Literacy standard will be able to answer the items just before your bookmark with probability just at or above .80 (80 percent). This same adult will be able to answer the items just after your bookmark with probability just below .80.

Next, to establish your **Intermediate Literacy** performance level:

Place your bookmark to identify those items which you believe adults with Intermediate Literacy skills should be able to answer correctly at least 80 percent of the time. Items coming before your bookmark will be answered correctly at least 80 percent of the time by adults in your Intermediate Literacy performance level. Items coming after your bookmark may be answered correctly, but they will be answered correctly less than 80 percent of the time by some adults in your Intermediate Literacy performance level. The least literate adult who meets your Intermediate Literacy standard will be able to answer the items just before your bookmark with probability just at or above .80 (80 percent). This same adult will be able to answer the items just after your bookmark with probability just below .80.

Finally, to establish your **Advanced Literacy** performance level:

Place your bookmark to identify those items which you believe adults with Advanced Literacy skills should be able to answer correctly at least 80 percent of the time. Items coming before your bookmark will be answered correctly at least 80 percent of the time by adults in your Advanced Literacy performance level. Items coming after your bookmark may be answered correctly, but they will be answered correctly less than 80 percent of the time by some adults in your Advanced Literacy performance level. The least literate adult who meets your Advanced Literacy standard will be able to answer the items just before your bookmark with probability just at or above .80 (80 percent). This same adult will be able to answer the items just after your bookmark with probability just below .80.

Satisfaction Questionnaire
Bookmark Standard-Setting Session
for the National Adult Literacy Survey (NALS)
National Research Council, Washington, DC
July 17-19, 2004

Thank you for participating in the standard-setting meeting for the National Adult Literacy Survey (NALS). In order to help improve future standard-setting meetings, please complete the following questionnaire about your experiences this weekend.

1. How satisfied were you with the advance information given to you about the standard-setting meeting (e.g., memos with information about the hotel, location of the meeting)?

Very Satisfied   Satisfied   Not Satisfied

Please explain:

2. How satisfied were you with the food provided during the meeting?

Very Satisfied   Satisfied   Not Satisfied

Please explain:

3. How satisfied were you with your hotel accommodations?

Very Satisfied   Satisfied   Not Satisfied

Please explain:

4. How satisfied were you with the training you received on Saturday morning?

Very Satisfied   Satisfied   Not Satisfied

Please explain:

5. How satisfied were you with the room assignments and table discussions?

Very Satisfied   Satisfied   Not Satisfied

Please explain:

6. How satisfied were you with the contributions and guidance of the table leaders?

Very Satisfied   Satisfied   Not Satisfied

Please explain:

7. How satisfied were you with the organization of the standard-setting meeting?

Very Satisfied   Satisfied   Not Satisfied

Please explain:

8. How satisfied were you with the cut scores decided by your table?

Very Satisfied   Satisfied   Not Satisfied

Please explain:

9. How valuable do you feel your contribution was to the outcomes of the standard-setting meeting?

Very Satisfied   Satisfied   Not Satisfied

Please explain:

10. How valuable was your participation in the standard-setting meeting to you?

Very Satisfied   Satisfied   Not Satisfied

Please explain:

Please feel free to add additional suggestions or comments about the standard-setting meeting.

Thank you!

TABLE C-1 Design of the Bookmark Standard Setting with NALS Data, July 2004

	RP 80			RP 67			RP 50		
	Table 1	Table 2	Table 3	Table 4	Table 5	Table 6	Table 7	Table 8	Table 9
First Literacy Area:	Prose	Quant.	Doc.	Prose	Quant.	Doc.	Prose	Quant.	Doc.
Second Literacy Area:	Doc.	Prose	Quant.	Doc.	Prose	Quant.	Doc.	Prose	Quant.

TABLE C-2A Participants' Bookmark Placements and Associated Cut Scores for Basic, Prose Literacy, July 2004

Response Participant[a]	Table	Probability	Occasion	Round 1 BK[b]	Round 1 SS[c]	Round 2 BK	Round 2 SS	Round 3 BK	Round 3 SS
1.1	1	0.80	1	11	262	11	262	6	226
1.2	1	0.80	1	14	276	11	262	10	256
1.3	1	0.80	1	6	226	6	226	6	226
1.4	1	0.80	1	8	250	8	250	6	226
2.1	2	0.80	2	6	226	6	226	6	226
2.2	2	0.80	2	11	262	11	262	12	263
2.3	2	0.80	2	8	250	8	250	8	250
2.4	2	0.80	2	6	226	6	226	6	226
2.5	2	0.80	2	3	208	5	224	6	226
4.1	4	0.67	1	5	197	6	211	5	197
4.2	4	0.67	1	5	197	6	211	5	197
4.3	4	0.67	1	7	225	7	225	6	211
4.4	4	0.67	1	10	241	7	225	5	197
4.5	4	0.67	1	11	242	7	225	5	197
5.1	5	0.67	2	5	197	6	211	6	211

5.2	5	0.67	2	7	225	6	211	6	211
5.3	5	0.67	2	5	197	6	211	6	211
5.4	5	0.67	2	7	225	6	211	6	211
5.5	5	0.67	2	7	225	6	211	6	211
7.1	7	0.50	1	5	171	10	217	10	217
7.2	7	0.50	1	10	217	10	217	10	217
7.3	7	0.50	1	10	217	10	217	10	217
7.4	7	0.50	1	12	230	12	230	12	230
8.1	8	0.50	2	6	194	6	194	6	194
8.2	8	0.50	2	6	194	6	194	6	194
8.3	8	0.50	2	7	195	6	194	6	194
8.4	8	0.50	2	5	171	6	194		
8.5	8	0.50	2	6	194	6	194	6	194

Missing data: Participant 8.4 left after Round 1 of Occasion 2 due to a schedule conflict.

[a]The first participant at each table (i.e. 1.1, 2.1, ..., 9.1) is the table leader.

[b]Denotes the item number in the ordered item booklet on which the bookmark was placed (see pg. 112 for explanation of bookmark placements).

[c]Denotes the cut score associated with the bookmark placement. It is the RP location for the last item before the bookmark placement, converted to a scale score.

TABLE C-2B Participants' Bookmark Placements and Associated Cut Scores for Intermediate, Prose Literacy, July 2004

Response				Round 1		Round 2		Round 3	
Participant[a]	Table	Probability	Occasion	BK[b]	SS[c]	BK	SS	BK	SS
1.1	1	0.80	1	20	289	23	316	23	316
1.2	1	0.80	1	23	316	23	316	22	314
1.3	1	0.80	1	23	316	23	316	23	316
1.4	1	0.80	1	18	287	23	316	24	317
2.1	2	0.80	2	20	289	20	289	20	289
2.2	2	0.80	2	20	289	20	289	20	289
2.3	2	0.80	2	22	314	20	289	20	289
2.4	2	0.80	2	20	289	20	289	20	289
2.5	2	0.80	2	15	277	15	277	20	289
4.1	4	0.67	1	20	270	24	300	20	270
4.2	4	0.67	1	24	300	24	300	24	300
4.3	4	0.67	1	20	270	24	300	20	270
4.4	4	0.67	1	24	300	24	300	20	270
4.5	4	0.67	1	23	297	24	300	20	270

Participant									
5.1	5	0.67	2	15	260	16	263	16	263
5.2	5	0.67	2	29	325	29	325	16	263
5.3	5	0.67	2	7	225	16	263	16	263
5.4	5	0.67	2	20	270	16	263	16	263
5.5	5	0.67	2	24	300	24	300	24	300
7.1	7	0.50	1	20	251	23	278	23	276
7.2	7	0.50	1	24	278	24	278	24	278
7.3	7	0.50	1	23	276	23	276	23	276
7.4	7	0.50	1	29	294	25	281	25	281
8.1	8	0.50	2	20	251	20	251	20	251
8.2	8	0.50	2	15	233	15	233	15	233
8.3	8	0.50	2	31	301	26	285	26	285
8.4	8	0.50	2	23	276				
8.5	8	0.50	2	23	276	26	285	26	285

Missing data: Participant 8.4 left after Round 1 of Occasion 2 due to a schedule conflict.

[a]The first participant at each table (i.e. 1.1, 2.1, ..., 9.1) is the table leader.

[b]Denotes the item number in the ordered item booklet on which the bookmark was placed (see pg. 112 for explanation of bookmark placements).

[c]Denotes the cut score associated with the bookmark placement. It is the RP location for the last item before the bookmark placement, converted to a scale score.

TABLE C-2C Participants' Bookmark Placements and Associated Cut Scores for Advanced, Prose Literacy, July 2004

Response Participant[a]	Table	Probability	Occasion	Round 1 BK[b]	Round 1 SS[c]	Round 2 BK	Round 2 SS	Round 3 BK	Round 3 SS
1.1	1	0.80	1	34	371	34	371	30	349
1.2	1	0.80	1	33	363	33	363	32	362
1.3	1	0.80	1	39	433	39	433	39	433
1.4	1	0.80	1	26	329	34	371	32	362
2.1	2	0.80	2	24	317	24	317	27	333
2.2	2	0.80	2	32	362	30	349	32	362
2.3	2	0.80	2	37	410	32	362	32	362
2.4	2	0.80	2	25	324	24	317	27	333
2.5	2	0.80	2	25	324	24	317	24	317
4.1	4	0.67	1	38	401	39	407	34	343
4.2	4	0.67	1	34	343	38	401	34	343
4.3	4	0.67	1	30	329	38	401	24	300
4.4	4	0.67	1	40	424	40	424	37	391
4.5	4	0.67	1	36	359	37	391	36	359

Participant	Table[a]			Item[b]	Score[c]	Item[b]	Score[c]	Item[b]	Score[c]
5.1	5	2	0.67	33	336	33	336	33	336
5.2	5	2	0.67	40	424	40	424	33	336
5.3	5	2	0.67	20	270	33	336	33	336
5.4	5	2	0.67	37	391	40	424	33	336
5.5	5	2	0.67	31	333	33	336	33	336
7.1	7	1	0.50	37	370	37	370	37	370
7.2	7	1	0.50	39	378	40	380	40	380
7.3	7	1	0.50	40	380	40	380	40	380
7.4	7	1	0.50	36	333	36	333	36	333
8.1	8	2	0.50	31	301	31	301	31	301
8.2	8	2	0.50	30	300	30	300	30	300
8.3	8	2	0.50	36	333	36	333	36	333
8.4	8	2	0.50	32	305				
8.5	8	2	0.50	38	378	37	370	37	370

Missing data: Participant 8.4 left after Round 1 of Occasion 2 due to a schedule conflict.

[a] The first participant at each table (i.e. 1.1, 2.1, ..., 9.1) is the table leader.

[b] Denotes the item number in the ordered item booklet on which the bookmark was placed (see pg. 112 for explanation of bookmark placements).

[c] Denotes the cut score associated with the bookmark placement. It is the RP location for the last item before the bookmark placement, converted to a scale score.

TABLE C-3 Summary Statistics for the Round 3 Judgments for Prose by Response Probability (RP) Level, July 2004

RP level	Basic			Intermediate			Advanced		
	0.50	0.67	0.80	0.50	0.67	0.80	0.50	0.67	0.80
Bookmark:									
Median	8.00	6.00	6.00	23.50	20.00	20.00	36.50	33.00	32.00
Mean	8.25	5.60	7.33	22.75	19.20	21.33	35.88	33.00	30.56
Std. Dev.	2.49	0.52	2.24	3.69	3.16	1.66	3.68	3.46	4.30
Cut Score:									
Median	205.61	210.58	226.09	277.1	269.52	289.34	351.6	336.25	362.36
Mean	207.21	205.25	236.24	270.88	273.01	301.03	345.76	341.59	357.25
Std. Dev.	14.33	6.88	15.53	18.70	14.28	13.89	33.73	22.66	32.98
Std. Error	5.07	2.18	5.18	6.61	4.52	4.63	11.93	7.17	10.99
N	8	10	9	8	10	9	8	10	9

TABLE C-4 FOLLOWS

TABLE C-4A Participants' Bookmark Placements and Associated Cut Scores for Basic, Document Literacy, July 2004

Response Participant[a]	Table	Probability	Occasion	Round 1 BK[b]	Round 1 SS[c]	Round 2 BK	Round 2 SS	Round 3 BK	Round 3 SS
1.1	1	0.80	2	12	211	12	211	12	211
1.2	1	0.80	2	15	217	14	215	14	215
1.3	1	0.80	2	12	211	12	211	12	211
1.4	1	0.80	2	10	202	10	202	10	202
3.1	3	0.80	1	21	233	18	224	18	224
3.2	3	0.80	1	18	224	18	224	18	224
3.3	3	0.80	1	12	211	12	211	12	211
3.4	3	0.80	1	12	211	18	224	18	224
4.1	4	0.67	2	10	185	10	185	10	185
4.2	4	0.67	2	10	185	10	185	10	185
4.3	4	0.67	2	13	190	10	185	10	185
4.4	4	0.67	2	10	185	10	185	10	185
4.5	4	0.67	2	10	185	10	185	10	185

6.1	6	0.67	1	15	193	17	202	17	202
6.2	6	0.67	1	17	202	17	202	17	202
6.3	6	0.67	1	11	187	15	193	15	193
6.4	6	0.67	1	24	215	19	206	19	206
6.5	6	0.67	1	14	191	15	193	15	193
7.1	7	0.50	2	11	159	22	191	22	191
7.2	7	0.50	2	23	184	22	191	22	191
7.3	7	0.50	2	18	176				
7.4	7	0.50	2	18	176	22	191	22	191
9.1	9	0.50	1	23	184	23	184		
9.2	9	0.50	1	15	173	20	182		
9.3	9	0.50	1	23	184	23	184		
9.4	9	0.50	1	8	157	23	184		
9.5	9	0.50	1	20	182	23	184		

Missing data: Participant 7.3 left after Round 1 of Occasion 2 due to a schedule conflict. Table 9 Round 3 data are missing due to a processing error.

[a]The first participant of each table (i.e. 1.1, 2.1, ..., 9.1) is the table leader.

[b]Denotes the item number in the ordered item booklet on which the bookmark was placed (see pg. 112 for explanation of bookmark placements).

[c]Denotes the cut score associated with the bookmark placement. It is the RP location for the last item before the bookmark placement, converted to a scale score.

TABLE C-4B Participants' Bookmark Placements and Associated Cut Scores for Intermediate, Document Literacy, July 2004

Response Participant[a]	Table	Probability	Occasion	Round 1		Round 2		Round 3	
				BK[b]	SS[c]	BK	SS	BK	SS
1.1	1	0.80	2	40	257	40	257	40	257
1.2	1	0.80	2	27	240	30	244	30	244
1.3	1	0.80	2	40	257	40	257	40	257
1.4	1	0.80	2	42	260	42	260	42	260
3.1	3	0.80	1	48	276	48	276	48	276
3.2	3	0.80	1	43	261	47	275	45	267
3.3	3	0.80	1	48	276	48	276	48	276
3.4	3	0.80	1	48	276	48	276	48	276
4.1	4	0.67	2	47	247	47	247	47	247
4.2	4	0.67	2	56	271	49	253	49	253
4.3	4	0.67	2	34	226	51	255	51	255
4.4	4	0.67	2	34	226	47	247	47	247

Participant	[a]			Item[b]	Cut score[c]	Item[b]	Cut score[c]	Item[b]	Cut score[c]
4.5	4	0.67	2	38	233	47	247	47	247
6.1	6	0.67	1	48	252	56	271	56	271
6.2	6	0.67	1	56	271	56	271	56	271
6.3	6	0.67	1	38	233	51	255	51	255
6.4	6	0.67	1	58	284	56	271	56	271
6.5	6	0.67	2	44	242	44	242	51	255
7.1	7	0.50	2	46	222	53	226	53	226
7.2	7	0.50	2	44	216	44	216	44	216
7.3	7	0.50	2	53	226				
7.4	7	0.50	2	42	221	46	222	46	222
9.1	9	0.50	1	55	211	55	211		
9.2	9	0.50	1	42	221	53	226		
9.3	9	0.50	1	46	222	55	211		
9.4	9	0.50	1	32	199	55	211		
9.5	9	0.50	1	47	227	55	211		

Missing data: Participant 7.3 left after Round 1 of Occasion 2 due to a schedule conflict. Table 9 Round 3 data are missing due to a processing error.

[a] The first participant of each table (i.e. 1.1, 2.1, ..., 9.1) is the table leader.

[b] Denotes the item number in the ordered item booklet on which the bookmark was placed (see pg. 112 for explanation of bookmark placements).

[c] Denotes the cut score associated with the bookmark placement. It is the RP location for the last item before the bookmark placement, converted to a scale score.

TABLE C-4C Participants' Bookmark Placements and Associated Cut Scores for Advanced, Document Literacy, July 2004

Response Participant[a]	Table	Probability	Occasion	Round 1 BK[b]	Round 1 SS[c]	Round 2 BK	Round 2 SS	Round 3 BK	Round 3 SS
1.1	1	0.80	2	58	310	58	310	58	310
1.2	1	0.80	2	41	259	48	276	48	276
1.3	1	0.80	2	58	310	58	310	58	310
1.4	1	0.80	2	64	330	64	330	64	330
3.1	3	0.80	1	68	378	70	386	70	386
3.2	3	0.80	1	64	330	64	330	64	330
3.3	3	0.80	1	71	388	69	380	69	380
3.4	3	0.80	1	66	343	66	343	66	343
4.1	4	0.67	2	65	296	65	296	66	324
4.2	4	0.67	2	69	324	69	324	69	324
4.3	4	0.67	2	57	279	69	324	69	324
4.4	4	0.67	2	65	296	65	296	65	296
4.5	4	0.67	2	58	284	69	324	69	324

6.1	6	0.67	1	73	378	73	378	73	378
6.2	6	0.67	1	73	378	73	378	73	378
6.3	6	0.67	1	71	359	72	363	72	363
6.4	6	0.67	1	72	363	72	363	72	363
6.5	6	0.67	1	73	378	73	378	73	378
7.1	7	0.50	2	65	279	67	286	67	286
7.2	7	0.50	2	69	327	68	305	68	305
7.3	7	0.50	2	72	358				
7.4	7	0.50	2	67	286	65	279	65	279
9.1	9	0.50	1	70	339	70	339		
9.2	9	0.50	1	65	279	68	305		
9.3	9	0.50	1	72	358	70	339		
9.4	9	0.50	1	55	211	68	305		
9.5	9	0.50	1	65	279	68	305		

Missing data: Participant 7.3 left after Round 1 of Occasion 2 due to a schedule conflict. Table 9 Round 3 data are missing due to a processing error.

[a]The first participant of each table (i.e. 1.1, 2.1, ..., 9.1) is the table leader.

[b]Denotes the item number in the ordered item booklet on which the bookmark was placed (see pg. 112 for explanation of bookmark placements).

[c]Denotes the cut score associated with the bookmark placement. It is the RP location for the last item before the bookmark placement, converted to a scale score.

TABLE C-5 Summary Statistics for the Round 3 Judgments for Document Literacy by Response Probability (RP) Level, July 2004

RP Level	Basic			Intermediate			Advanced		
	0.50	0.67	0.80	0.50	0.67	0.80	0.50	0.67	0.80
Bookmark:									
Median	8.00	6.00	6.00	23.50	20.00	20.00	36.50	33.00	32.00
Mean	22.25	13.30	14.25	52.00	51.10	42.63	68.00	70.40	62.13
Std. Dev.	1.04	3.65	3.28	4.44	3.75	6.16	1.60	2.63	7.22
Cut Score:									
Median	190.17	188.96	213.00	232.80	254.96	263.50	304.89	343.38	330.00
Mean	189.49	192.28	215.25	230.16	257.30	264.14	306.68	345.05	333.13
Std. Dev.	2.55	8.54	8.10	5.10	10.27	11.68	21.30	29.70	36.73
Std. Error	0.90	2.70	2.86	1.80	3.25	4.13	7.53	9.39	12.99
N	8	10	8	8	10	8	8	10	8

TABLE C-6 FOLLOWS

TABLE C-6A Participants' Bookmark Placements and Associated Cut Scores for Basic, Quantitative Literacy, July 2004

Response Participant[a]	Table	Probability	Occasion	Round 1 BK[b]	Round 1 SS[c]	Round 2 BK	Round 2 SS	Round 3 BK	Round 3 SS
2.1	2	0.80	1	14	283	18	300	16	287
2.2	2	0.80	1	18	300	18	300	16	287
2.3	2	0.80	1	13	282	15	284	15	284
2.4	2	0.80	1	16	287	18	300	16	287
2.5	2	0.80	1	17	295	14	283	14	283
3.1	3	0.80	2	8	277	14	283	8	277
3.2	3	0.80	2	14	283	14	283	6	251
3.3	3	0.80	2	6	251	8	277	8	277
3.4	3	0.80	2	8	277	8	277	8	277
5.1	5	0.67	1	5	216	5	216	5	216
5.2	5	0.67	1	6	217	6	217	6	217
5.3	5	0.67	1	5	216	5	216	5	216
5.4	5	0.67	1	1		5	216	5	216
5.5	5	0.67	1	4	211	4	211	4	211
6.1	6	0.67	2	16	272	16	272	16	272

6.2	6	0.67	2	15	271	15	271	15	271
6.3	6	0.67	2	15	271	15	271	15	271
6.4	6	0.67	2	15	271	15	271	15	271
6.5	6	0.67	2	15	271	15	271	15	271
8.1	8	0.50	1	7	222	11	235	11	235
8.2	8	0.50	1	11	235	11	235	8	225
8.3	8	0.50	1	15	258	11	235	11	235
8.4	8	0.50	1	7	222	8	225	8	225
8.5	8	0.50	1	14	250	11	235	11	235
9.1	9	0.50	2	11	235	15	258	15	258
9.2	9	0.50	2	11	235				
9.3	9	0.50	2	15	258	15	258	15	258
9.4	9	0.50	2	6	185	14	250	14	250
9.5	9	0.50	2	14	250	14	250	14	250

Missing data: Scale score cutpoint is undefined for bookmark placed on the first item (Participant 5.4, Round 1); Participant 9.2 left after Round 1 of Occasion 2 due to a schedule conflict.

[a]The first participant of each table (i.e., 1.1, 2.1, ..., 9.1) is the table leader.

[b]Denotes the item number in the ordered item booklet on which the bookmark was placed (see pg. 112 for explanation of bookmark placements).

[c]Denotes the cut score associated with the bookmark placement. It is the RP location for the last item before the bookmark placement, converted to a scale score.

TABLE C-6B Participants' Bookmark Placements and Associated Cut Scores for Intermediate, Quantitative Literacy, July 2004

Response					Round 1		Round 2		Round 3	
Participant[a]	Table	Probability	Occasion		BK[b]	SS[c]	BK	SS	BK	SS
2.1	2	0.80	1		30	349	36	369	30	349
2.2	2	0.80	1		36	369	36	369	32	355
2.3	2	0.80	1		27	342	30	349	30	349
2.4	2	0.80	1		21	322	36	369	30	349
2.5	2	0.80	1		32	355	27	342	27	342
3.1	3	0.80	2		22	326	29	346	22	326
3.2	3	0.80	2		26	334	29	346	20	309
3.3	3	0.80	2		30	349	30	349	30	349
3.4	3	0.80	2		16	287	22	326	16	287
5.1	5	0.67	1		25	307	18	276	18	276
5.2	5	0.67	1		14	271	25	307	25	307
5.3	5	0.67	1		14	271	17	272	17	272
5.4	5	0.67	1		14	271	18	276	18	276
5.5	5	0.67	1		18	276	18	276	18	276
6.1	6	0.67	2		25	307	25	307	25	307
6.2	6	0.67	2		37	347	27	311	27	311

6.3	6	0.67	2	25	307	25	307	25	307
6.4	6	0.67	2	27	311	26	309	27	311
6.5	6	0.67	2	34	338	26	309	26	309
8.1	8	0.50	1	21	263	30	299	30	299
8.2	8	0.50	1	26	284	30	299	26	284
8.3	8	0.50	1	34	310	30	299	30	299
8.4	8	0.50	1	27	288	30	299	29	298
8.5	8	0.50	2	29	298	29	298	29	298
9.1	9	0.50	2	28	289	25	282	25	282
9.2	9	0.50	2	25	282				
9.3	9	0.50	2	34	310	25	282	25	282
9.4	9	0.50	2	25	282	25	282	25	282
9.5	9	0.50	2	25	282	25	282	25	282

Missing data: Participant 9.2 left after Round 1 of Occasion 2 due to a schedule conflict.

[a]The first participant of each table (i.e., 1.1, 2.1, ..., 9.1) is the table leader.

[b]Denotes the item number in the ordered item booklet on which the bookmark was placed (see pg. 112 for explanation of bookmark placements).

[c]Denotes the cut score associated with the bookmark placement. It is the RP location for the last item before the bookmark placement, converted to a scale score.

TABLE C-6C Participants' Bookmark Placements and Associated Cut Scores for Advanced, Quantitative Literacy, July 2004

Participant[a]	Table	Probability	Occasion	Round 1 BK[b]	Round 1 SS[c]	Round 2 BK	Round 2 SS	Round 3 BK	Round 3 SS
2.1	2	0.80	1	39	389	39	389	39	389
2.2	2	0.80	1	41	421	41	421	41	421
2.3	2	0.80	1	43	436	41	421	41	421
2.4	2	0.80	1	39	389	39	389	39	389
2.5	2	0.80	1	42	433	38	382	38	382
3.1	3	0.80	2	39	389	38	382	35	366
3.2	3	0.80	2	35	366	35	366	30	349
3.3	3	0.80	2	42	433	39	389	39	389
3.4	3	0.80	2	31	351	39	389	31	351
5.1	5	0.67	1	41	387	37	347	37	347
5.2	5	0.67	1	37	347	37	347	37	347
5.3	5	0.67	1	25	307	25	307	25	307
5.4	5	0.67	1	30	324	37	347	37	347
5.5	5	0.67	1	32	329	32	329	32	329
6.1	6	0.67	2	43	410	43	410	43	410

6.2	6	2	0.67	43	410	43	410	43	410
6.3	6	2	0.67	39	356	39	356	39	356
6.4	6	2	0.67	43	410	43	410	43	410
6.5	6	2	0.67	43	410	43	410	43	410
8.1	8	1	0.50	39	323	40	351	40	351
8.2	8	1	0.50	40	351	40	351	37	321
8.3	8	1	0.50	43	384	43	384	43	384
8.4	8	1	0.50	35	316	41	359	37	321
8.5	8	1	0.50	41	359	41	359	41	359
9.1	9	2	0.50	39	323	39	323	39	323
9.2	9	2	0.50	37	321				
9.3	9	2	0.50	42	360	40	351	40	351
9.4	9	2	0.50	38	322	39	323	39	323
9.5	9	2	0.50	39	323	39	323	39	323

Missing data: Participant 9.2 left after Round 1 of Occasion 2 due to a schedule conflict.

[a]The first participant of each table (i.e., 1.1, 2.1, ..., 9.1) is the table leader.

[b]Denotes the item number in the ordered item booklet on which the bookmark was placed (see pg. 112 for explanation of bookmark placements).

[c]Denotes the cut score associated with the bookmark placement. It is the RP location for the last item before the bookmark placement, converted to a scale score.

TABLE C-7 Summary Statistics for the Round 3 Judgments for Quantitative Literacy by Response Probability (RP) Level, July 2004

RP level	Basic			Intermediate			Advanced		
	0.50	0.67	0.80	0.50	0.67	0.80	0.50	0.67	0.80
Bookmark:									
Median	11.00	10.50	14.00	26.00	25.00	30.00	39.00	38.00	39.00
Mean	11.89	10.10	11.89	27.11	22.60	26.33	39.44	37.90	37.00
Std. Dev.	2.76	5.40	4.26	2.32	4.25	5.61	1.88	5.86	4.09
Cut Score:									
Median	235.05	244.34	283.36	283.52	307.18	348.64	323.45	351.40	389.15
Mean	241.14	243.59	279.13	289.43	295.22	334.9	339.92	367.46	384.23
Std. Dev.	12.85	29.51	11.45	8.66	17.64	23.10	22.51	39.28	26.33
Std. Error	4.28	9.33	3.82	2.89	5.58	7.70	7.50	12.42	8.78
N	9	10	9	9	10	9	9	10	9

TABLE C-8 Summary of Round 1 Bookmark Placements and Cut Scores for Prose Literacy by Response Probability (RP) Level and Occasion, July 2004

	Basic			Intermediate			Advanced		
RP Level	0.80	0.67	0.50	0.80	0.67	0.50	0.80	0.67	0.50
Occasion 1									
Median bookmark placement	9.5	7.0	10.0	21.5	23.0	23.5	33.5	36.0	38.0
Median cut score	256.0	225.0	217.0	302.5	297.0	277.0	367.0	359.0	374.0
N	4	5	4	4	5	4	4	5	4
Occasions 1 and 2									
Median bookmark placement	8.0	7.0	6.0	20.0	21.5	23.0	32.0	35.0	36.0
Median cut score	250.0	225.0	194.0	289.0	283.0	276.0	362.0	351.0	333.0
N	9	10	9	9	10	9	9	10	9

TABLE C-9 Summary of Round 1 Bookmark Placements and Cut Scores for Document Literacy by Response Probability (RP) Level and Occasion, July 2004

	Basic			Intermediate			Advanced		
RP Level	0.80	0.67	0.50	0.80	0.67	0.50	0.80	0.67	0.50
Occasion 1									
Median bookmark placement	15.0	15.0	20.0	48.0	48.0	46.0	67.0	73.0	65.0
Median cut score	217.5	193.0	182.0	276.0	252.0	221.0	360.5	378.0	279.0
N	4	5	5	4	5	5	4	5	5
Occasions 1 and 2									
Median bookmark placement	12.0	12.0	18.0	42.5	45.5	46.0	64.0	70.0	67.0
Median cut score	211.0	188.5	176.0	260.5	244.5	221.0	330.0	341.5	286.0
N	8	10	9	8	10	9	8	10	9

TABLE C-10 Summary of Round 1 Bookmark Placements and Cut Scores for Quantitative Literacy by Response Probability (RP) Level and Occasion, July 2004

	Basic			Intermediate			Advanced		
RP Level	0.80	0.67	0.50	0.80	0.67	0.50	0.80	0.67	0.50
Occasion 1									
Median bookmark placement	19.0	5.0	11.0	30.0	14.0	27.0	41.0	32.0	40.0
Median cut score	287.0	216.0	235.0	349.0	271.0	288.0	421.0	329.0	351.0
N	5	4	5	5	5	5	5	5	5
Occasions 1 and 2									
Median bookmark placement	14.0	10.5	11.0	27.0	25.0	26.5	39.0	40.0	39.0
Median cut score	283.0	271.0	235.0	342.0	307.0	286.0	389.0	371.5	323.0
N	9	9	10	9	10	10	9	10	10

TABLE C-11 Regression Results for Bookmark Placements for Prose Literacy, July 2004

	Occasion 1	Occasions 1 and 2
Number of Panelists	13	28
Basic		
RP50	1.65^a $(2.06)^b$	0.54 (1.25)
RP80	2.15 (2.06)	1.21 (1.25)
Constant	7.60 (1.37)	6.90 (0.86)
R^2	0.11	0.04
Intermediate		
RP50	1.80 (1.86)	2.51 (2.18)
RP80	−1.20 (1.86)	−0.49 (2.18)
Constant	22.2 (1.24)	20.60 (1.50)
R^2	0.19	0.07
Advanced		
RP50	2.40 (2.64)	1.54 (2.41)
RP80	−2.6 (2.64)	−3.34 (2.41)
Constant	35.6 (1.76)	33.9 (1.66)
R^2	0.24	0.14

[a]Regression coefficient.
[b]Standard error.

TABLE C-12 Regression Results for Bookmark Placements for Document Literacy, July 2004

	Occasion 1	Occasions 1 and 2
Number of Panelists	13	27
Basic		
RP50	1.60^a $(3.40)^b$	4.27^* (2.13)
RP80	−0.45 (3.61)	0.60 (2.20)
Constant	16.20 (2.41)	13.40 (1.46)
R^2	0.03	0.16
Intermediate		
RP50	−4.40 (4.58)	−0.08 (3.59)
RP80	−2.05 (4.86)	−3.30 (3.70)
Constant	48.8 (3.23)	45.3 (2.47)
R^2	0.08	0.04
Advanced		
RP50	$−7.0^*$ (2.72)	−0.93 (3.20)
RP80	−5.15 (2.89)	$−6.35^*$ (3.31)
Constant	72.4 (1.92)	67.6 (2.20)
R^2	0.39	0.15

[a]Regression coefficient.
[b]Standard error.
$^*p < .10$.

TABLE C-13 Regression Results for Bookmark Placements for Quantitative Literacy, July 2004

Number of Panelists	Occasion 1	Occasions 1 and 2
	14	29
Basic		
RP50	6.60^{a**} $(2.10)^{b}$	1.40 (1.72)
RP80	11.40** (2.16)	2.97 (1.72)
Constant	4.20 (1.49)	9.70 (1.22)
R^2	0.79	0.07
Intermediate		
RP50	10.40* (2.87)	4.1 (3.20)
RP80	12.20** (2.95)	3.37 (3.20)
Constant	17.00 (2.03)	23.3 (2.27)
R^2	0.58	0.08
Advanced		
RP50	6.60* (2.05)	1.70 (2.59)
RP80	7.80* (2.11)	1.40 (2.59)
Constant	33.00 (1.45)	37.6 (1.83)
R^2	0.46	0.03

[a]Regression coefficient
[b]Standard error
*p < .10
**p < .01

TABLE C-14 Regression Results for Cut Scores for Prose Literacy, July 2004

	Occasion 1	Occasions 1 and 2
Number of Panelists	13	28
Basic		
RP50	-11.65^a $(16.37)^b$	$-18.99*$ (8.91)
RP80	$33.10*$ (14.62)	$25.70*$ (9.46)
Constant	220.40 (10.22)	217.10 (5.85)
R^2	0.45	0.47
Intermediate		
RP50	-12.65 (11.39)	-11.03 (11.54)
RP80	14.60 (10.80)	14.52 (10.25)
Constant	287.40 (7.27)	281.70 (8.99)
R^2	0.35	0.18
Advanced		
RP50	-5.95 (21.21)	-19.00 (19.39)
RP80	2.80 (28.12)	-1.78 (20.62)
Constant	371.20 (18.24)	361.00 (15.51)
R^2	0.01	0.04

[a]Regression coefficient.
[b]Standard error.
*p < .10.

TABLE C-15 Regression Results for Cut Scores for Document Literacy, July 2004

	Occasion 1	Occasions 1 and 2
Number of Panelists	14	28
Basic		
RP50	-21.60^{a*} $(7.25)^{b}$	$-16.80**$ (4.67)
RP80	22.15** (7.28)	23.20** (4.57)
Constant	197.60 (5.04)	191.80 (3.10)
R^2	0.76	0.74
Intermediate		
RP50	$-40.40**$ (10.69)	$-30.17**$ (7.17)
RP80	15.85 (10.12)	14.38* (7.92)
Constant	256.40 (9.44)	248.50 (6.56)
R^2	0.76	0.61
Advanced		
RP50	$-78.00*$ (26.52)	-31.72 (20.81)
RP80	-11.45 (14.17)	-2.50 (19.56)
Constant	371.20 (4.25)	333.50 (13.33)
R^2	0.52	0.11

[a]Regression coefficient.
[b]Standard error.
*p < .10.
**p < .01.

TABLE C-16 Regression Results for Cut Scores for Quantitative Literacy, July 2004

	Occasion 1	Occasions 1 and 2
Number of Panelists	14	29
Basic		
RP50	22.20[a]** (7.37)[b]	−8.20 (11.67)
RP80	74.20** (3.66)	38.47** (10.42)
Constant	215.20 (1.07)	243.20 (9.36)
R^2	0.92	0.46
Intermediate		
RP50	9.40 (10.51)	−11.80 (9.92)
RP80	68.20** (10.45)	36.40* (11.85)
Constant	279.20 (7.02)	300.60 (8.85)
R^2	0.80	0.47
Advanced		
RP50	7.80 (18.41)	−30.80* (14.97)
RP80	74.80** (17.12)	31.78* (16.64)
Constant	338.80 (13.63)	369.00 (13.01)
R^2	0.65	0.40

[a]Regression coefficient.
[b]Standard error.
*p < .10.
**p < .01.

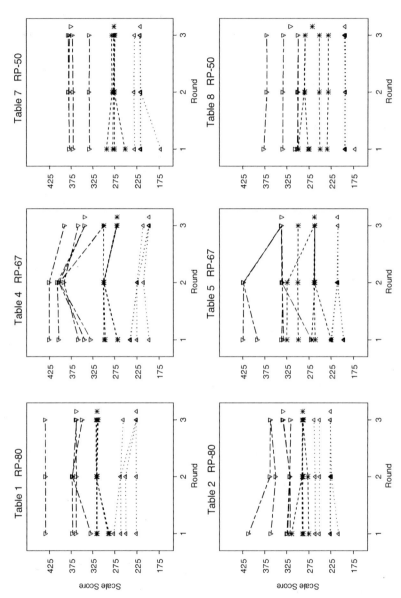

FIGURE C-1 Prose literacy cut scores by round for participants at each table, July 2004. Symbols indicate basic (△), intermediate (*), and advanced (▽) cut-score judgments. Round 3 medians are depicted by standalone symbols.

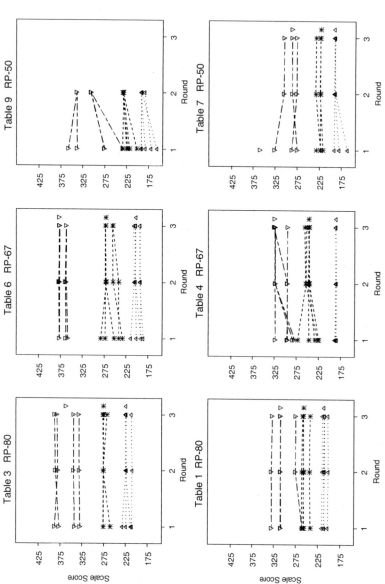

FIGURE C-2 Document literacy cut scores by round for participants at each table, July 2004. Symbols indicate basic (△), intermediate (*), and advanced (▽) cut-score judgments. Round 3 medians are depicted by standalone symbols.

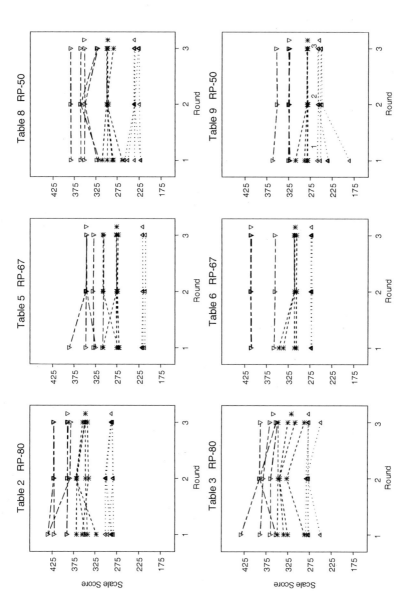

FIGURE C-3 Quantitative literacy cut scores by round for participants at each table, July 2004. Symbols indicate basic (Δ), intermediate (*), and advanced (∇) cut-score judgments. Round 3 medians are depicted by standalone symbols.

Appendix D

September 2004 Bookmark Standard-Setting Session with the 2003 NAAL Data

his appendix details how the bookmark procedure was implemented and reports results for the committee's September session. Following the text are the background materials, which include the agenda, participant questionnaires, tables, and figures for the September session.

A total of 30 panelists from the fields of adult education, middle and high school English language arts, industrial and organizational psychology, and state offices of adult education participated in the second standard setting, held over three days in September 2004. Six of the panelists had participated in the July standard setting. These six individuals returned in September as table leaders, which added continuity of process and familiarity of material to the second session (the agenda is included in Background Materials at the end of this appendix).

BOOKMARK STANDARD SETTING WITH THE 2003 NAAL DATA

As in July, panelists were given a questionnaire to collect background information (a blank questionnaire is included in Background Materials at the end of this appendix). Almost half (46.7 percent, n = 14) of the September participants had managerial responsibilities for adult education in their states or regional areas, although several (20 percent, n = 6) were also instructors in adult education. Half (50 percent, n = 14) of the participants who completed the questionnaire reported they were somewhat familiar with NAAL prior to participating in the standard-setting activities; five (17.9 percent) reported that they were very familiar with NAAL, and nine (32.1 percent) said they were unfamiliar with NAAL prior to the standard setting. In addition, participants responded that their work environments were predominantly urban (48.1 percent, n = 13) or suburban (37 percent, n = 10).

On the basis of the primary responsibilities listed on their resumes, the 29 panelists were classified into five areas of expertise: Adult Basic Education (ABE), General Educational Development (GED), English for Speakers of Other Languages (ESOL), middle or high school language arts (grades 6-12), and industrial and organizational psychology. Participants were randomly assigned to one of six tables of five people. Four of the six tables had a representative from each of the five areas of expertise; one table included a workplace and labor force literacy expert.

Once panelists were assigned to tables, the groups were then randomly assigned to literacy areas using the same counterbalancing design used in July (Table D-1). Two tables worked on prose literacy first; one of these tables was then assigned to work on document literacy and the other to work on quantitative literacy. Two tables worked on document literacy first; one of these tables was assigned to work on quantitative literacy and the other to work on prose literacy. The remaining two tables that worked on quantitative literacy first were similarly divided for the second content area: one table was assigned to work on prose literacy while the other was assigned to work on document literacy. Again, the bookmark placements were designated as Occasion 1 or Occasion 2 to indicate the order with which the table work on each assigned literacy area.

Ordered Item Booklets

The ordered item booklets used for the second standard setting were organized in the same way as for the first standard setting. One small change, however, was that some of the NAAL test questions were scored according to a partial credit scheme. This means that answers were scored as wrong, partially correct, or fully correct. When a partial credit scoring scheme is used, a difficulty value is estimated for both the partially correct score and the fully correct score. As a result, the test questions have to appear multiple times in the ordered item booklet, once for the difficulty value associated with partially correct and a second time for the difficulty value associated with fully correct. The ordered item booklets included the scoring rubric for determining partial credit and full credit scores.

Training Procedures

Training procedures in September were similar to those used in July. Table leader training was held the day before the standard setting, and panelist training was held on the first day of the standard setting. The majority of materials presented to the September panelists during the three-hour training session were the same as those presented in July, and most of the procedures were the same.

Conducting the Standard Setting

The procedures used in September were similar to those used in July, with the exception that the committee decided that all panelists in September should use the instructions for a response probability of 67 percent. This meant that the design for the standard setting could follow more typical bookmark procedures. That is, groups of panelists usually work on the same ordered item booklet at different tables during Rounds 1 and 2 but join each other for Round 3 discussions. Therefore, in September, the two tables working on the same literacy area were merged for the Round 3 discussion.

During Round 3, panelists received data summarizing bookmark placements for the two tables combined. This included a listing of each panelist's bookmark placements and the median bookmark placements by table. In addition, the combined median scale score (based on the data from both tables) was calculated for each level, and impact data provided about the percentages of adults who would fall into the below basic, basic, intermediate, and advanced categories if the combined median values were used as cut scores. (Because the full 2003 NAAL data set was not ready in time for the standard setting, the impact data used for Round 3 were based on the 1992 NALS results.) Panelists from both tables discussed their reasons for choosing different bookmark placements, after which each panelist independently made his or her final judgments about bookmark placements for the basic, intermediate, and advanced literacy levels.

As in July, panelists in September were asked to complete a satisfaction questionnaire about their perception of the standard-setting process at the end of the session.[1] The majority (93 percent, n = 28) reported that they were very satisfied with the organization of the event (Question 7) and that they were either satisfied (30 percent, n = 9) or very satisfied (63 percent, n = 19) with the cut score decisions of their table (Question 8).

As in July, panelists were also asked, questions about their background experiences with adult education and their familiarity with NAAL prior to the standard-setting session. Questions added to the panelist professional and personal information questionnaire (see page 299) based on feedback

---

[1]The satisfaction questionnaire given in September was identical to the one given in July (see page 246).

from the July participants included a series of three questions on how well participants understood the context of the test, the meaning of the performance levels, and the meaning of the bookmark placement. Results from this questionnaire were positive. A total of 28 panelists (93 percent) reported that they were very comfortable with the context of the test, the meaning of the performance levels, and the meaning of the bookmark placement (the remaining two individuals did not complete this part of the questionnaire).

Revising the Performance-Level Descriptions

At the conclusion of the September standard setting, 12 of the panelists were asked to stay for an extended session to write performance-level descriptions for the NAAL items. The panelists represented a cross-section of the larger group, in that at least one member from each of the six tables particpated in the extended session and there was representation as well from each of the three areas of expertise (adult education, middle and high school English language arts, and industrial and organizational psychology). The 12 participants were split into 3 groups of 4, with each group focusing on one of the three NAAL literacy areas. A period of approximately two hours was allotted for the panelists to discuss and suggest revisions to the performance-level descriptions. At this point, specific examples of, and references to, items and stimuli in the released NALS items were incorporated into the performance-level descriptions.[2]

RESULTS OF STANDARD SETTING WITH 2003 DATA

The methods for the September standard setting were, for the most part, the same as those used during the July session with respect to the sequencing of the standard-setting activities. The primary difference between the July and September sessions was that the committee had decided, partly on the basis of the analyses of the July standard-setting data, that panelists would use only a response probability of 67 percent (rp67) in the September session. This decision allowed the standard-setting design to be fully counterbalanced (Table D-1). That is, panelists at Tables 1 and 2 worked with prose items during Occasion 1; during Occasion 2, panelists at Table 1 worked with the document literacy items while Table 2 panelists worked with the quantitative items. Another difference between the July and September sessions was that, in July, use of multiple rp assignments

---

[2]The final performance-level descriptions and exemplars are presented in Table 5-4 of the report.

precluded having panelists from different tables join each other during Round 3. Because all panelists in September used the same rp level, those working on the same literacy area at two different tables were able to merge into one table for the Round 3 discussion, a practice advocated by the developers of the bookmark procedure (Mitzel et al., 2001). Results from this session are reported below.

Prose

A complete listing of all judgments made by each panelist who reviewed the prose literacy scale at the September standard-setting session is presented in Tables D-2A, D-2B, and D-2C. The information included in the table consists of each participant's bookmark placement for each round, as well as the corresponding scale score.[3] The table number used by each panelist is provided, as well as an indication of whether a given literacy scale was reviewed by the panelist first (i.e., Occasion 1) or second (i.e., Occasion 2).

Figure D-1 provides a visual depiction of the cut scores associated with panelists' bookmark placement decisions across the three rounds. These graphs are presented in a slightly different manner than for the July standard setting. Tables 1 and 2 examined the prose ordered item booklets in Occasion 1 (top two graphs), and unlike the July standard setting, panelists at these two tables joined each other after Round 2. Therefore, the graphs are presented as mirror opposites—the top left-hand graph shows the placements moving from Round 1 to Round 3; the top right-hand graph shows the placements moving from Round 3 to Round 1. This provides a means for easily comparing the extent of agreement across the two tables after Round 3. The bottom two graphs show the same information for Tables 4 and 5 working with prose items during Occasion 2.

Overall, the variability in panelists' cut scores tended to decrease across the rounds, particularly for the basic and intermediate performance levels. At Tables 1 and 2, considerable variability was evident in the advanced level cut scores, even at Round 3; agreement about the advanced level cut scores was better for Tables 4 and 5.

A summary of the Round 3 combined (Occasion 1 and 2) cut scores for prose literacy from July and September is given in Table D-3. The variability in the advanced cut score is evident in the standard deviations in this table.

---

[3]The item parameters used for the September standard setting were those provided to the committee in August 2004. The transformation constants used to convert theta estimates to scaled scores follow—prose: 54.973831 and 284.808948; document: 55.018198 and 279.632461; quantitative: 58.82459 and 284.991949.

Document

A complete listing of all judgments made by each panelist who reviewed the document literacy scale at the September standard setting session is presented in Tables D-4.

Figure D-2 portrays the cut scores associated with panelists' bookmark placements for each of the three rounds. Here, Tables 3 and 4 reviewed the document items during Occasion 1 (top two graphs); and Tables 1 and 6 reviewed the document items during Occasion 2 (bottom two graphs). Again, convergence in the cut scores is apparent by Round 3 for the basic and intermediate performance levels. Considerable disparity is present for the advanced level at all tables except Table 4.

A summary of the Round 3 combined (Occasion 1, Occasion 2) cut scores for document literacy for July and September is given in Table D-5. Again, the divergence in opinion about the advanced cut scores is evident in the size of the standard deviation.

Quantitative

A complete listing of all judgments made by each panelist who reviewed the quantitative literacy scale at the September standard setting session is presented in Tables D-6A, D-6B, D-6C. Figure D-3 presents the cut scores associated with panelists' bookmark decisions across the three rounds. Table 5 and 6 reviewed the quantitative literacy items during Occasion 1 (top two graphs); Tables 2 and 3 reviewed the items during Occasion 2 (bottom two graphs). Overall, there was a trend toward consensus by Round 3, although there was notable variability in cut scores for the advanced level at Table 5 and the basic level at Table 6, even at Round 3. Panelists verbally reported after the standard-setting session that they had more difficulty placing bookmarks for the quantitative section than they did for the prose or document section. A summary of the Round 3 combined (Occasion 1, Occasion 2) cut scores for document literacy from the July and September sessions is given in Table D-7.

Examination of Interrater Agreement

Although the bookmark method does not require panelists to reach consensus on the cut scores, agreement is encouraged. One indication of the quality of the standard-setting process is an examination of the extent to which they agreed with regard to their bookmark placements. This level of agreement is evaluated through estimates of interrater agreement.

To calculate the interrater agreement, we used the reliability feature in Statistical Package for the Social Sciences (SPSS) to estimate the intraclass correlations among the Round 3 scaled cut scores for each literacy area. These intraclass correlations appear below.

July	Prose	Document	Quantitative
rp50	.94	.95	.92
rp67	.94	.97	.95
rp80	.91	.92	.95

September	Prose	Document	Quantitative
rp67	.94	.94	.88

These values are all quite high and indicate that rater agreement was at acceptable levels.

ADDITIONAL MATERIALS TO ASSIST IN FUTURE ANALYSES

During the course of our analytic work on the 2003 NAAL data, we received several versions of the data files from NCES and its contractor. The timing of the receipt of these files did not always coincide with the schedule for the committee's work, and this may necessitate that NCES and its contractors repeat some of the committee's analyses. To facilitate replication, should it be necessary, we provide additional details from the bookmark standard setting and specify which data files we used for the different stages of our work.

Tables D-8 through D-13 provide additional information from the bookmark standard setting. Each table gives the Round 3 bookmark placements and corresponding cut score by participant, table, response probability value, and occasion for each of the six standard-setting groups (prose, document, and quantitative literacy from July and September sessions). Also included is the identification number of each item on which a bookmark was placed. On these tables, the cut score is the scale score corresponding to the proficiency estimate (given the specified response probability criterion) for the item just before the bookmark placement.

The item parameters used for the July bookmark standard setting were those in the publicly available data file. The transformation constants used to convert IRT proficiency estimates to scaled scores appeared in footnote 3 of Appendix C (p. 228).

The item parameters used for the September bookmark standard setting were those on the file forwarded to us in August 2004, which was based on data for the main NAAL sample but did not include the additional state and inmate samples. The transformation constants used to convert IRT proficiency estimates to scaled scores appeared in footnote 3 of Appendix D (p. 289).

All of the analyses of 2003 test takers (e.g., the population percentages at each performance level, the median literacy scores derived for the quasi-contrasting group procedure) were based on the file delivered to us on January 21, 2005. The transformation constants (scale and location) used to convert IRT proficiency estimates to scaled scores were for prose, 58.480557 and 280.704956; for document, 58.755463 and 274.881560; and for quantitative, 63.311586 and 280.488425.

ACKNOWLEDGMENTS

The committee wishes to acknowledge the assistance and contributions of the individuals who served as panelists for the two bookmark standard settings and provided valuable input on the performance-level descriptions.

Eunice Askov, Pennsylvania State University
Marjorie Ball, Mississippi State Penitentiary, Parchman
Roxanne Bauer, Indianapolis Public Schools, Indiana
Michelle Blantz, South Georgia Technical College
Rhodella Brown, Daytona Beach Community College, Florida
Miriam Burt, Center for Applied Linguistics, Washington, DC
Laura Chenven, AFL-CIO Working for America Institute, Washington, DC
Suzanne Cimochowski, EASTCONN, Hampton, Connecticut
Marie Cora, Hotspur Partners, LLC, Boston
Christopher Coro, Northampton Community College, Pennsylvania
Susan Cowles, Oregon State Department of Community Colleges and
    Workforce Development
Shari Crockett, Regional Office of Education, Monroe/Randolph
    Counties, Illinois
Lansing Davis, New Jersey State Employment and Training Commission
Kim Donehower, University of North Dakota
Suzanne Elston, Bradley County Adult Education, Tennessee
Leslie Farr, Ohio State University
Sharon Floyd, Saginaw Public Schools, Michigan
Janet Geary, North Kansas City School District, Missouri
Karen Gianninoto, Salisbury State University, Maryland
Kimberly Gibson, Sierra College, California
Suzanne Grant, Arlington Public Schools, Virginia
Anne Greenwell, Jefferson County Public Schools, Kentucky
Christina Gutierrez, T.C. Williams High School, Alexandria, Virginia
Nancy Hampson, San Diego Community College District, California
James Harris, Caliber Associates, Fairfax, Virginia
Roberta Hawkins, Shorewood High School, Shoreline, Washington

Fran Holthaus, Upper Valley Joint Vocational School, Piqua, Ohio
Sally House, Central Mississippi Correctional Facility, Pearl
Brenda Jeans, Beauregard Parish School Board, Louisiana
Paul Jurmo, New York University
Judy Kihslinger, Waukesha County Technical College, Wisconsin
Terry Kinzel, Big Bend Community College, Washington
Jaqueline Korengel, Commonwealth of Kentucky, Frankfort
Nathan Kuncel, University of Illinois at Urbana-Champaign
Diane Lindahl, Western Wisconsin Technical College
Ardith Loustalet, St. Vrain Valley School District, Colorado
Alfredo Lujan, Monte del Sol Charter School, New Mexico
Sanford Marks, Community College of Southern Nevada
Peggy McGuire, University of Tennessee
Maureen Meehan, University of Illinois at Chicago
Doug Molitor, 3M, St. Paul, Minnesota
Donald Mott, Wilson Mott & Associates, Greenville, North Carolina
Vivian Mott, East Carolina University
Bill Muth, U.S. Federal Bureau of Prisons, Washington, DC
Connie Nelson, Massachusetts Worker Education Roundtable, Boston
Donna Nola-Ganey, Louisiana Department of Education, Baton Rouge
Peg Perri, Western Wisconsin Technical College
Rebecca Rogers, Washington University in St. Louis
Teresa Russell, Independent Consultant, Minnesota
Sally Sandy, Parkway School District, Missouri
Kathleen Santopietro Weddel, Colorado Department of Education
Diane Schroeder, St. Charles Community College, Missouri
Don Seaman, Texas Center for the Advancement of Literacy and
    Learning, College Station
Jane Siveria, Florida Department of Education, Tallahassee
Cristine Smith, World Education, Inc., Boston
Maggie Sokolik, University of California, Berkeley
Linda Stacy, Owens Community College, Ohio
Linda Taylor, Comprehensive Adult Student Assessment System, San Diego
Ray Thompson, Middle Georgia Technical College
Patricia Thorpe, University of Phoenix
Fran Tracy-Mumford, Delaware Department of Education, Dover
Karen Valbrun, Georgia State Department of Technical and Adult
    Education
Denise Weiner, Delaware Department of Education, Dover
Lynne Weintraub, Jones Library, Amherst, Massachusetts
Ira Yankwitt, Literacy Assistance Center, New York
Linda Young, Oklahoma State Department of Education

BACKGROUND MATERIALS

September Standard-Setting Session

Item	Page

Tables

Figures

Agenda
Standard-Setting Session for the
National Assessment of Adult Literacy (NAAL)
National Research Council, Washington, DC
September 17-20, 2004

Friday, September 17, 2004—The Day Before the Standard Setting

3:00–3:15 PM	Welcome, Introductions Stuart Elliott, Judy Koenig, *NRC* Rich Patz, *Consultant to NRC*
3:15–5:00 PM	Training for Table Leaders

Saturday, September 18, 2004—Day 1 of Standard Setting

8:00–8:30 AM	Participant registration Continental breakfast
8:30–9:00 AM	Welcome, Introductions Stuart Elliott, Judy Koenig, *NRC* Rich Patz, *Consultant to NRC*
9:00–10:20 AM	Training
10:20–10:30 AM	Break
10:30 AM–Noon	Training continued
Noon–1:00 PM	Lunch
1:00–2:00 PM	Round 1 (1st subject area) Participants review all items of NAAL (1st subject area) *individually*
2:00–4:00 PM	Participants at each table, *as a group*, study and discuss items in the ordered item booklets
4:00–5:00 PM	Bookmark directions given and Round 1 judgments made (judgments are made *individually*)
5:00 PM	First day adjourned

Sunday, September 19, 2004—Day 2 of Standard Setting

8:00–8:30 AM	**Continental breakfast**
8:30–8:45 AM	**Large-group meeting**
8:45–10:00 AM	**Round 2 (1st subject area)** Tables receive their Round 1 judgments Bookmark directions given for Round 2 *As a group*, discussion about Round 1 data Round 2 judgments made *individually*
10:00–10:45 AM	**Break**
10:45–Noon	**Round 3 (1st subject area, both tables merge)** Tables receive impact data from their Round 2 judgments Bookmark directions given for Round 3 *Both tables, as a group*, discussion about Round 2 data Round 3 judgments made *individually*
Noon–1:00 PM	**Lunch**
1:00–1:30 PM	**Large-group meeting**
1:30–2:30 PM	**Round 1 (2nd subject area)** Participants review all items of NAAL (2nd subject area) *individually*
2:30–4:30 PM	Participants at each table, *as a group*, study and discuss items in the ordered item booklets
4:30–5:30 PM	Bookmark directions given and Round 1 judgments made (judgments are made *individually*)
5:30 PM	**Second day adjourned**

Monday, September 20, 2004—Day 3 of Standard Setting

8:00–8:30 AM	Continental breakfast
8:30–8:45 AM	Large-group meeting
8:45–9:45 AM	Round 2 (2nd subject area) Tables receive data from their Round 1 judgments Bookmark directions given for Round 2 *As a group*, discussion about Round 1 data Round 2 judgments made *individually*
9:45–10:30 AM	Break
10:30–11:30 AM	Round 3 (2nd subject area, both tables merge) Tables receive impact data from their Round 2 judgments Bookmark directions given for Round 3 *Both tables, as a group*, discussion about Round 2 data Round 3 judgments made *individually*
11:30 AM–Noon	Large-group discussion
Noon	Standard setting meeting adjourned
12:00–12:30 PM	Box Lunch
12:30–3:30 PM	Extended session on writing Performance-level descriptions

Professional and Personal Information Questionnaire
Bookmark Standard-Setting Session for NAAL
September 18-20, 2004
National Research Council, Washington, DC

Please answer the following questions so we better understand the characteristics of our group of standard setting participants.

1. Do your professional responsibilities include direct or managerial responsibilities 'for the education of adults? _____

____ Yes. I am directly involved as an instructor. For how many years have you had such responsibilities? _____

___Yes. I am involved in a managerial capacity. For how many years have you had such responsibilities? _____

___Yes. I am directly involved with the education of adults but not as an instructor or a manger. In what way are you involved with the education of adults? For how many years have you had such responsibilities? _____

___No. Please characterize your professional responsibilities:

_____

2. How would you characterize the educational setting for these adults (check any and all that apply):

___Middle or elementary school   ___4-year college or university
___Traditional high school   ___Graduate or professional school
___Vocational high school   ___Community college
___Alternative high school   ___Workplace education setting
___Adult basic education   ___GED program
   program
___English language instruction
___Other. Please describe: _____

3. How familiar were you with the National Assessment of Adult Literacy (a.k.a. NAAL) before your participation in the standard-setting activities?

_____ Unfamiliar   _____Somewhat familiar   _____Very familiar

4. Standard-setting judgments require one to understand: (A) the content of the test (i.e., literacy), (B) the performance-level descriptions, and (C) the standard-setting task (i.e., what it means to place a bookmark in an ordered item book).

A. How well did you understand the content of the test? Please circle one number for each area of literacy for which you set a standard:

	Did not understand at all			Understood completely	
Prose literacy:	1	2	3	4	5
Document literacy:	1	2	3	4	5
Quantitative literacy:	1	2	3	4	5

B. How well did you understand the meaning of the performance levels as explained in the performance-level descriptions?

	Did not understand at all			Understood completely	
Performance Levels:	1	2	3	4	5

C. How well did you understand the meaning of bookmark placement based on your training and the bookmark placement instructions?

	Did not understand at all			Understood completely	
Bookmark Instructions:	1	2	3	4	5

5. Please tell us about yourself (optional)

Gender: ___ Male   _____ Female

Age: ____ 20-29 ___30-39 ___40-49 _ 50-59 _ 60-69 __70+

Race/Ethnicity: _____

Type of community in which you work:

Rural   Suburban   Urban

TABLE D-1 Design of the Bookmark Standard Setting with NAAL Data, September 2004[a]

	Table 1	Table 2	Table 3	Table 4	Table 5	Table 6
First Literacy Area:	Prose	Prose	Doc.	Doc.	Quant.	Quant.
Second Literacy Area:	Doc.	Quant.	Quant.	Prose	Prose	Doc.

[a]All panelists used rp 67 instructions.

TABLE D-2A Participants' Bookmark Placements and Associated Cut Scores for Basic, Prose Literacy, September 2004

Response				Round 1		Round 2		Round 3	
Participant[a]	Table	Probability	Occasion	BK[b]	SS[c]	BK	SS	BK	SS
1.1	1	0.67	1	8	206	8	206	8	206
1.2	1	0.67	1	8	206	8	206	8	206
1.3	1	0.67	1	15	229	8	206	12	217
1.4	1	0.67	1	6	199	8	206	8	206
1.5	1	0.67	1	8	206	8	206	8	206
2.1	2	0.67	1	11	210	11	210	12	217
2.2	2	0.67	1	11	210	11	210	11	210
2.3	2	0.67	1	11	210	11	210	11	210
2.4	2	0.67	1	12	217	12	217	12	217
2.5	2	0.67	1	14	225	12	217	8	206
4.1	4	0.67	2	14	225	13	221	13	221
4.2	4	0.67	2	15	229	13	221	13	221
4.3	4	0.67	2	18	233	14	225	15	229
4.4	4	0.67	2	11	210	13	221	13	221
4.5	4	0.67	2	14	225	14	225	14	225
5.1	5	0.67	2	17	232	18	233	18	233
5.2	5	0.67	2	14	225	18	233	13	221
5.3	5	0.67	2	18	233	18	233	18	233
5.4	5	0.67	2	14	225	17	232	18	233
5.5	5	0.67	2	18	233	18	233	18	233

[a]The first participant at each table (i.e. 1.1, 2.1, ..., 6.1) is the table leader.
[b]Denotes the item number in the ordered item booklet on which the bookmark was placed (see pg. 112 for explanation of bookmark placements).
[c]Denotes the cut score associated with the bookmark placement. It is the RP location for the last item before the bookmark placement, converted to a scale score.

TABLE D-2B Participants' Bookmark Placements and Associated Cut Scores for Intermediate, Prose Literacy, September 2004

Participant[a]	Table	Probability	Occasion	Round 1 BK[b]	Round 1 SS[c]	Round 2 BK	Round 2 SS	Round 3 BK	Round 3 SS
1.1	1	0.67	1	27	245	31	260	37	270
1.2	1	0.67	1	31	260	27	245	31	260
1.3	1	0.67	1	41	287	30	251	37	270
1.4	1	0.67	1	22	237	31	260	37	270
1.5	1	0.67	1	15	229	27	245	27	245
2.1	2	0.67	1	27	245	29	249	29	249
2.2	2	0.67	1	37	270	37	270	37	270
2.3	2	0.67	1	32	265	29	249	32	265
2.4	2	0.67	1	29	249	29	249	29	249
2.5	2	0.67	1	37	270	37	270	37	270
4.1	4	0.67	2	42	288	45	293	45	293
4.2	4	0.67	2	51	314	45	293	45	293
4.3	4	0.67	2	37	270	45	293	45	293
4.4	4	0.67	2	45	293	45	293	45	293
4.5	4	0.67	2	37	270	45	293	45	293
5.1	5	0.67	2	44	292	44	292	44	292
5.2	5	0.67	2	31	260	44	292	45	293
5.3	5	0.67	2	45	293	44	292	44	292
5.4	5	0.67	2	31	260	45	293	45	293
5.5	5	0.67	2	32	265	45	293	45	293

[a]The first participant at each table (i.e. 1.1, 2.1, ..., 6.1) is the table leader.

[b]Denotes the item number in the ordered item booklet on which the bookmark was placed (see pg. 112 for explanation of bookmark placements). It is the RP location for the last item before the bookmark placement.

[c]Denotes the cut score associated with the bookmark placement. It is the RP location for the last item before the bookmark placement, converted to a scale score.

TABLE D-2C Participants' Bookmark Placements and Associated Cut Scores for Advanced, Prose Literacy, September 2004

Response Participant[a]	Table	Probability	Occasion	Round 1 BK[b]	Round 1 SS[c]	Round 2 BK	Round 2 SS	Round 3 BK	Round 3 SS
1.1	1	0.67	1	56	345	56	345	56	345
1.2	1	0.67	1	60	368	60	368	60	368
1.3	1	0.67	1	45	293	51	314	55	336
1.4	1	0.67	1	49	310	56	345	56	345
1.5	1	0.67	1	39	275	60	368	56	345
2.1	2	0.67	1	53	332	48	307	48	307
2.2	2	0.67	1	64	405	53	332	56	345
2.3	2	0.67	1	45	293	48	307	53	332
2.4	2	0.67	1	48	307	45	293	55	336
2.5	2	0.67	1	51	314	51	314	60	368
4.1	4	0.67	2	60	368	48	307	56	345
4.2	4	0.67	2	64	405	53	332	56	345
4.3	4	0.67	2	64	405	48	307	56	345
4.4	4	0.67	2	64	405	45	293	56	345
4.5	4	0.67	2	53	332	51	314	56	345
5.1	5	0.67	2	65	420	65	420	65	420
5.2	5	0.67	2	65	420	65	420	65	420
5.3	5	0.67	2	65	420	65	420	65	420
5.4	5	0.67	2	63	405	65	420	65	420
5.5	5	0.67	2	53	332	65	420	65	420

[a]The first participant at each table (i.e. 1.1, 2.1, ..., 6.1) is the table leader.

[b]Denotes the item number in the ordered item booklet on which the bookmark was placed (see pg. 112 for explanation of bookmark placements).

[c]Denotes the cut score associated with the bookmark placement. It is the RP location for the last item before the bookmark placement, converted to a scale score.

TABLE D-3 Summary Statistics for Round 3 Cut Scores for Prose Literacy Scale, July and September 2004

	July (RP67)			Sept. (RP67)		
	Basic	Intermediate	Advanced	Basic	Intermediate	Advanced
Median	211.00	270.00	336.00	219.00	281.00	345.00
Mean	205.40	273.20	341.60	218.55	277.30	362.60
Std. Dev	7.23	14.51	22.69	10.13	17.42	36.10
Std. Error	2.29	4.59	7.18	2.27	3.90	8.07
N	10	10	10	20	20	20

TABLE D-4A Participants' Bookmark Placements and Associated Cut Scores for Basic, Document Literacy, September 2004

Response				Round 1		Round 2		Round 3	
Participant[a]	Table	Probability	Occasion	BK[b]	SS[c]	BK	SS	BK	SS
1.1	1	0.67	2	12	194	12	194	12	194
1.2	1	0.67	2	10	192	13	198	13	198
1.3	1	0.67	2	23	223	17	204	17	204
1.4	1	0.67	2	18	210	12	194	18	210
1.5	1	0.67	2	11	193	18	210	12	194
3.1	3	0.67	1	20	215	18	210	18	210
3.2	3	0.67	1	8	182	17	204	18	210
3.3	3	0.67	1	18	210	18	210	18	210
3.4	3	0.67	1	15	201	18	210	19	215
3.5	3	0.67	1	17	204	17	204	18	210
4.1	4	0.67	1	19	215	19	215	18	210
4.2	4	0.67	1	19	215	19	215	19	215
4.3	4	0.67	1	18	210	19	215	18	210
4.4	4	0.67	1	10	192	10	192	10	192
4.5	4	0.67	1	19	215	19	215	19	215
6.1	6	0.67	2	18	210	5	170	5	170
6.2	6	0.67	2	5	170	5	170	5	170
6.3	6	0.67	2	19	215	19	215	19	215
6.4	6	0.67	2	19	215	19	215	19	215
6.5	6	0.67	2	19	215	19	215	19	215

[a]The first participant of each table (i.e. 1.1, 2.1, ..., 6.1) is the table leader.
[b]Denotes the item number in the ordered item booklet on which the bookmark was placed (see pg. 112 for explanation of bookmark placements).
[c]Denotes the cut score associated with the bookmark placement. It is the RP location for the last item before the bookmark placement, converted to a scale score.

TABLE D-4B Participants' Bookmark Placements and Associated Cut Scores for Intermediate, Document Literacy, September 2004

Response				Round 1		Round 2		Round 3	
Participant[a]	Table	Probability	Occasion	BK[b]	SS[c]	BK	SS	BK	SS
1.1	1	0.67	2	36	243	36	243	36	243
1.2	1	0.67	2	36	243	36	243	36	243
1.3	1	0.67	2	50	280	42	266	38	254
1.4	1	0.67	2	40	256	36	243	40	256
1.5	1	0.67	2	29	235	36	243	36	243
3.1	3	0.67	1	31	236	29	235	38	254
3.2	3	0.67	1	22	216	32	236	38	254
3.3	3	0.67	1	42	266	29	235	42	266
3.4	3	0.67	1	25	224	30	235	40	256
3.5	3	0.67	1	31	236	31	236	36	243
4.1	4	0.67	1	36	243	41	260	41	260
4.2	4	0.67	1	48	274	41	260	39	256
4.3	4	0.67	1	42	266	41	260	41	260
4.4	4	0.67	1	36	243	41	260	41	260
4.5	4	0.67	1	36	243	41	260	41	260
6.1	6	0.67	2	29	235	29	235	29	235
6.2	6	0.67	2	31	236	32	236	38	254
6.3	6	0.67	2	40	256	38	254	36	243
6.4	6	0.67	2	38	254	38	254	38	254
6.5	6	0.67	2	36	243	38	254	38	254

[a]The first participant of each table (i.e. 1.1, 2.1, ..., 6.1) is the table leader.
[b]Denotes the item number in the ordered item booklet on which the bookmark was placed (see pg. 112 for explanation of bookmark placements).
[c]Denotes the cut score associated with the bookmark placement. It is the RP location for the last item before the bookmark placement, converted to a scale score.

TABLE D-4C Participants' Bookmark Placements and Associated Cut Scores for Advanced, Document Literacy, September 2004

Response Participant[a]	Table	Probability	Occasion	Round 1 BK[b]	Round 1 SS[c]	Round 2 BK	Round 2 SS	Round 3 BK	Round 3 SS
1.1	1	0.67	2	62	371	52	283	57	318
1.2	1	0.67	2	57	318	57	318	57	318
1.3	1	0.67	2	57	318	57	318	62	371
1.4	1	0.67	2	52	283	52	283	52	283
1.5	1	0.67	2	40	256	57	318	57	318
3.1	3	0.67	1	55	301	59	332	59	332
3.2	3	0.67	1	61	358	59	332	61	358
3.3	3	0.67	1	56	302	56	302	56	302
3.4	3	0.67	1	42	266	59	332	59	332
3.5	3	0.67	1	53	285	59	332	59	332
4.1	4	0.67	1	63	386	62	371	62	371
4.2	4	0.67	1	63	386	62	371	62	371
4.3	4	0.67	1	61	358	62	371	62	371
4.4	4	0.67	1	62	371	62	371	62	371
4.5	4	0.67	1	59	332	62	371	62	371
6.1	6	0.67	2	41	260	41	260	48	274
6.2	6	0.67	2	62	371	62	371	62	371
6.3	6	0.67	2	62	371	62	371	62	371
6.4	6	0.67	2	59	332	59	332	59	332
6.5	6	0.67	2	59	332	61	358	62	371

[a]The first participant of each table (i.e. 1.1, 2.1, ..., 6.1) is the table leader.
[b]Denotes the item number in the ordered item booklet on which the bookmark was placed (see pg. 112 for explanation of bookmark placements).
[c]Denotes the cut score associated with the bookmark placement. It is the RP location for the last item before the bookmark placement, converted to a scale score.

TABLE D-5 Summary Statistics for Round 3 Cut Scores for Document Literacy Scale, July and September 2004

	July (RP67)			Sept. (RP67)		
	Basic	Intermediate	Advanced	Basic	Intermediate	Advanced
Median	189.00	255.00	343.50	210.00	254.00	345.00
Mean	192.10	257.20	345.20	204.10	252.40	341.90
Std. Dev	8.45	10.09	29.96	13.90	8.00	32.17
Std. Error	2.67	3.19	9.47	3.11	1.79	7.19
N	10	10	10	20	20	20

TABLE D-6A Participants' Bookmark Placements and Associated Cut Scores for Basic, Quantitative Literacy, September 2004

Response Participant[a]	Table	Probability	Occasion	Round 1 BK[b]	Round 1 SS[c]	Round 2 BK	Round 2 SS	Round 3 BK	Round 3 SS
2.1	2	0.67	2	6	215	6	215	10	230
2.2	2	0.67	2	6	215	10	230	16	245
2.3	2	0.67	2	10	230	10	230	10	230
2.4	2	0.67	2	17	250	17	250	17	250
2.5	2	0.67	2	4	203	10	230	16	245
3.1	3	0.67	2	18	252	16	245	16	245
3.2	3	0.67	2	16	245	16	245	16	245
3.3	3	0.67	2	16	245	16	245	16	245
3.4	3	0.67	2	22	265	16	245	16	245
3.5	3	0.67	2	22	265	18	252	16	245
5.1	5	0.67	1	23	266	15	244	15	244
5.2	5	0.67	1	17	250	23	266	15	244
5.3	5	0.67	1	15	244	15	244	15	244
5.4	5	0.67	1	16	245	17	250	15	244
5.5	5	0.67	1	7	224	23	266	23	266
6.1	6	0.67	1	5	211	5	211	5	211
6.2	6	0.67	1	11	233	9	226	4	203
6.3	6	0.67	1	16	245	15	244	15	244
6.4	6	0.67	1	12	240	14	242	12	240
6.5	6	0.67	1	14	242	15	244	14	242

[a]The first participant of each table (i.e., 1.1, 2.1, ..., 6.1) is the table leader.
[b]Denotes the item number in the ordered item booklet on which the bookmark was placed (see pg. 112 for explanation of bookmark placements). It is the RP location for the last item before the bookmark placement.
[c]Denotes the cut score associated with the bookmark placement, converted to a scale score.

TABLE D-6B Participants' Bookmark Placements and Associated Cut Scores for Intermediate, Quantitative Literacy, September 2004

Response Participant[a]	Table	Probability	Occasion	Round 1 BK[b]	Round 1 SS[c]	Round 2 BK	Round 2 SS	Round 3 BK	Round 3 SS
2.1	2	0.67	2	20	260	29	288	30	289
2.2	2	0.67	2	17	250	29	288	35	298
2.3	2	0.67	2	34	298	29	288	29	288
2.4	2	0.67	2	53	400	35	298	35	298
2.5	2	0.67	2	29	288	29	288	35	298
3.1	3	0.67	2	34	298	30	304	29	288
3.2	3	0.67	2	21	264	38	304	30	289
3.3	3	0.67	2	38	304	35	298	35	298
3.4	3	0.67	2	29	288	35	298	29	288
3.5	3	0.67	2	35	298	35	298	32	295
5.1	5	0.67	1	43	324	43	324	41	312
5.2	5	0.67	1	29	288	43	324	41	312
5.3	5	0.67	1	37	302	41	312	37	302
5.4	5	0.67	1	34	298	37	302	37	302
5.5	5	0.67	1	34	298	43	324	43	324
6.1	6	0.67	1	27	273	24	267	24	267
6.2	6	0.67	1	21	264	23	266	12	240
6.3	6	0.67	1	42	319	33	295	32	295
6.4	6	0.67	1	29	288	31	290	29	288
6.5	6	0.67	1	35	298	33	295	31	290

[a]The first participant of each table (i.e., 1.1, 2.1, ..., 6.1) is the table leader.
[b]Denotes the item number in the ordered item booklet on which the bookmark was placed (see pg. 112 for explanation of bookmark placements).
[c]Denotes the cut score associated with the bookmark placement. It is the RP location for the last item before the bookmark placement, converted to a scale score.

TABLE D-6C Participants' Bookmark Placements and Associated Cut Scores for Advanced, Quantitative Literacy, September 2004

Response				Round 1		Round 2		Round 3	
Participant[a]	Table	Probability	Occasion	BK[b]	SS[c]	BK	SS	BK	SS
2.1	2	0.67	2	35	298	35	298	42	319
2.2	2	0.67	2	35	298	49	356	49	356
2.3	2	0.67	2	49	356	49	356	49	356
2.4	2	0.67	2	54	461	49	356	49	356
2.5	2	0.67	2	54	461	49	356	49	356
3.1	3	0.67	2	44	327	46	338	46	338
3.2	3	0.67	2	41	312	47	343	47	343
3.3	3	0.67	2	49	356	49	356	49	356
3.4	3	0.67	2	50	369	45	331	45	331
3.5	3	0.67	2	45	331	46	338	47	343
5.1	5	0.67	1	49	356	54	461	54	461
5.2	5	0.67	1	54	461	54	461	54	461
5.3	5	0.67	1	54	461	54	461	54	461
5.4	5	0.67	1	54	461	54	461	51	393
5.5	5	0.67	1	53	400	54	461	53	400
6.1	6	0.67	1	49	356	49	356	49	356
6.2	6	0.67	1	51	393	50	369	50	369
6.3	6	0.67	1	50	369	51	393	49	356
6.4	6	0.67	1	48	355	51	393	47	343
6.5	6	0.67	1	51	393	51	393	45	331

[a]The first participant of each table (i.e., 1.1, 2.1, ..., 6.1) is the table leader.
[b]Denotes the item number in the ordered item booklet on which the bookmark was placed (see pg. 112 for explanation of bookmark placements).
[c]Denotes the cut score associated with the bookmark placement. It is the RP location for the last item before the bookmark placement, converted to a scale score.

TABLE D-7 Summary Statistics for Round 3 Cut Scores for Quantitative Literacy Scale, July and September 2004

	July (RP67)			Sept. (RP67)		
	Basic	Intermediate	Advanced	Basic	Intermediate	Advanced
Median	244.00	307.00	351.50	244.00	295.00	356.00
Mean	243.20	295.20	367.30	240.35	293.05	369.25
Std. Dev	29.56	17.49	39.10	13.46	17.14	43.82
Std. Error	9.85	5.83	13.03	3.01	3.83	9.80
N	10	10	10	20	20	20

TABLE D-8 Item ID Table for Prose Literacy Bookmark Placements, Round 3, July 2004

Participant[a]	Table	Response Probability	Occasion
4.1	4	0.67	1
4.2	4	0.67	1
4.3	4	0.67	1
4.4	4	0.67	1
4.5	4	0.67	1
5.1	5	0.67	2
5.2	5	0.67	2
5.3	5	0.67	2
5.4	5	0.67	2
5.5	5	0.67	2

[a]The first participant of each table (i.e. 1.1, 2.1, ..., 9.1) is the table leader.

[b]Denotes the item number in the ordered item booklet on which the bookmark was placed (see pg. 112 for explanation of bookmark placements).

[c]Denotes the cut score associated with the bookmark placement. It is the RP location for the last item before the bookmark placement, converted to a scale score.

TABLE D-9 Item ID Table for Document Literacy Bookmark Placements, Round 3, July 2004

Participant[a]	Table	Response Probability	Occasion
4.1	4	0.67	2
4.2	4	0.67	2
4.3	4	0.67	2
4.4	4	0.67	2
4.5	4	0.67	2
6.1	6	0.67	1
6.2	6	0.67	1
6.3	6	0.67	1
6.4	6	0.67	1
6.5	6	0.67	1

[a]The first participant of each table (i.e. 1.1, 2.1, ..., 9.1) is the table leader.

[b]Denotes the item number in the ordered item booklet on which the bookmark was placed (see pg. 112 for explanation of bookmark placements).

[c]Denotes the cut score associated with the bookmark placement. It is the RP location for the last item before the bookmark placement, converted to a scale score.

Basic			Intermediate			Advanced		
Item Identification	Round 3 BK[b]	SS[c]	Item Identification	Round 3 BK	SS	Item Identification	Round 3 BK	SS
N080101	5	197	AB60601	20	270	N130301	34	343
N080101	5	197	AB40901	24	300	N130301	34	343
N100101	6	211	AB60601	20	270	AB40901	24	300
N080101	5	197	AB60601	20	270	N120501	37	391
N080101	5	197	AB60601	20	270	N110601	36	359
N100101	6	211	AB60201	16	263	N090801	33	336
N100101	6	211	AB60201	16	263	N090801	33	336
N100101	6	211	AB60201	16	263	N090801	33	336
N100101	6	211	AB60201	16	263	N090801	33	336
N100101	6	211	AB40901	24	300	N090801	33	336

Basic			Intermediate			Advanced		
Item Identification	Round 3 BK[b]	SS[c]	Item Identification	Round 3 BK	SS	Item Identification	Round 3 BK	SS
N120601	10	185	AB50901	47	247	N010901	69	324
N120601	10	185	N090501	49	253	N010901	69	324
N120601	10	185	AB70701	51	255	N010901	69	324
N120601	10	185	AB50901	47	247	AB60502	65	296
N120601	10	185	AB50901	47	247	N010901	69	324
AB31301	17	202	AB31001	56	271	N/A[d]		378
AB31301	17	202	AB31001	56	271	N/A		378
AB50801	15	193	AB70701	51	255	N100701	72	363
AB40101	19	206	AB31001	56	271	N100701	72	363
AB50801	15	193	AB70701	51	255	N/A		378

[d]Some panelists placed their bookmarks for the advanced level after the final item in the booklet. When this occurred, SS is the scale score associated with the RP location for the final item in the booklet.

TABLE D-10 Item ID Table for Quantitative Literacy Bookmark Placements, Round 3, July 2004

Participant[a]	Table	Response Probability	Occasion
5.1	5	0.67	1
5.2	5	0.67	1
5.3	5	0.67	1
5.4	5	0.67	1
5.5	5	0.67	1
6.1	6	0.67	2
6.2	6	0.67	2
6.3	6	0.67	2
6.4	6	0.67	2
6.5	6	0.67	2

[a]The first participant of each table (i.e. 1.1, 2.1, ..., 9.1) is the table leader.

[b]Denotes the item number in the ordered item booklet on which the bookmark was placed (see pg. 112 for explanation of bookmark placements).

[c]Denotes the cut score associated with the bookmark placement. It is the RP location for the last item before the bookmark placement, converted to a scale score.

[d]Some panelists placed their bookmarks for the advanced level after the final item in the booklet. When this occurred, SS is the scale score associated with the RP location for the final item in the booklet.

Basic			Intermediate			Advanced		
Item Identification	Round 3 BK[b]	SS[c]	Item Identification	Round 3 BK	SS	Item Identification	Round 3 BK	SS
N100801	5	216	N130601	18	276	N080901	37	347
AB50404	6	217	N011101	25	307	N080901	37	347
N100801	5	216	N110801	17	272	N011101	25	307
N100801	5	216	N130601	18	276	N080901	37	347
LC00601	4	211	N130601	18	276	N010601	32	329
AB40704	16	272	N011101	25	307	N/A[d]		410
AB40601	15	271	N081001	27	311	N/A		410
AB40601	15	271	N011101	25	307	N121101	39	356
AB40601	15	271	N081001	27	311	N/A		410
AB40601	15	271	N121001	26	309	N/A		410

TABLE D-11 Item ID Table for Prose Literacy Bookmark Placements, Round 3, September 2004

Participant[a]	Table	Response Probability	Occasion
1.1	1	0.67	1
1.2	1	0.67	1
1.3	1	0.67	1
1.4	1	0.67	1
1.5	1	0.67	1
2.1	2	0.67	1
2.2	2	0.67	1
2.3	2	0.67	1
2.4	2	0.67	1
2.5	2	0.67	1
4.1	4	0.67	2
4.2	4	0.67	2
4.3	4	0.67	2
4.4	4	0.67	2
4.5	4	0.67	2
5.1	5	0.67	2
5.2	5	0.67	2
5.3	5	0.67	2
5.4	5	0.67	2
5.5	5	0.67	2

[a]The first participant of each table (i.e. 1.1, 2.1, ..., 9.1) is the table leader.

[b]Denotes the item number in the ordered item booklet on which the bookmark was placed (see pg. 112 for explanation of bookmark placements).

[c]Denotes the cut score associated with the bookmark placement. It is the RP location for the last item before the bookmark placement, converted to a scale score.

[d]Some panelists placed their bookmarks for the advanced level after the final item in the booklet. When this occurred, SS is the scale score associated with the RP location for the final item in the booklet.

Basic			Intermediate			Advanced		
Item Identification	Round 3 BK[b]	SS[c]	Item Identification	Round 3 BK	SS	Item Identification	Round 3 BK	SS
C061001	8	206	C080301	37	270	N130301	56	345
C061001	8	206	C071101	31	260	N110601	60	368
N100101	12	217	C080301	37	270	N090801	55	336
C061001	8	206	C080301	37	270	N130301	56	345
C061001	8	206	C020501	27	245	N130301	56	345
N100101	12	217	C040301	29	249	C080701	48	307
C050801	11	210	C080301	37	270	N130301	56	345
C050801	11	210	N120401	32	265	C080701	53	332
N100101	12	217	C040301	29	249	N090801	55	336
C061001	8	206	C080301	37	270	N110601	60	368
C020901	13	221	N130301	45	293	N130301	56	345
C020901	13	221	N130301	45	293	N130301	56	345
C080401	15	229	N130301	45	293	N130301	56	345
C020901	13	221	N130301	45	293	N130301	56	345
C040101	14	225	N130301	45	293	N130301	56	345
C020401	18	233	N120301	44	292	N/A[d]		420
C020901	13	221	N130301	45	293	N/A		420
C020401	18	233	N120301	44	292	N/A		420
C020401	18	233	N130301	45	293	N/A		420
C020401	18	233	N130301	45	293	N/A		420

TABLE D-12 Item ID Table for Document Literacy Bookmark Placements, Round 3, September 2004

Participant[a]	Table	Response Probability	Occasion
1.1	1	0.67	2
1.2	1	0.67	2
1.3	1	0.67	2
1.4	1	0.67	2
1.5	1	0.67	2
3.1	3	0.67	1
3.2	3	0.67	1
3.3	3	0.67	1
3.4	3	0.67	1
3.5	3	0.67	1
4.1	4	0.67	1
4.2	4	0.67	1
4.3	4	0.67	1
4.4	4	0.67	1
4.5	4	0.67	1
6.1	6	0.67	2
6.2	6	0.67	2
6.3	6	0.67	2
6.4	6	0.67	2
6.5	6	0.67	2

[a]The first participant of each table (i.e. 1.1, 2.1, ..., 9.1) is the table leader.

[b]Denotes the item number in the ordered item booklet on which the bookmark was placed (see pg. 112 for explanation of bookmark placements).

[c]Denotes the cut score associated with the bookmark placement. It is the RP location for the last item before the bookmark placement, converted to a scale score.

Basic			Intermediate			Advanced		
Item Identification	Round 3 BK[b]	SS[c]	Item Identification	Round 3 BK	SS	Item Identification	Round 3 BK	SS
C030701	12	194	C030601	36	243	C021101	57	318
C030702	13	198	C030601	36	243	C021101	57	318
C080501	17	204	N090501	38	254	N100701	62	371
C030708	18	210	C080201	40	256	C020201	52	283
C030701	12	194	C030601	36	243	C021101	57	318
C030708	18	210	N090501	38	254	N010901	59	332
C030708	18	210	N090501	38	254	N110901	61	358
C030708	18	210	C060901	42	266	N100601	56	302
C020101	19	215	C080201	40	256	N010901	59	332
C030708	18	210	C030601	36	243	N010901	59	332
C030708	18	210	C030501	41	260	N100701	62	371
C020101	19	215	C030708	39	256	N100701	62	371
C030708	18	210	C030501	41	260	N100701	62	371
N090301	10	192	C030501	41	260	N100701	62	371
C020101	19	215	C030501	41	260	N100701	62	371
C071001	5	170	C021001	29	235	N100501	48	274
C071001	5	170	N090501	38	254	N100701	62	371
C020101	19	215	C030601	36	243	N100701	62	371
C020101	19	215	N090501	38	254	N010901	59	332
C020101	19	215	N090501	38	254	N100701	62	371

TABLE D-13 Item ID Table for Quantitative Literacy Bookmark
Placements, Round 3, September 2004

Participant[a]	Table	Response Probability	Occasion
2.1	2	0.67	2
2.2	2	0.67	2
2.3	2	0.67	2
2.4	2	0.67	2
2.5	2	0.67	2
3.1	3	0.67	2
3.2	3	0.67	2
3.3	3	0.67	2
3.4	3	0.67	2
3.5	3	0.67	2
5.1	5	0.67	1
5.2	5	0.67	1
5.3	5	0.67	1
5.4	5	0.67	1
5.5	5	0.67	1
6.1	6	0.67	1
6.2	6	0.67	1
6.3	6	0.67	1
6.4	6	0.67	1
6.5	6	0.67	1

[a]The first participant of each table (i.e. 1.1, 2.1, ..., 9.1) is the table leader.

[b]Denotes the item number in the ordered item booklet on which the bookmark
was placed (see pg. 112 for explanation of bookmark placements).

[c]Denotes the cut score associated with the bookmark placement. It is the RP location
for the last item before the bookmark placement, converted to a scale score.

[d]Some panelists placed their bookmarks for the advanced level after the final item in the
booklet. When this occurred, SS is the scale score associated with the RP location for the
final item in the booklet.

Basic			Intermediate			Advanced		
Item Identification	Round 3 BK[b]	SS[c]	Item Identification	Round 3 BK	SS	Item Identification	Round 3 BK	SS
C070301	10	230	N090101	30	289	N010701	42	319
C020301	16	245	C080801	35	298	C050701	49	356
C070301	10	230	N130601	29	288	C050701	49	356
N120701	17	250	C080801	35	298	C050701	49	356
C020301	16	245	C080801	35	298	C050701	49	356
C020301	16	245	N130601	29	288	N010601	46	338
C020301	16	245	N090101	30	289	C020801	47	343
C020301	16	245	C080801	35	298	C050701	49	356
C020301	16	245	N130601	29	288	N120801	45	331
C020301	16	245	C070301	32	295	C020801	47	343
C020601	15	244	C020801	41	312	N/A[d]		461
C020601	15	244	C020801	41	312	N/A		461
C020601	15	244	C030709	37	302	N/A		461
C020601	15	244	C030709	37	302	N130701	51	393
N110801	23	266	C040601	43	324	C040801	53	400
C050301	5	211	C060701	24	267	C050701	49	356
C030706	4	203	C030704	12	240	N121101	50	369
C020601	15	244	C070301	32	295	C050701	49	356
C030704	12	240	N130601	29	288	C020801	47	343
N090901	14	242	C080101	31	290	N120801	45	331

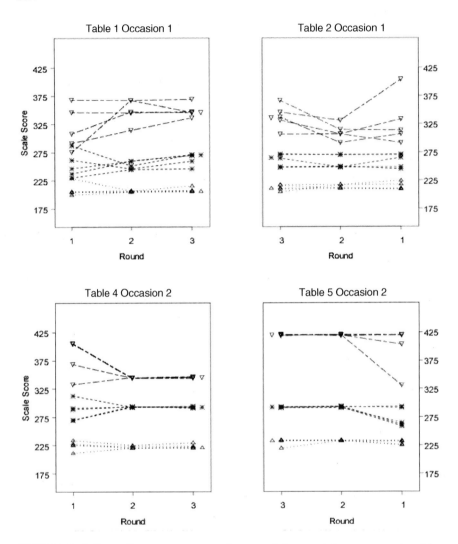

FIGURE D-1 Prose literacy cut scores by round for participants at each table, September 2004. Symbols indicate basic (Δ), intermediate (*), and advanced (∇) cut-score judgments. Round 3 medians are depicted by standalone symbols.

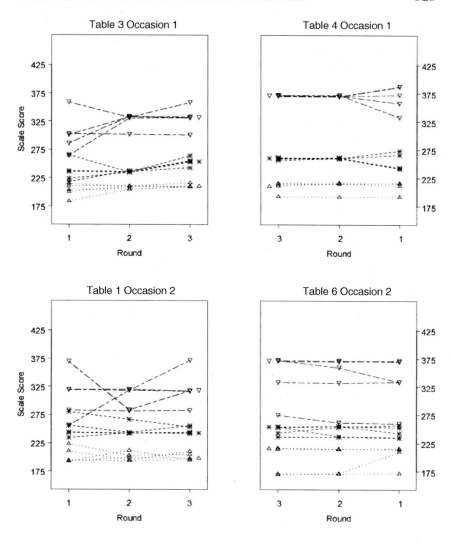

FIGURE D-2 Document literacy cut scores by round for participants at each table, September 2004. Symbols indicate basic (Δ), intermediate (*), and advanced (∇) cut-score judgments. Round 3 medians are depicted by standalone symbols.

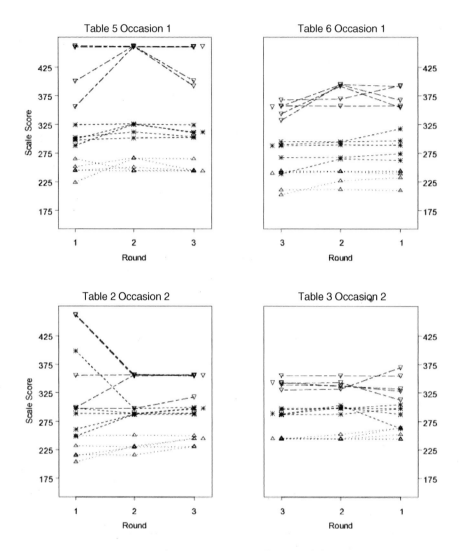

FIGURE D-3 Quantitative literacy cut scores by round for participants at each table, September 2004. Symbols indicate basic (Δ), intermediate (*), and advanced (∇) cut-score judgments. Round 3 medians are depicted by standalone symbols.

Appendix E

Biographical Sketches of Committee Members and Staff

Christopher F. Edley, Jr. (*Co-Chair*), is dean and professor of law at the University of California, Berkeley. Prior to his recent move to Berkeley, he spent 23 years on the law faculty at Harvard University. His work is primarily related to civil rights and education, and he has a long history of public service. In the Clinton administration, he worked as associate director for economics and government at the Office of Management and Budget, as special counsel to the president directing a White House review of affirmative action, and as a consultant to the president's advisory board on the race initiative. Edley's academic work is primarily in the area of civil rights, with additional concentrations in public policy and administrative law. He has taught federalism, budget policy, Defense Department procurement law, national security law, and environmental law. He is a cofounder of the Civil Rights Project, a multidisciplinary research and policy think tank focused on issues of racial justice. From 1999 to early in 2005, he served on the bipartisan U.S. Commission on Civil Rights. He is a member of the National Commission on Federal Election Reform. He has an M.A. in public policy from Harvard University and a J.D. from Harvard Law School.

Robert M. Hauser (*Co-Chair*) is Vilas research professor of sociology at the University of Wisconsin-Madison, where he has directed the Center for Demography and Ecology and the Institute for Research on Poverty. He currently directs the Center for Demography of Health and Aging, which is supported by the National Institute on Aging. He is a member of the National Academy of Sciences and a fellow of the American Statistical Association, the Center for Advanced Study in the Behavioral Sciences, and the American Academy of Arts and Sciences. He has served on the National Research Council's Committee on National Statistics, Commission on Behavioral and Social Sciences and Education, and Board on Testing and Assessment. He has worked on the Wisconsin Longitudinal Study since 1969 and directed it since 1980. His current research interests include trends in educational progression and social mobility in the United States among racial and ethnic groups, the uses of educational assessment as a policy tool, the effects of families on social and economic inequality, and changes in socioeconomic standing, health, and well-being across the life course. He has a Ph.D. in sociology from the University of Michigan.

Judith A. Alamprese is a principal associate at Abt Associates Inc., where she directs research, evaluation, policy, and technical assistance projects in adult education and workforce development. She is conducting a multiyear national study to investigate the organizational, instructional, and individual-level factors associated with adults' capacity to improve their decoding and fluency skills. Her other research includes evaluations of states' adult education programs with a focus on program improvement and development of leadership skills, design of family literacy programs, studies of the effectiveness of family literacy programs and programs aimed at preparing parents with low basic skills for work, and evaluations of workplace literacy programs. She was a codeveloper of the National External Diploma Program, the first competency-based applied performance assessment system for adults. She currently serves on the National Institute for Literacy/ National Center for the Study of Adult Learning and Literacy's Adult Literacy Research Working Group and the Verizon University Board of Advisors, and she is an adviser on several adult literacy studies. She has an M.A. in sociology from Syracuse University's Maxwell School of Citizenship and Public Affairs.

Michael X. Delli Carpini is dean of the Annenberg School for Communication at the University of Pennsylvania. Previously he was director of the public policy program of the Pew Charitable Trusts (1999-2003) and a member of the Political Science Department at Barnard College and graduate faculty of Columbia University (1987-2002), serving as chair of the Barnard department from 1995 to 1999. His research explores the role of the citizen in American politics, with particular emphasis on the impact of the mass media on public opinion, political knowledge, and political participation. He is the author of two books as well as numerous articles, essays, and edited volumes on political communications, public opinion, and political socialization. He has B.A. and M.A. degrees from the University of Pennsylvania (1975) and a Ph.D. from the University of Minnesota (1980).

Constance F. Citro (*Senior Program Officer*) is director of the Committee on National Statistics at the National Academies. She is a former vice president and deputy director of Mathematica Policy Research, Inc., and was an American Statistical Association/National Science Foundation research fellow at the U.S. Census Bureau. At the National Research Council, she has served as study director for numerous projects, including the Panel to Review the 2000 Census, the Panel on Estimates of Poverty for Small Geographic Areas, the Panel on Poverty and Family Assistance, the Panel to Evaluate the Survey of Income and Program Participation, the Panel to Evaluate Microsimulation Models for Social Welfare Programs, and the Panel on Decennial Census Methodology. Her research has focused on the quality and accessibility of large, complex microdata files, as well as analysis related to income and poverty measurement. She is a fellow of the American Statistical Association. She has a B.A. from the University of Rochester and M.A. and Ph.D. degrees in political science from Yale University.

Stuart W. Elliott (*Senior Program Officer*) is director of the Board on Testing and Assessment at the National Research Council, where he has worked on projects related to science assessment, citizenship examinations, incentives and accountability, and information technology. Before coming to the National Research Council, he worked as an economic consultant for several private-sector consulting firms. He was also a research fellow in cognitive psychology and economics at Carnegie Mellon University and a visiting scholar at the Russell Sage Foundation. He has a Ph.D. in economics from the Massachusetts Institute of Technology.

Vivian L. Gadsden is director and senior research scientist for the National Center on Fathers and Families and senior research scientist for the National Center on Adult Literacy in the Graduate School of Education at the University of Pennsylvania. She is also an associate professor of education for the graduate school. Her research examines intergenerational learning in families and in diverse social and cultural contexts. Her current research projects include a longitudinal study on intergenerational learning within African American and Latino families and a school-based study with second graders. A third project involves young, urban fathers, mothers, and children in school. Her work has appeared in numerous journals, edited books, and monograph series. Among her awards are a Spencer–National Academy of Engineering postdoctoral fellowship, the outstanding early career achievement award from the American Educational Research Association, and several major research grants. She has an Ed.D. in educational psychology and policy from the University of Michigan.

Andrew J. Hartman is currently an elementary school teacher-intern in the Denver Public Schools. Prior to entering this program, he was director of policy and research at the Bell Policy Center in Denver. He is the former executive director of the National Institute for Literacy in Washington, DC, a position he held for eight years. Prior to that, he served as staff director for the U.S. House Committee on Education and Labor. He was the recipient of the national 2001 literacy leadership award. He was a member of the National Advisory Committee for the development of national standards in civics education. He has a Ph.D. in child development from the University of Illinois at Champaign-Urbana.

Glynda A. Hull is the area chair of language, literacy, and culture and associate professor in the Graduate School of Education at the University of California, Berkeley. Her research interests include sociocultural studies of how writers' and readers' constructions of texts are shaped by past schooling, current instruction, institutions, and communities; use of multimedia technologies with at-risk students; understanding the roles that literacy plays in the workplace, particularly for low-income and at-risk populations; how new information technologies are affecting the nature of work and the literacy skills that workers are expected to have; and literacy skills in at-risk students. She has twice received the Richard Braddock memorial award for the best article of the year in college composition and communication. In 2001 she also received the National Council of Teachers of English award for best article reporting qualitative or quantitative research related to technical or scientific communication. Her most recent books include *School's Out! Bridging Out-of-School Literacies with Classroom Practice* and *Changing Work, Changing Workers: Critical Perspectives on Language, Literacy, and Skills.* She has a Ph.D. in English from the University of Pittsburgh.

Judith Anderson Koenig (*Study Director*) is a senior program officer with the National Research Council's Board on Testing and Assessment. She has worked on the board's projects related to the National Assessment of Educational Progress, assessing students with special needs, and teacher licensing and advanced certification. Previously she was a senior research associate with the Association of American Medical Colleges, where she led a research program on the Medical College Admission Test. She has also worked as a special education teacher and diagnostician with school systems in Michigan and Virginia. She has a Ph.D. in educational measurement, statistics, and evaluation from the University of Maryland.

Rebecca A. Maynard is university trustee professor of education and social policy at the University of Pennsylvania and senior program associate at the

William T. Grant Foundation. Prior to 1993, she was senior vice president and director of Princeton Research at Mathematica Policy Research, Inc. Her research has included numerous large-scale demonstration program evaluations on issues related to teenage parenthood, teenage pregnancy prevention, and child care, employment, and welfare policies. Currently she is principal investigator for three major projects: the National Evaluation of Title V Abstinence Education Programs, the Project to Improve and Disseminate Guidelines for Conducting Systematic Reviews of Research in Education and Social Welfare Policy, and the ACCESS program for science and technology studied. She has a Ph.D. in economics from the University of Wisconsin.

Lorraine McDonnell is professor of political science at the University of California, Santa Barbara. Her research focuses on the design and implementation of education reform initiatives, the politics of student testing, and the development and use of educational accountability systems. Her most recent book is *Politics, Persuasion, and Educational Testing* (2004). At the National Research Council, she was cochair of the Committee on Goals 2000 and the Inclusion of Students with Disabilities and vice chair of the Board on Testing and Assessment. Currently she cochairs the Committee on the U.S. Naturalization Test Redesign. She has a Ph.D. in political science from Stanford University.

Larry J. Mikulecky is professor of education at Indiana University. His research examines adolescent and adult literacy issues. His most recent research focuses on the uses of technology for language and literacy learning as well as for professional development. His recent publications have focused on literacy in the workplace, in terms of the literacy skills required in the workplace as well as workplace literacy programs. He has served as principal investigator on more than 20 research projects funded by the federal government as well as foundations and corporations. He is a member of Phi Beta Kappa and has been awarded Indiana University's Gorman teaching award as well as its highest teaching award, the Frederic Bachman Lieber distinguished teaching award. He is also the recipient of Laubach of Canada's distinguished service award and the state of Indiana's community service award for literacy work. He has a Ph.D. in reading curriculum and instruction from the University of Wisconsin-Madison.

Robert J. Mislevy is a professor in the University of Maryland's Department of Educational Measurement, Statistics, and Evaluation. Previously he worked at the Educational Testing Service for 16 years, where he was distinguished research scientist in the Division of Statistics and Psychometrics Research. His research interests center on applying recent developments in statistical methodology and cognitive research to practical problems in educational and psychological measurement. His current projects include developing an assessment design system, with applications in simulation-based assessments. He has published dozens of journal articles and book chapters and has been the recipient of the American Educational Research Association's Raymond B. Cattell early career award for programmatic research as well as the National Council of Measurement in Education's triennial award for technical contributions to educational measurement. He is currently a member of the National Research Council's Board on Testing and Assessment. He has a Ph.D. in methodology of behavioral research from the University of Chicago (1981).

Norman G. Peterson is research director at the Satisfaction Performance Research Center in Minneapolis, Minnesota. He contributes to research design, development, and evaluation of individual and organizational measures, statistical analyses, and application of research findings to organizational issues. Previously he was a senior research fellow at the American Institutes for Research. His research interests include occupational analysis, the development and validation of measures of individual differences, employee selection and classification systems, and the prediction of human performance in occupational and training settings. He is a fellow of the Society for Industrial and Organizational Psychology, the American Psychological Association, and the American Psychological Society. He has a Ph.D. in psychology, specializing in industrial and organizational psychology, from the University of Minnesota.

John P. Poggio is a professor in the Department of Educational Psychology and Research and director of development of the Kansas Assessment Programs at the University of Kansas, where he teaches courses in measurement, statistics, and research methodology. He served on the editorial boards of *Applied Measurement in Education* from 1986 to 1991 and the *Journal of Personnel Evaluation in Education* from 1985 to 1995. He has served on numerous advisory committees, particularly to state education agencies, and he currently serves on the technical advisory committee for the Kansas and Kentucky state assessment programs, where he has been extensively involved in test development, test design, and standard-setting procedures. He has conducted a number of studies that involved comparisons of various standard-setting procedures. He is the author of numerous publications, including journal articles, book chapters, and books, on educational measurement. He has a Ph.D. in educational research from Boston College.

Rima E. Rudd is senior lecturer on society, human development, and health at the Harvard University School of Public Health. She serves as director of educational programs for her department and teaches graduate courses on health literacy, innovative strategies in health education, and program planning. Her current work focuses on health literacy, and she works closely with the adult education, public health, and medical sectors. She is a research fellow of the National Center for the Study of Adult Learning and Literacy and is principal investigator or co-principal investigator for three studies of adult literacy and health. She authored the action plan for the health literacy objective in Healthy People 2010 *Communicating Health: Priorities and Strategies for Progress (2003)* and the Educational Testing Services report, *Literacy and Health in America* (2004). She served on the Institute of Medicine's Committee on Health Literacy, which produced the report *Health Literacy: Prescription to End Confusion* (2004). She has an Sc.D. in public health from the Johns Hopkins University School of Hygiene and Public Health.

Mary Jane Schmitt is the project director responsible for oversight of a comprehensive mathematics curriculum development project for adults and out-of-school youth at TERC in Cambridge, Massachusetts. In addition, she works at Harvard University with dining service and maintenance workers whose goals include job skill enhancement and high school equivalency certification. She served on the National Institute for Literacy's expert review panel for the development and validation of the Equipped for the Future standards. She has served as a consultant for Statistics Canada, the Adult Literacy Media Alliance, the Texas State Department of Education, and the GED Testing Service of the American Council on Education. Her research interests are in the area of adults' acquisition of numeracy skills. She has an M.A. in human development and psychology from Harvard University, where she is currently a doctoral candidate in the Graduate School of Education.

Lynne Steuerle Schofield (*Research Assistant*) is special assistant to the dean at the College of Education at Temple University, where she is responsible for new project development and partnership building. She has an M.A. in statistics and an M.A. in public policy from Carnegie Mellon University. She is certified to teach mathematics in Pennsylvania and New Jersey. She is a doctoral candidate at Carnegie Mellon University and expects to receive a Ph.D. in statistics and public policy in spring 2007.

David M. Thissen is professor of psychology at the Department of Psychology and the L.L. Thurstone Psychometric Laboratory of the University of

North Carolina, Chapel Hill. From 1999 to 2002, he served as an officer for the Psychometric Society and was president of the group from 2000 to 2001. He has been an associate editor for *Psychometrika* and an advisory editor for the *Journal of Educational Measurement* and has served on the editorial board for *Psychological Methods*; he is currently editor of the *Journal of Educational and Behavioral Statistics*. He has numerous publications in the area of item response theory, including journal articles, book chapters, and books. He serves on the technical advisory committees for the state assessment programs in North Carolina and Louisiana, and on the validity studies panel of the National Assessment of Educational Progress. His research interests lie in the areas of psychometrics, item response theory, models for human growth and development, and graphics and statistics in psychological contexts. He has a Ph.D. in behavioral sciences from the University of Chicago.

Andrew E. Tompkins (*Research Assistant*) is a research assistant for the National Research Council's Board on Testing and Assessment, where he has worked in various capacities, aiding committees in their research in such areas as testing equity and access, test design, advanced study of mathematics and science in high schools, performance assessments for adult education, and the redesign of the naturalization test. He has an M.A. in history from the State University of New York at Albany.

Lori Houghton Wright (*Program Officer*) is a program officer with the National Research Council's Board on Testing and Assessment, where she is working on projects related to appropriate uses of school-level education data and evaluation of advanced teacher certification programs. Prior to joining the National Research Council, she worked with the Student Assessment Services unit of the Massachusetts Department of Education, where she was involved with the development, scoring, and range-finding for the state mathematics criterion-referenced assessment (MCAS) for grades 4, 6, 8, and 10. She also spent one year as a visiting assistant professor at the University of the Virgin Islands, St. Croix. She has a Ph.D. in educational leadership and policy analysis from the University of Missouri-Columbia.

Heide Spruck Wrigley is a senior research associate for Aguirre International in California. Her work has involved research and evaluation in all areas of adult literacy education and training, with a special emphasis on minority populations. As the Aguirre manager of a national study entitled What Works in Adult ESL Literacy, she is responsible for the overall design of a framework for literacy development and language acquisition and is involved in all aspects of implementation. As part of two current projects